BLACK
LAW
QUESTIONS
& ANSWERS

QA

LAW OF TORTS

Questions and Answers Series

Titles in the Series

Other titles in preparation

BLACKSTONE'S LAW QUESTIONS & ANSWERS

LAW OF TORTS

SECOND EDITION

DAVID OUGHTON

Professor of Commercial Law, De Montfort University, Leicester

JOHN LOWRY

Deputy Director, Centre for Consumer and Commercial Law
Research, Brunel University

BLACKSTONE
PRESS LIMITED

First published in Great Britain 1994 by Blackstone Press Limited, Aldine Place, London W12 8AA. Telephone: 0181-740 2277

© D. W. Oughton and J. Lowry, 1994

ISBN: 1 85431 810 1

First edition, 1994
Second edition, 1999

British Library Cataloguing in Publication Data
A CIP catalogue record for this book is available from the British Library

Typeset by Montage Studios Limited, Tonbridge, Kent
Printed by Bell & Bain Limited, Glasgow

Contents

Preface

As the authors stated in the first edition of this book, the task of preparing sample examination questions and answers is a task not undertaken lightly and the same degree of fear, apprehension and circumspection applies to this updated edition as applied to the last. It is accepted that others may disagree with the approach and style adopted by the authors, but this is simply a reflection of the fact that the mind of one lawyer may differ from that of another and that, in truth, there is no such thing as a 'right answer' to many hypothetical problem questions on the issues raised by the law of tort(s). We hope, however, that what has been produced covers an acceptable range of issues and demonstrates the types of question which a student may encounter in a tort examination.

In this edition, considerable emphasis is given to the tort of negligence and its off-shoots, such as the position of an occupier of premises, the liability of an employer and the position of a producer of a defective product, but chapters are also devoted to defamation, economic torts, trespass, nuisance and the rule in *Rylands* v *Fletcher*. Attention is also given to the status of the right of privacy and the extent to which it is protected by tort law. Recent developments such as the House of Lords' decisions in *Hunter* v *Canary Wharf Ltd*; *Bolitho* v *City & Hackney Health Authority*; *Cambridge Water Co.* v *Eastern Counties Leather* and *White* v *Chief Constable of South Yorkshire Police*, are all dealt with in a number of the questions, as are statutory developments such as the Defamation Act 1996. Although the book is divided into chapters dealing with distinct areas of the law of tort, it will be found that many of the questions cross boundaries into other areas of tort law.

As with the previous edition of this book, the lion's share of responsibility for any criticisms or defects in the questions or answers lies with David Oughton, who extends his deep gratitude to John Lowry and L'Angelo Mysterioso for their very much appreciated contributions. As ever, the unwitting support of students at the institutions at which the authors teach is acknowledged and appreciated.

Last, but far from least, we would like to apologise to and thank our families (Sue, Gareth, Karen, Yasmin, Alastair and Alex) for their patience and forbearance over lost weekends, etc.

David Oughton
John Lowry
January 1999

Table of Cases

Table of Statutes

1 Introduction

PREPARATION

How you prepare your own revision work is a matter for you to decide, but it is important to read as widely as possible. In general, you should gather together the materials you have accumulated in a logical order and learn both the principles of law and what you have picked up on how to apply that law to the questions.

It is impossible to say how much time you will need to revise for the examination, because the requirements for each individual will differ. But it is worth remembering that while too little revision is fatal, too much is also dangerous since it is possible to reach a peak before the date of the examination. It is no use knowing everything perfectly two weeks before the examination, especially if you become stale thereafter. The key is to reach your peak on the day of the examination, which is all very well to say, but very difficult to put into practice.

THE EXAMINATION

The most important general note of guidance is not to panic. If you have revised well there will always be a sufficient number of questions on the paper for you to answer if you think in a cool, calm and collected manner. Moreover, the easy part about taking an examination for which you have prepared well is getting to pass standard. It becomes progressively more difficult to go from a pass mark to upper second or first class standard.

You are now sitting in front of a collection of pens, chewing gum, (Valium?), a watch, an answer book and an examination paper and the invigilator says you may commence. Remember, do not panic.

In a typical tort examination, you will have to answer four or five questions out of a total of about nine or ten. The questions you will encounter may be of two different types. Some will be hypothetical problem questions and some will be essay questions, usually based on quotations either from an academic text or from a judgment, followed by the unhelpful instruction, 'Discuss'.

You need to read the whole paper and decide which questions you wish to answer. Many institutions now give students reading time before the examination commences, but you will only have a limited time in which to answer these questions. It will usually pay dividends to sketch out a brief plan of each of your preferred choices. At this stage do not worry about the candidate next to you who has already filled two reams of paper. Content yourself that he or she is not only writing irrelevant rubbish in a totally unplanned fashion, but will also have to reconsider what has been written because he or she has no plan to work from and may have omitted important details.

The plan is time consuming, but is worthwhile. The advantage of planning the questions you propose to answer is that what you write should be directly relevant and you will avoid the serious problem of writing irrelevant material about issues which do not form part of the answer to the question. Moreover, if you have time left at the end, you can check your answer against the plan you prepared earlier.

Time management is crucial. If you take ten minutes to read the paper and plan your campaign, this leaves around 35 minutes *per* question in a five question examination and 42 minutes *per* question in a four question examination. Do not be tempted to substantially overrun this time allocation. It is far better to hand in a script in which you have completed the required number of questions, albeit incompletely, than to spend two hours on question one, 45 minutes on question two and then find you have 15 minutes in which to complete two further questions.

THE QUESTIONS YOU WILL ENCOUNTER

The examination in the law of tort will consist of two types of question — essay questions and hypothetical problems.

Essay questions

The key issue here is that if you do not understand precisely what the question asks you to do, do not answer it. Be honest with yourself when you ask what the question means. It is far too easy for a single word to be picked up from the quotation, taken in isolation and misinterpreted. Not infrequently candidates take the opportunity to write everything they know on a topic regardless of its relevance. Candidates who do this invariably fail on the question on which that sort of approach is adopted. It is important to answer the question the examiner has set rather than the question you would have liked to have been set!

In answering an essay question, you should produce a very brief introduction, identifying no more than the issues you propose to cover and any line of argument you propose to adopt. The main body of the essay will develop on those introductory issues and arguments, and should relate them to the question which has been set and, at all costs, you should use cases to support your argument. Finally, you need to conclude your essay by relating your arguments to the specific question set.

Hypothetical problem questions

Problem questions are often easier to answer than essay questions since, if you are prepared to look carefully, much of the answer is actually discoverable from the question itself. There are clues telling you what you must or must not write about — these are usually in the rubric at the end of each question. For example, if you are told to advise Dick, do not be tempted to advise Dora instead! Moreover, in many instances the facts of the problem will preclude a discussion of certain issues but highlight the importance of discussing other issues. For example, if you are told that a particular individual has done something negligently, there appears little point in discussing the issues of duty of care and breach of duty: the question is likely to be on remedies, defences, remoteness or causation.

When answering problem questions, it helps to state the relevant law in relation to particular issues and then apply that law to the relevant issue, making reference to the relevant facts of the problem. Do not be tempted to discuss legal principles which bear no relevance to the question. Here a plan of your intended answer is particularly useful.

As you go along, it helps to relate each point you make to the question set. In practice, it is far better to state a legal principle and immediately apply it than to regurgitate all the law first and then apply it at the end of your answer. The importance of applying the law as you go along is that you can demonstrate to the examiner that you know what the law is, you understand it and you can relate it to the problem. The last two stages are easily lost if you separate the law from its application. Moreover, the law first, application later approach is distinctly 'examiner-unfriendly' because the examiner has to flip back two pages to discover what was said about the law when it was stated to see if it has been accurately applied.

At all stages, you must support your argument with references to relevant case law or statutory authority. Do not be tempted to say, 'See *Donoghue* v *Stevenson*' since the examiner has 'seen' the case on many previous occasions. What you must do is to show that you understand the principle of law established by a case and why it is relevant to the question. In this process it may be necessary to relate the facts of the case, but more often than not the facts of the case will not be relevant. Moreover, do not use an ability to tell stories about what happened in a particular case to disguise your lack of knowledge of the law. From an examiner's point of view there is little more annoying than having to wade through pages of case facts, only to discover, at the end, that the candidate has little or no knowledge of the legal principle established by the case referred to.

Having stated the law and applied it, you may come to a definite conclusion, but you do not have to. The nature of problem questions is that they will be riddled with ambiguities. The important point is that you must be able to see all the various possibilities raised by the question, explain them and show how they affect the particular facts of the problem. It is far better to present several possible arguments than to dogmatically insist that there is a right answer which does not permit any alternatives. Given that you may have several lines of argument, reaching a definitive conclusion may be difficult, but this does not matter. If you have presented the arguments for each of the alternative lines of thinking and you have applied your argument to the question in a logical fashion, that will suffice. Occasionally, you can be forgiven if you decide to sit on the fence. After all, if the right answer is so obvious, we would not need courts or lawyers and you would not be revising for this examination! As you will have appreciated by following a tort law course, there are endless problems of policy which make the subject very uncertain at times.

Showing that you appreciate what law is relevant is an important feature. You can do this by highlighting, in block capitals, the cases you use. But examiners should also read what comes between the case names, so that has to be accurate and relevant as well.

2 The Role of the Law of Tort

INTRODUCTION

This chapter seeks to place the law of tort in context. The first question examines the relationship between tort law and its common law partner, the law of contract. While the teaching of law conventionally pigeonholes these major areas of study, it has to be appreciated that there are areas of overlap between the various core subjects. Of prime importance for the purposes of the relationship between the law of contract and the law of tort is the limited use of the tort of negligence as a means of dealing with the problem of economic loss.

Questions two, three and four seek to consider the various functions served by tort law. In particular, question two deals with the role of tort law as a system of accident compensation. Many of the criticisms of the role of the law of tort in this regard must be read in the light of the more detailed consideration of remedies for breach of tortious obligations in **Chapter 12**. Although tort law does play a minor role in the overall picture of accident compensation, it should be appreciated that it is only a very small part of a broader range of state-provided compensation schemes, albeit somewhat more generous to those who are successful. Question three deals with the law of tort as a deterrent to harm-causing activities. In part, this raises the matter of the relationship between the law of tort and the criminal law, but also considers the increasing interest of economists in the use of tortious rules as a means of achieving efficient results. Conversely, the law is not the marketplace, and other factors such as justice are relevant in ascertaining the role of tort law.

Although the tort of negligence has dominated in the twentieth century, it has to be noted that there are many torts other than the tort of negligence which serve to protect particular individual interests. As an example of the range of interests protected by various torts, question four considers the extent to which privacy and the right to bodily integrity is a protected interest, demonstrating the difficulties which may be caused in attempting to slot the privacy interest into existing torts, which may have been conceived with a slightly different interest in mind. This last matter also impinges on the issues raised in **Chapter 3** (Trespass to the Person) and **Chapter 8** (Torts in Relation to Land).

QUESTION 1

Contract and tort are like cheese and biscuits: different but complementary.

(*Holyoak.*)

Discuss.

Commentary

This question requires consideration of the following:

(a)   the major differences between contractual and tortious liability;

(b)   the generalisations which are said to distinguish the two branches of the common law, including the difference between the expectation interest and the *status quo* interest, the difference between fault-based and strict liability and the view that contractual obligations are voluntarily assumed whereas tortious obligations are imposed by law;

(c)   whether there can be a concurrent liability in both contract and tort and whether contractual obligations override those which may be imposed by the law of tort.

Suggested Answer

There are undoubtedly differences between liability in tort and contractual liability, but the differences may, at times, pale into near insignificance because of the interplay between these two branches of a broader law of obligations. The major differences can be found in the law of limitation of actions where different rules apply to the accrual of the cause of action, although, even in this area, the courts have been faced with acute problems where a limitation defence has been raised in a case where there is concurrent contractual and tortious liability. Other areas where different rules apply according to whether the action is framed in contract or in tort include the issues of remoteness of damage; quantification of damages and the difference between non-feasance and misfeasance.

A number of generalisations are said to distinguish tortious and contractual liability. A primary distinction is said to be that tort is protective whereas the law of contract is productive: T. Weir, *Casebook on Tort*, 7th edn (London:

Sweet & Maxwell, 1992). Another way of stating this distinction is to say that the law of contract protects the plaintiff's expectation interest by casting the plaintiff forward into the position he would have been in had the defendant performed his contractual promises (*Robinson* v *Harman* (1854) 1 Exch 850). In contrast, tort law is concerned with restoring the *status quo* by returning the plaintiff to the position he was in before the defendant committed his wrongful act (*Livingstone* v *Rawyards Coal Co.* (1880) 5 App Cas 25). As with all generalisations, it is bound to break down from time to time. There are circumstances in which contractual remedies compensate *status quo* losses and in which tortious remedies protect a person's expectations.

While the typical loss complained of by a plaintiff suing for breach of contract is the failure to make a gain which might otherwise have been made had the contract been performed, it should be appreciated that the loss of profit representing the plaintiff's expectation of gain also includes simple expenditure loss which, if included in the plaintiff's award of damages, will involve returning the plaintiff to the position he was in before the contract with the defendant was entered into. Moreover, in some instances, where the contract entered into is of a highly speculative nature, such as the production of a film, the expectation loss suffered by the plaintiff may be incapable of calculation, in which case a more appropriate measure of damages may be compensation in respect of the expense incurred by the plaintiff, thereby protecting the *status quo* interest alone (*Anglia TV Ltd* v *Reed* [1972] 1 QB 60).

The rule that the law of tort only returns the plaintiff to the position he was in before the defendant's wrong was committed is also one which is subject to exceptions. In particular, there are duties to exercise reasonable care which arise out of a contractual relationship, in which case it can be said that there is an expectation that such care will be exercised. The clearest example of this kind of duty can be found in the field of occupiers' liability where the occupier is liable not only for acts which cause physical harm but also for a failure to act, such as a failure to maintain a fence, which makes the plaintiff's position worse.

Moreover, there is a line of authority which establishes that a solicitor who negligently advises his client with the result that the intended beneficiary of a will fails to receive the bequest it was intended by the now deceased client that he should receive, may be liable, in the tort of negligence, for the failure to take reasonable care (*Ross* v *Caunters* [1980] Ch 297; *White* v *Jones* [1995] 1 All ER 691). In these circumstances, the intended beneficiary has an expectation of gain (the intended bequest) which is not capable of protection by way of contractual rules, due to the restrictive effect of the doctrine of privity of contract. However, despite proposals for the reform of the doctrine of privity of contract (Law Commission: *Privity of Contract: Contracts for the Benefit of Third Parties* (Law Com No. 242, 1996, Cmnd 3329) it seems unlikely that a person in the position of the intended beneficiary will have a contractual action in the future, since it is not the *contract* between the solicitor and his client which confers a benefit on the beneficiary, but the *will*, had it been correctly drafted. In contrast, the tort of negligence has been adapted to protect the intended beneficiary on the basis that it is reasonably foreseeable that such loss might be suffered by the plaintiff, that the relationship of proximity between the solicitor and the beneficiary is sufficiently close to justify the finding of liability, and that the solicitor has voluntarily undertaken responsibility towards the beneficiary by undertaking to advise the client in such a manner as to ensure the effectiveness of the intended bequest (*Ross* v *Caunters* [1980] Ch 297; *White* v *Jones* [1995] 1 All ER 691).

Furthermore, even in relation to what is often regarded as the classic tort action, an action for damages for negligently inflicted personal injury, a substantial element of the plaintiff's action for damages will be in respect of expected future gains in the form of damages for lost earnings.

A second distinction between tort and contract is said to be that contractual duties are fixed by the parties to the contract, whereas tortious duties are fixed by law. To advance on this distinction it can be said that duties in tort are owed to persons generally, whereas contractual duties are owed specifically to the other party or parties to the relevant contract. While tortious duties are fixed by law, it should not be forgotten that many such duties arise out of a contractual relationship. This will often be the case where there is a contract for the provision of services under which there will be an implied term that the supplier will exercise reasonable care and skill in performing the contract (Supply of Goods and Services Act 1982, s. 13). Here, determining the extent of the supplier's duty to exercise reasonable care will require close attention to the specific undertakings which form the basis of the contract and it is important that any tortious duty found to exist should not undermine the express contractual undertakings of the parties (*Johnstone* v *Bloomsbury Health Authority* [1991] 2 All ER 293; *Reid* v *Rush & Tompkins plc* [1990] 1 WLR 212).

Services contracts apart, the liability of an occupier to his visitors will also depend on any contractual relationship which exists between the parties (Occupiers' Liability Act 1957, s. 2(1)), so that regard must be had to the extent to which the occupier agrees to extend, limit or vary the duty normally owed to a lawful visitor under the general law of tort. Under the original version of the rule in *Hedley Byrne & Co. Ltd* v *Heller & Partners Ltd* [1964] AC 465 it was a requirement, on the particular facts of that case, that the defendant should have voluntarily assumed responsibility for the accuracy of a statement communicated to the plaintiff. Accordingly, since in *Hedley Byrne* the defendant had disclaimed responsibility for the accuracy of a financial reference, it was considered by the House of Lords that the defendant would owe the plaintiff no duty of care. In time, the requirement of voluntary assumption of responsibility came to be replaced by a requirement of reasonable reliance as the key indicator of liability on the part of the maker of a statement. The principal reason for the apparent abandonment of the requirement of voluntary assumption of responsibility seems to have been that it did not fit with the normal understanding of the basis for the imposition of liability in tort, namely that it was a responsibility imposed by law and that whether or not the defendant voluntarily undertook a responsibility towards the plaintiff could have no bearing on whether a legally imposed duty could be said to exist (*Smith* v *Bush (Eric S.)* [1990] 1 AC 831). Thus in *Smith* v *Bush (Eric S.)* the defendants, a firm of surveyors carrying out a building society valuation, could still owe a duty of care to an impecunious consumer buyer of a house surveyed by them despite the fact that they disclaimed responsibility for the accuracy of the advice they gave. The basis of the decision was that regardless of the disclaimer, the advice given by the defendants was something which a person in the position of the plaintiffs would reasonably rely upon.

However, more recently the requirement of voluntary assumption of responsibility has seen a revival, albeit explained in a somewhat different way to the way in which it appeared to be explained in *Hedley Byrne & Co.* v *Heller & Partners Ltd.* For example, in *Hedley Byrne* Lord Devlin considered the required relationship between the plaintiff and the defendant to be 'equivalent to contract' with the result that but for the absence of consideration there would have been a contractual relationship between the parties. More recently, in *Henderson* v *Merrett Syndicates Ltd* [1994] 3 All ER 506, it was considered that a defendant (in this case a Lloyd's managing agent) providing professional or quasi-professional services whose advice was relied upon by the plaintiff would owe a tortious duty of care to the plaintiff whether or not there existed between the parties a contractual relationship, provided the defendant had voluntarily assumed responsibility for the accuracy of the advice given. Moreover, it seems that this duty of care can be imposed despite the fact that the parties had chosen to structure their obligations through their contractual relationships. The difficulty this analysis presents, on the face of it, is that tortious duties are imposed by law rather than by way of any contractual arrangements. However, in *White* v *Jones* [1995] 1 All ER 691 a more detailed explanation of the nature of the voluntary assumption of responsibility test was given by Lords Goff and Browne-Wilkinson. In particular, in order to get round the criticism of the requirement in *Smith* v *Bush*, Lord Browne-Wilkinson explained that it was not the duty which was voluntarily assumed, since this must be imposed by law. Instead, in his Lordship's opinion, what has been voluntarily assumed is the relationship between the defendant and the plaintiff, from which relationship the duty can be inferred, especially in circumstances in which the plaintiff has reasonably relied upon the advice given by the defendant. The main problem with this particular analysis is that it is just as capable of applying to negligent acts, such as that of getting into a motor vehicle and driving it in a negligent fashion, which have been traditionally dealt with on the basis of an imposed duty not affected by considerations relating to the voluntariness of the defendant's conduct. Perhaps the developments unleashed in *Henderson* v *Merrett Syndicates Ltd* and *White* v *Jones* are best considered relevant only in the context of actions for negligently caused economic loss.

A further distinction between contractual and tortious liability is said to be that contractual duties are strict whereas tortious duties are, generally, fault-based. However, there are numerous exceptions to this generalisation. In particular, many contractual duties are fault-based, particularly those which are implied into contracts for the supply of services (Supply of Goods and Services Act 1982, s. 13). Moreover, the device of the collateral contract has been used in the past to impose liability on the maker of a misleading pre-contractual statement at a time when there was no liability in damages for negligent misrepresentation (*Esso Petroleum Ltd* v *Mardon* [1976] QB 801). In tort law the meaning of the term 'fault' is not easy to ascertain, but there are a number of torts which are apparently those of strict liability. Examples include the liability of a keeper of an animal belonging to a dangerous species (Animals Act 1971, s. 2(1)), the rule in *Rylands* v *Fletcher* (1868) LR 3 HL 330, the provisions of the Consumer Protection Act 1987, Part I and the Nuclear Installations Act 1965 and the rules relating to the vicarious liability of an employer for the tortious acts of his employees. In relation to the last mentioned, it should be observed that while the employer may not be personally at fault, he is held liable for those torts committed by his employees in the course of their employment. Accordingly, there will usually have been a fault-based wrong committed by someone for whom the employer is held responsible. Furthermore, the way in which some so-called strict liability torts have been interpreted by the courts is such as to inject into them elements of fault. In particular, the interpretation of the non-natural use requirement of the rule in *Rylands* v *Fletcher* suggests that it is necessary to consider the general benefit to the community of the defendant's activity, the locality in which the accumulation took place and the reasonableness of the precautions taken by the defendant to guard against the risk of harm to others (*Mason* v *Levy Auto Parts of England* [1967] 2 QB 530). These requirements sound suspiciously similar to those relevant to an enquiry into the issue of breach of duty of care and whether there is an actionable nuisance; both of which are substantially fault-based enquiries. The presence of a development risks defence in the Consumer Protection Act 1987, s. 4(1)(e) substantially reduces the impact of the Act, since it is a defence for a producer to show that the state of scientific and technological development at the time a product was put into circulation was not such as to allow a product defect to be discovered. Moreover, the definition of defectiveness in s. 3(2) of the Act takes into account factors well known in fault-based torts such as consumer misuse, warnings and instructions as to use and the general manner in which a product is marketed.

The best illustration of the complementary nature of contractual and tortious liability can be found in cases in which a person is concurrently liable in contract and in tort. Since tortious liability is regarded as parasitic (*Pacific Associates Inc* v *Baxter* [1990] QB 993), there is no sense in searching for liability in tort where the parties are in a contractual relationship (*Tai Hing Cotton Mill* v *Liu Chong Bank Ltd* [1986] 1 AC 801). It follows that liability in tort cannot be any greater than that expressly or impliedly created by the contract between the parties. Conversely, the mere fact that a contract exists between the parties and that they have chosen to structure their obligations by reference to that contract will not preclude the existence of a tortious duty of care where the contract remains silent on the matter which is in dispute (*Henderson* v *Merrett Syndicates Ltd* [1994] 3 All ER 506; c.f. *National Bank of Greece SA* v *Pinios SA* [1990] 1 AC 637). As Lord Goff noted, it may be that the facts of *Henderson*, considered above, are unusual, since in most cases where there is a chain of contractual relationships, the imposition of a tortious duty of care might be inconsistent with the contractual undertakings contained in the contractual structure. Thus it has been observed that in the case of a building contract under which there are contractual arrangements between the building owner and the main contractor and arrangements between the main contractor and the various sub-contractors, it will not normally be the case that a sub-contractor will owe any tortious duty of care to the building owner, since the sub-contractor will not normally voluntarily undertake responsibility to the owner (*Barclays Bank plc* v *Fairclough Building Ltd* [1995] 1 All ER 289). How the *Barclays* case differs from *Henderson* v *Merrett* is not entirely clear, but it seems that the distinction cannot lie in the difference between physical damage and economic loss. (See *Marc Rich & Co.* v *Bishop Rock Marine Co. Ltd* [1995] 3 All ER 307.)

Furthermore, there may be circumstances in which the contractual undertakings of the parties are consistent with general tortious duties, especially those requiring the exercise of reasonable care. Thus if an employer fails to provide a safe system of work by requiring an employee to be available for work for an average of 88 hours a week, the contractual term requiring attendance may amount to a limitation of liability in respect of negligently caused personal injury, so that the provisions of the Unfair Contract Terms Act 1977, s. 2(1) may be invoked (*Johnstone* v *Bloomsbury Health Authority* [1991] 2 All ER 293).

In conclusion, it is clear that there are differences between contractual and tortious liability, but the two branches of the common law of obligations work together towards the provision of adequate remedies for the plaintiff. However, where tort and contract intermix, the generality of the tort system will normally give way to the more specific inter-party obligations undertaken by way of contract.

QUESTION 2

Consider the defects, if any, in the fault system of accident compensation and the case for reform of the means of accident compensation.

Commentary

This question requires consideration of the role of tort law as a system of compensation for accident victims. In particular, regard should be had to the following:

(a) criticisms of the tort system based on cost, delay, the lump sum method of compensation and general unpredictability of outcome;

(b) alternatives to the tort system such as state insurance, no-fault accident compensation schemes and private insurance.

Suggested Answer

In practice, much of the law of tort is concerned with compensating the victim of the defendant's accidental wrongdoing. Accordingly, at a general level, the function of a remedy in the law of tort is to relieve the plaintiff in respect of the loss or damage he has suffered rather than to punish the defendant.

Generally, the tort system is concerned with *wrongs* in the sense that the defendant is required to compensate the plaintiff in respect of damage caused by some fault-based or culpable conduct on his (the defendant's) part. In this sense, tort liability rules are concerned with *loss shifting* in that they make the defendant responsible for the loss suffered by the plaintiff because he (the defendant) is in some way to blame for that loss.

The growth of the practice of insurance has introduced the notion of *loss distribution* under which the question is not who is to blame for an accident, but who can most easily bear the loss caused by a particular accident? For example, it was once observed by Lord Griffiths in *Smith* v *Bush (Eric S.)* [1989] 2 WLR 790 that:

> There was once a time when it was considered imprudent even to mention the possible existence of insurance cover in a lawsuit. But those days are long past. . . . The availability and cost of insurance must be a relevant factor when considering which of two parties should be required to bear the risk of a loss.

Where a potential cause of accidents is identified, such as the motor car or the work accident, insurance against the risk created may become compulsory or a regime of strict tort liability may be introduced by Parliament. Moreover, in relation to motor vehicle accidents, there is also a safety net provided by the Motor Insurers' Bureau (MIB) which has an agreement with the Department of Transport that they will provide additional cover in cases in which an accident is caused by an uninsured or untraced driver. Strangely, although employers are also subject to a compulsory insurance scheme, there is no equivalent of the MIB agreement, which is regarded as a relevant factor by the courts in such cases (*Dunbar* v *A & B Painters Ltd* [1986] 2 Lloyd's Rep 38, 42–3 *per* Balcombe LJ).

Where an accident victim is able to satisfy the legal requirements necessary to make out a claim in tort, he stands to recover much more than will be available to a person who is unable to pursue a tort claim. The reason for this is that English law adopts a system of 'full compensation'. In personal injury cases, this means that tort compensation should be related to the actual earnings of the plaintiff. Moreover, the full compensation system pays damages in respect of both pecuniary loss (e.g., expense incurred) and non-pecuniary loss (e.g., pain and suffering). Conversely, the number of successful tort claimants is relatively small for a number of reasons. For example, in order to be able to recover, the plaintiff must be the victim of an 'accident', which may be either the result of the fault of the defendant or due to the commission of a wrong, in respect of which liability is strict. For these purposes, an 'accident' may include congenital disability and disease, where they are man-made, but there are a number of such conditions which may occur by accident but which are not attributable to the fault of an identified defendant. In such circumstances, for example where disease occurs naturally, the tort system is likely to fail as a means of accident compensation by allowing a number of plaintiffs to fall through the compensation net.

Other criticisms of the tort system as a means of accident compensation are those of cost, delay, unpredictability of outcome, the unbalanced way in which payments are made and the problem of how compensation payments are used by the plaintiff after an award has been made.

So far as cost is concerned, it was established by the Pearson Report (Report of the Royal Commission on Compensation for Personal Injuries, Cmnd 7054, 1978) that the administrative cost of tort compensation was 85 per cent of the total amount paid out in 1977. In contrast, the equivalent cost of compensation under the social security system came to only 11 per cent. Moreover, since the outcome in a tort action is dependent on litigation commenced by the plaintiff, the litigant must be in a position, subject to the limited availability of legal aid, to be able to fund the process of litigation. The cost of the tort system is intimately associated with the requirement of fault. Much expense is incurred in identifying who is at fault and therefore potentially responsible for the harm suffered by the plaintiff. Costs are incurred in assessing how much compensation should be paid, since there must be an investigation into the consequences of an accident, involving the preparation of expert reports, etc. Moreover, because of the adversary system, these costs are duplicated since each party will have to call his own experts.

The tort system is also very slow in delivering compensation, again due in part to the adversary system. The more complicated the case, the greater will be the likelihood of delay. The Civil Justice Review (Cm 394, 1988) has revealed that the average time from accident to trial in the case of a High Court action is five years and in the case of a county court trial, three years. Moreover, defendants and their insurers have every incentive to throw obstacles in the path of a plaintiff in the hope that litigation will be suspended. The review of the Civil Justice system undertaken by Lord Woolf (*Access to Justice*, 1996) has suggested radical reforms designed to speed up the whole system of dispensing civil justice. Under the Woolf proposals, there would be a fast track procedure for personal injury actions involving a sum not more than £10,000. In addition, it is also proposed to extend the jursidiction of the county court small claims procedure to cover personal injury cases up to a value of £3,000. Under the proposals, a trial would have to take place within 30 weeks of the date on which the writ was issued and trials are expected to last hours rather than days. In the case of complex claims, such as those for medical negligence (whether above or below the £10,000 threshold) and all claims valued at more than £10,000, it is proposed that there should be a multi-track system subject to close judicial scrutiny for the purposes of time management. The notion of judicial case management is intended to cut out the possibility of proceedings being unduly lengthened by time wasting tactics on the part of large corporate defendants and their insurers. Moreover, there are also proposals to allow a plaintiff to make an offer of settlement, similar to the present system whereby a defendant may make a payment into court. Under the Woolf proposals, an unreasonable refusal by a defendant to accept the offer of settlement would work against him.

The unpredictability of the tort system is also notorious. Even assuming that a duty is established in a typical negligence action, the problems of establishing breach of duty, factual causation and that the damage suffered is not too remote are such that few plaintiffs can ever be assured of success. Even where the plaintiff is successful, the unpredictability of the tort system is such that the final award may be considerably less than may have been anticipated at the outset, which must be offset against the cost of bringing the action in the first place. Because of this pressure, plaintiffs will often settle out of court, resulting in under-compensation in more complicated cases. At the same time, the administrative cost to insurance companies in processing smaller claims may lead to an over-generous out of court settlement, thereby resulting in over-compensation in order to settle a claim as quickly as possible, demonstrating the unbalanced way in which compensation may be paid to individual litigants.

The means of paying compensation in the form of a lump sum has also attracted criticism. When assessing how much should be paid, the court will have to have regard to possible future events at the time of trial. However, later events which were not in mind at the time of trial cannot be taken into account at a later stage unless the circumstances of the case are such that an award of provisional damages can be made so as to take account of the possible future onset of disease or other physical or mental deterioration in the plaintiffs condition (Supreme Court Act 1981, s. 32A). Given the uncertainty of the lump sum payment, it is not surprising that in the case of traumatic, long-term injuries, the accountancy driven system of structured settlements has begun to prove popular (see the Damages Act 1996, s. 5). Although increasingly common in the case of long-term accident damage, it should be noted that a plaintiff cannot be compelled to agree to a structured settlement in place of a lump sum payment (Damages Act 1996, s. 2). Under this system, the plaintiff is guaranteed periodic compensation during his lifetime based on the purchase of an annuity by the defendant's liability insurers. The annuity can make provision for events which may affect the need for increased compensation at various stages in the continued life of the accident victim and avoids the problem of profligacy on the part of plaintiffs following the receipt of an award of lump sum damages. The advantages of the structured settlement fall on both sides. Not only does the annuity system avoid payment of tax by accident victims (Taxes Act 1988, ss. 329A and 329B, added by the Finance Act 1995, s. 142) but it also results in substantial savings over the normal lump sum system so far as insurers are concerned. An immediate lump sum can be paid to the victim, however, to meet identified need, e.g., the adaptation of a house for the purposes of a quadriplegic accident victim. However probably the most serious criticism of the system of structured settlements is that a very small percentage of accident victims are deriving a substantial benefit at the expense of ordinary taxpayers, which effectively benefits such victims to an even greater extent than is already the case where an accident victim is successful in an action for damages. By way of contrast, there may be ordinary taxpayers who have subsidised the award to such a victim who are themselves injured, but unable to maintain an action for damages themselves because they have suffered a non-tortious injury (see *Hodgson* v *Trapp* [1988] 3 All ER 870 at 876 per Lord Bridge).

Alternatives to the fault-based tort system include private insurance by the victim and the tortfeasor; the greater use of rules of strict liability based on an assumption that the potential tortfeasor should be insured against the possible risk of damage to others; public insurance schemes such as the social security system and more wide-ranging public insurance schemes such as that employed in New Zealand by virtue of the Accident Rehabilitation and Compensation Insurance Act 1992 which effectively eliminates the need to have recourse to the law of tort as a system of accident compensation.

Some types of accident damage can be insured against by both the victim and the tortfeasor. In particular, life, permanent health and personal accident policies are readily available to all potential accident victims. Moreover, some employers will take out occupational sick pay policies which go beyond state provision for short-term income replacement. At present, the likelihood that such policies will exist depends greatly on the social class into which the accident victim falls and the nature of his employment. Before private insurance can replace the tort system, there must be a distinct change in taxation policy so that all members of society are paid in such a way that they can afford to take out private insurance. There still remains the problem that the low paid will not have the resources to cover themselves adequately against all possible eventualities. The fact that private insurance policies exist does not, at present, make any difference to an award of tort damages since the courts do not wish to discourage thrift, so payments out of privately arranged insurance will not be deducted from an award of tort damages (*Bradburn* v *Great Western Railway* (1874) LR 10 Ex 1).

The present social security system provides for payment in respect of a number of injuries which may or may not result from the fault of an identified defendant. Roughly, benefits can be divided into those which relate to non-industrial injuries and those which relate to injury suffered at work. The former include sickness benefit or statutory sick pay and invalidity benefit or allowance. In respect of industrial injuries, disablement benefit may be awarded to an injured employee. The important consideration concerning these benefits is that, at present, they are deductible from an award of tort damages, but they are not based on the principle of full compensation since the amount payable is based on average earnings rather than on the actual earnings of the accident victim. However as has been observed, the social security system is more effeicient in terms of the cost of making payments to individuals and can be geared to the needs of the claimant as and when new financial difficulties might arise.

Dissatisfaction with the tort system of compensation has led to the introduction of a comprehensive no-fault scheme of compensation in New Zealand. This system replaces the victim's earnings at 80 per cent of his pre-accident earnings, subject to a maximum ceiling. In addition, a lump sum can be awarded in respect of permanent disablement, but payments for pain and suffering and loss of amenity are minimal. Also, the cost of the scheme must be related to the type of economy which exists in New Zealand, which is largely agricultural. It is arguable that the same system would not translate to a more industrialised economy in which there are substantial numbers of industrial injuries resulting from production processes. Also there still remains the political problem that public schemes have to be paid for out of public funds, which tends to make them less popular with those who have the resources to make private arrangements.

QUESTION 3

While economic efficiency may be '... one of several and sometimes contradictory objectives of tort. The marketplace and efficiency must always be subordinated to justice to individuals' (*Street on Torts.*)

In the light of this statement, discuss the extent to which efficiency and justice are objectives of the law of tort.

Commentary

This question involves consideration of the role of the law of tort as a means of deterring accident-causing activities. Regard should be had to the following:

(a) the primary objectives of economic analysis of legal rules;

(b) efficiency versus justice as objectives of the law of tort;

(c) the distinction between loss shifting and loss distribution and the role of private insurance;

(d) the different notions of justice across the whole range of tortious liability.

Suggested Answer

The law of tort is primarily concerned with accidents which result in physical harm to the person or to property, although it may also protect the economic interests of the plaintiff in a limited number of cases. The law of tort may serve a number of different purposes. Liability rules may serve to deter wrongdoers from engaging in activities which harm others, while the law should also seek to provide a remedy for those who are harmed as a result of the defendant's wrongs.

On an economic analysis, the desire to deter a person from engaging in activities which cause harm to others is seen as a primary objective. A legal rule is perceived to be efficient if it deters wrongdoing in a cost effective manner, but while the deterrent effect of a rule of the law of tort may be important, it should not be promoted to the extent that the plight of an injured person is forgotten. Somehow, in applying legal rules, the courts have to reach a suitable balance between efficiency and justice. The conflict between efficiency and justice can be seen most clearly in cases of negligence, especially when it comes to be determined whether the defendant's actions constitute an actionable breach of duty. The goal of efficiency is probably best served by the rule that an act is only negligent if reasonable precautions have not been taken by the defendant (*Latimer* v *AEC Ltd* [1953] AC 643), since it is clear that taking every possible precaution to guard against a minor risk of harm would be uneconomic. For example, it might be possible to reduce the number of road traffic accidents by requiring vehicle manufacturers to produce cars which could not travel any faster than 10 m.p.h., but this would hardly be acceptable in terms of economic efficiency, nor would this solution be socially acceptable.

It should be appreciated that virtually every activity has some capacity for causing harm, but to take every possible precaution to guard against minimal risks would not make sense. Thus when the evidence shows that in a period of 30 years, only six cricket balls have been struck from the defendant's cricket ground to the outside, the excessive precaution of substantially raising the height of the perimeter fence is not necessary to guard against such a minimal risk of harm to others (*Bolton* v *Stone* [1951] AC 850). However, the rule that the magnitude of risk created by the defendant should be considered is based on the notion that a particularly vulnerable plaintiff should be treated more carefully than others by the tortfeasor (*Paris* v *Stepney Borough Council* [1951] AC 367), thereby illustrating the importance of practical justice in special cases.

If the law imposes liability in damages for certain acts, this would appear to serve a deterrent purpose, since few people will wish to engage in conduct which they realise is likely to result in them having to pay another in respect of the harm which has been caused. There are occasions, however, on which there may be little the defendant can do to avoid causing harm to others. For example, since the test of liability is objectively based, the defendant who does his incompetent best may still be liable since he is judged by the standards of the reasonable man and not by reference to his own ability (*Nettleship* v *Weston* [1971] 2 QB 691). Moreover, in many cases the defendant's fault amounts to little more than inadvertence, so that the defendant may not have foreseen the danger he creates, but the law may state that he has not acted in the same way as a reasonable man would have acted and is therefore liable.

The view that tort rules serve a deterrent purpose is readily understandable where liability is based on the notion of loss shifting. Loss shifting as a method of compensation has its roots in the nineteenth century notion that there should be no liability without proof of fault and that a person who is at fault should pay for the losses he has caused. Modern tort law is now dominated by the presence of an insurance market and there has been a move from loss shifting as a system of compensation to one based on the notion of loss distribution. The insurance market is such that major causes of accidents can be identified and those who engage in accident causing activities, such as employers, drivers and manufacturers, may be required or encouraged to take out insurance to cover potential risks of loss. Moreover, in most cases, the insured accident causer can pass on the cost of insurance to the consumers of his product or his service, thereby spreading the costs associated with the accident risk more broadly. Since the accident causer must be or ought to be insured the problem is that it is not the tortfeasor who pays damages, but his insurer. The widespread availability of insurance also serves to undermine the argument that tort rules serve a deterrent purpose, since it is rarely the defendant, but his insurers who foot the bill where an award of damages is made. Insurers themselves might appear to be able to deter tortious misconduct, but there is little evidence that they do. It is possible to raise premiums in the case of bad risks, but this is never likely to deter mere inadvertence.

Even in professional negligence cases where tort rules might conceivably have a deterrent effect, the inadvertence argument once more becomes relevant. It is also arguable that the threat of liability based on the notion of fault is likely to result in the adoption of over-defensive practices which might prove detrimental to the interests of the client or patient. A further consideration is that if tort rules do operate in a deterrent fashion, then steps may be taken by potential defendants to guard against being sued which may be out of proportion to what is considered reasonably necessary. The possibility that such disproportionate steps may be taken is often put forward as a reason for not imposing a duty of care. Thus if there is a danger that doctors may engage in 'defensive medicine' this may be a reason for declining to hold that a duty of care exists in particular circumstances. But the concept of defensive practices is not confined to cases of medical malpractice and may extend into other areas such as the exercise of statutory powers by a public authority charged with a responsibility for protecting others (see *X (minors)* v *Bedfordshire County Council* [1995] 3 WLR 152), the police (see *Hill* v *Chief Constable of West Yorkshire* [1988] 2 All ER 238), the Crown Prosecution Service (see *Elguzouli-Daf* v *Metropolitan Police Commissioner* [1995] 1 All ER 833), a coastguard service (see *Skinner* v *Secretary of State for Transport, The Times*, 3 January 1995) or a ship classification society (see *Marc Rich & Co.* v *Bishop Rock Marine Co. Ltd* [1995] 3 All ER 307).

The deterrent effect of tort rules is closely related to the economic efficiency argument that if an activity imposes costs on others, those costs should be reflected in the true cost of the harm causing activity: see Calabresi, *The Cost of Accidents*, 1970, p. 69. For example, on this theory the cost of a car not fitted with seatbelts, or one which is to be driven by a 17-year-old, would have to reflect the increased accident costs associated with the use of such a vehicle. The main difficulty with this theory is that it is often difficult to identify the true cause of an accident. For example, if a collision occurs at a road intersection, is the true cause of the accident the fact that the cars have been driven carelessly, the fact that the traffic lights are not working properly, the fact that the road surface is unduly worn, or the fact that the tyres on one of the vehicles are defective? In each case the answer reveals a different defendant.

The principal problem with rules based on efficiency is that what is an efficient solution is not necessarily a fair solution. For example, the person whom an economist might regard as being in the best position to avoid the risk of a particular loss might be the accident victim himself.

Fairness or justice is seen by lawyers as the main reason for the existence of tort rules. The notion of justice takes a number of different forms. For example, there is a rights-based justice under which the plaintiff is entitled to protection against unjustifiable interferences with his civil rights. Prime examples of such tortious rules are those which protect against battery, assault and false imprisonment.

A second notion of justice is based on a balance of competing interests such as those of neighbouring landowners, best represented by the rule in *Rylands* v *Fletcher* (1868) LR 3 HL and the tort of private nuisance. Both torts seek to achieve a fair balance between competing ownership rights; private nuisance, in particular, is said to be based on the notion of give and take. What is important is whether the defendant's use of his land is reasonable, having regard to matters such as the locality in which the nuisance is caused, the duration of the nuisance, whether the plaintiff's land use is unduly sensitive and, in so far as remedies are concerned, whether the defendant's activity is socially useful.

Perhaps the most important notion of justice in tort law is that of needs or compensation based justice. Where a plaintiff is injured as a result of the defendant's tort, there is a primary need that the harm he has suffered should be adequately compensated. It is here that the tort of negligence plays a partial role, although there are other methods of compensation. It is generally accepted that victims of modern social conditions should not be left to bear all the costs. Thus in addition to liability rules under which most of the costs are borne by insurance, there are public compensation schemes to deal with matters such as invalidity payments, sickness benefit and other forms of social security payment. The principal issue has become not who is to blame for a particular variety of harm, but who is in the best position to pay for the consequences of that harm? Instead of simply shifting losses from the plaintiff to the wrong-doing defendant, modern tort law and its accompaniments work on the basis of loss spreading. This notion is well reflected in modern tortious rules on vicarious liability and product liability under which it has been recognised that employers and producers are in a unique position to be able to spread the cost of accidents by charging higher prices for the products they produce or the services they provide or by other cost cutting measures within their own businesses, combined with the secure knowledge that relevant insurance will cover any award of damages which might be ordered.

QUESTION 4

The trouble with English tort law is that it fails to provide sufficient protection to each citizen's inalienable right to bodily integrity and freedom from interference.

Discuss.

Commentary

This question centres upon the limits of the torts of assault, battery, intimidation and the rule in *Wilkinson* v *Downton*. It also considers the stringent 'property' test for the right to sue in private nuisance, reasserted by the House of Lords in *Hunter* v *Canary Wharf*.

Suggested Answer

For a long time, there has been a recognition that harassment and pestering of a person fall outside the remit of the recognised intentional torts against the person. This recognition has been coupled with an almost equally consistent rejection of the existence of harassment as a discrete tort in English law (*Kaye* v *Robertson* [1991] FSR 62; *Patel* v *Patel* [1988] 2 FLR 179). The only window of opportunity for the emergence of such a tort came with the Court of Appeal's decision in *Khorasandjian* v *Bush* [1993] 3 All ER 669. But very shortly after *Khorasandjian* had given birth to the potential for such a tort to develop, the House of Lords, in *Hunter* v *Canary Wharf* [1997] 2 All ER 426, closed any such avenue to the inferior courts. In *Hunter* it was held that, so far as suits for harassing conduct were concerned, the only basis upon which they may be mounted was in the law of private nuisance which, in turn, required that the plaintiff should have a proprietary interest in the premises in which the harassment took place.

It is also clear that nuisance is not alone in restricting the number of citizens to whom protection from non-tangible interferences is afforded. To begin with, assault is said to depend upon the direct infliction of a reasonable apprehension of a battery (*Thomas* v *NUM* [1986] Ch 20). This, of course, means that if the defendant's wrongdoing consists of persistent abusive telephone calls (as in *Khorasandjian*) then it would not be possible for the plaintiff to allege that he or she was reasonably fearful of the immediate infliction of a battery, as he or she must (*Cole* v *Turner* (1704) 6 Mod 149). It was for this reason that, in *Thomas*, the plaintiff, who was on a coach and behind a police cordon, failed to make out reasonable fear of an impending battery. It is the absence of any prospect of violation of the plaintiff's physical integrity which dictates that assault fails to cover a clear interference.

Similarly, the tort known as the rule in *Wilkinson* v *Downton* insists that the defendant must have 'wilfully done an act calculated to cause harm to the plaintiff' (*Wilkinson* v *Downton* [1897] 2 QB 57). This fails to cover cases in which harm is indirectly inflicted where the defendant occasions the plaintiff harm through good intentions (albeit according to *Wilkinson* an objective view of the defendant's intention is taken). Imagine that the facts of *Khorasandjian* had been slightly different. For example, if the defendant had intended only to convey words of affection and love, it could be argued that although the effect of the words was to cause considerable distress to the plaintiff, there was a material absence (even on an objective construction) of any 'calculation to cause harm'. The annoyance/harm would, on this argument, be merely incidental to the pleas to the plaintiff to be accepted as her partner. The absence of malice in the conduct complained of would be fatal to any suggestion that the clear wrong done could be brought within the *Wilkinson* v *Downton* principle.

Next, it is important to understand why an action based on intimidation has limits for the purposes set out in the title. Traditionally, intimidation may be invoked only in the context of interference with trade. It is uncertain therefore, whether the courts would be willing to extend its ambit to protect non commercial interests such as the kind of interference we have considered so far. Moreover, intimidation has also been held to depend upon the existence of a 'threat to commit a tort' (*Rookes* v *Barnard* [1964] AC 1129). It has also been held that the threat must be made with the intention of coercing the person to whom it is addressed into doing or refraining from doing something (*Hodges* v *Webb* [1920] 2 Ch 70). On the basis of the hypothetical posited earlier, therefore, an action for intimidation would be unavailable since although serious threats to commit a battery would be relevant, the requisite element of coercion would be absent.

Thus far we have seen that interferences in the nature of harassing conduct fall outside the ambit of all the relevant (that is, non-contact based) intentional torts against the person. Harassment has, however, recently received limited protection under statute. The Protection from Harassment Act 1997 provides for the civil law remedies of damages or an injunction for harassing conduct but only where that conduct has proven injurious effects (either in terms of health or in terms of resulting financial loss (s. 392)). Similarly, one-off incidents are not protected by the Act, for 'harassment', for the purposes of the statute, demands that the conduct complained of should have occurred on at least two occasions (s. 7(3)).

Leaving aside non-tangible forms of harm, we must also consider the limits of the torts of false imprisonment and battery. In relation to the former, it has never been authoritatively settled whether the plaintiff needs to be conscious of the fact of his or her imprisonment in order to be able to sue. The authorities that are directly in point are divided on the matter (compare *Herring* v *Boyle* (1834) 1 Cr M & R 377 and *Meering* v *Graham-White Aviation* (1920) 122 LT 44) and there is only obiter authority from the House of Lords that such knowledge is not required (*Murray* v *MOD* [1988] 2 All ER 521). Technically, then, the matter is still open to resolution at common law. On this basis, it is legitimate to argue that English law does not at present cater adequately for the insane, unconscious or immature plaintiff who is 'wrongly' imprisoned by another.

On the final point — the shortcoming in the law of battery — the matter is again one in which English law flounders in the absence of clear authority. It is this. Where A attempts to strike B but instead strikes C, it is, technically, unresolved whether A commits a battery against C. The problem centres on the fact that while it is clear that battery is an intentional tort (*Stephens* v *Myers* (1830) 4 C & P 349) it is by no means clear whether the intention must relate to the conduct (that is, striking out) or the outcome (in this case, making violent contact with C). Although it is possible that the notion of transferred intent which exists in the criminal law may be adapted to fit the tortious counterpart of a criminal assault (that is, a tortious battery), on present authorities English law is uncertain in the extent to which it would protect C in the hypothetical case advanced.

3   Trespass to the Person

INTRODUCTION

Trespass to the person is perhaps one of the oldest torts and illustrates the relationship between the law of tort and the criminal law. This is so especially since many of the wrongs which amount to a trespass to the person also amount to the commission of a crime. Because of the close relationship with the criminal law these torts require proof of a hostile intention and are also actionable *per se*; that is, there is no need for the plaintiff to prove that damage has been suffered. Instead, it is sufficient that the defendant has infringed the plaintiff's interest in bodily integrity, However, the fact that there has been no damage may be relevant in determining what remedy is given. The interest primarily protected by the torts of battery, assault and false imprisonment is the right of the individual to bodily integrity. As such these are 'civil liberties' torts and have lost a lot of their importance due to the rise of the tort of negligence in the field of accident compensation. The three questions which follow cover a range of issues arising out of all three of the torts amounting to trespass to the person.

QUESTION 1

Harry, a 20-year-old young man of dishevelled appearance, is passing the time of day with his friend Terry, both sharing a bottle of cooking sherry.

Gino, an Italian businessman, accompanied by his 15-year-old daughter, Bella, passes by on the other side of the street and makes derogatory comments on Harry's and Terry's appearance. Harry moves towards Gino in a menacing manner, shouting obscenities, but is unable to cross the road due to the volume of traffic.

Gino returns ten minutes later, carrying a pickaxe handle. Gino flails at Harry, but misses and strikes Terry instead, rendering him unconscious. Harry, fearing for his own safety, strikes Gino over the head with his bottle of sherry and a splinter of glass from the bottle badly cuts Bella who runs home. Harry then locks the unconscious Gino in a nearby shed in which there is an open skylight. David, a witness to these events, grabs Harry by the neck and restrains him by means of a stranglehold until PC Plod arrives who then takes Harry to the local police station. PC Plod arranges for Terry to be taken to hospital. In a semi-conscious state, Terry makes amorous advances involving contact towards Sarah, a nurse. Subsequently, Terry slips and falls heavily on his head. Doctor John decides that emergency surgery is necessary, entailing a blood transfusion, to which Terry would have objected on religious grounds, had he been conscious.

Bella is taken to hospital by her mother, Sophia. Dr John advises Sophia that it would be wise for Bella to have an X-ray of her head taken. Bella objects, but Sophia informs Dr John to ignore her daughter's objections. Accordingly, Dr John arranges for the X-ray to be taken.

Advise all the parties of their rights and liabilities.

Commentary

The principal issues raised by this question relate to the torts of assault, battery and false imprisonment. Answers should consider:

(a) do abusive words amount to an assault?

(b) in order to amount to an assault must a threat be capable of being carried out?

(c)   what are the ingredients of self-defence?

(d)   can a person be falsely imprisoned without his knowledge?

(e)   in what circumstances is medical battery committed?

Suggested Answer

Gino v *Harry*

Harry's threatening attitude towards Gino requires a consideration of what constitutes an assault, which is defined as an act which causes another person to apprehend the infliction of immediate, unlawful, force on his person (*Collins* v *Wilcock* [1984] 3 All ER 374)).

Harry utters threatening words. Dicta in the cases can both support and refute any suggestion that words alone cannot constitute an assault (*Meade's case* (1823) 1 Lew CC 184) (no assault); *R* v *Wilson* [1955] 1 WLR 493 (assault)). What is clear is that where there are words accompanied by a threatening act or gesture, as in the question, there can be an assault (*Read* v *Coker* (1853) 13 CB 850).

Even if words alone are capable of amounting to an assault, there remains the problem that there cannot be an assault unless the threat is immediate and gives rise to a reasonable apprehension of the infliction of a battery. Thus a threat, no matter how violent, cannot be an assault if the plaintiff does not fear for his own safety because he is sitting safely on board a moving bus (*Thomas* v *NUM (South Wales Area)* [1986] Ch 20). This case also emphasised the requirement that an imminent battery must be reasonably apprehended. The volume of traffic on the road dividing Harry from Gino may suggest that there is no reason to fear.

Subsequently, Gino returns with a weapon. It is unlikely that Gino can successfully plead self-defence as the use of an offensive weapon is probably out of proportion to the threat posed by a sherry bottle in the hands of two abusive delinquents (*Cockcroft* v *Smith* (1705) 11 Mod 43). The fact that Gino comes prepared to respond does not affect his position (*Beckford* v *R* [1988] AC 130) provided it is reasonable for him to act in the way he does. But since Gino was at liberty to leave, is impossible to argue that he has acted reasonably in self-defence.

There remain the issues of consent and public policy, which are relevant to the actions by Gino and Harry against each other. It has been said that in the case of an ordinary fight with fists, none of the participants will be permitted an action for damages on the ground that they all consent to their injuries (*Lane* v *Holloway* [1968] 1 QB 379). Moreover, where the plaintiff's husband and the defendant are participants to an affray in which the former is killed by the latter, it seems that the deceased will not be able to sue if he 'gets more than he bargained for' because he may be taken to have assumed the risk of injury or death or because it would be contrary to public policy to allow a successful action for damages (*Murphy* v *Culhane* [1977] QB 94). However, if the plaintiff's conduct is trivial and the defendant's conduct is totally out of proportion the defences referred to will not be available (*Lane* v *Holloway* [1968] 1 QB 379; *Barnes* v *Nayer*, *The Times*, 19 December 1986). Gino and Harry appear to be of roughly similar standing which might suggest that both may be denied damages on public policy grounds. Moreover, despite the fact that it was disputed whether the defence of contributory negligence applied to the tort of trespass prior to the enactment of the Law Reform (Contributory Negligence) Act 1945, it has been held in *Barnes* v *Nayer* that a plaintiff's contributory negligence can amount to fault for the purposes of the 1945 Act.

Harry/Terry v *Gino*

Gino's actions may constitute assault and battery if they do not fall within the defences considered above. A battery is the actual infliction of unlawful force on another person (*Collins* v *Wilcock* [1984] 3 All ER 374, 377). Assault has been defined above and it would be fair to assume that Harry may reasonably apprehend the infliction of a battery when faced with an irate person flailing a pickaxe handle.

Terry, in fact, receives the blow, but if he does not see it coming there can be no assault. However, there is a battery, provided Gino's act is hostile in the sense explained by Lord Goff in *F* v *West Berkshire Health Authority* [1989] 2 All ER 545, that there should be a touching to which the plaintiff can reasonably object. The problem in the question is one of intention. Gino intends to hit Harry, but in fact strikes Terry. It is important to remember that for trespass, the intention should relate to the act rather than to the consequences of the act. But there still remains the undecided issue whether English tort law recognises the notion of transferred intent. This concept is recognised in English criminal law (*R* v *Latimer* (1886) 17 QBD 359) and in the civil law of the USA, but there is no direct authority for the purposes of tort law, save for the indecisive and old decision in *Scott* v *Shepherd* (1773) 2 Bl R 892 (which is equally an authority on negligence) and dicta in the Northern Irish case, *Livingstone* v *Ministry of Defence* [1984] NI 356. But it seems logical that if Gino intends to strike Harry he should also be liable in damages for the infringement of Terry's civil liberties.

Finally, there is the issue of self-defence. Gino's position in this regard has been considered above, but Harry's response to the threat posed by Gino must be considered. Striking someone with a bottle is a battery, but in the light of the threat posed by a person wielding a pickaxe handle, the use of a bottle may be regarded as proportionate under the rule in *Cockcroft* v *Smith* (1705) 11 Mod 43 and although he lands his blow first, he may still be taken to have acted reasonably (*Dale* v *Wood* (1822) 7 Moore CP 33).

Gino may also complain that he has been falsely imprisoned by Harry. False imprisonment is defined as the unlawful restraint of a person against his will (*Meering* v *Grahame-White Aviation* (1920) 122 LT 44). Two main issues arise. First, can a person be falsely imprisoned when he is unconscious, and therefore unaware of the act of the defendant? On this issue, the authorities are divided, although the better view is that a person is not to be denied the right of suit in such cases (*Meering* v *Grahame-White Aviation* (1920) 122 LT 44; *Murray* v *Ministry of Defence* [1988] 2 All ER 521), but the unawareness may result in an award of nominal damages only (*Murray* v *Ministry of Defence* [1988] 2 All ER 521). To the contrary, there is also authority which suggests that a person cannot be falsely imprisoned if unaware of the restraint (*Herring* v *Boyle* (1834) 1 Cr M & R 377), but this case can be explained on the ground that the restraint was not complete. This may be an issue here since there is an open window in the shed through which Gino might be able to escape, depending on its height and accessibility (*Bird* v *Jones* (1845) 7 QB 742).

Harry v *David*

Applying a stranglehold is capable of amounting to a battery, and if it constitutes an 'unlawful imposition of constraint on another's freedom of movement from a particular place' (*Collins* v *Wilcock* [1984] 3 All ER 374), it is a false imprisonment. The circumstances suggest that David does this by way of a citizen's arrest and a trespass is only actionable if unlawful. The Police and Criminal Evidence Act 1984 (PACE) excuses a private individual who makes an arrest when an arrestable offence has been committed (PACE, s. 24). An assault on an individual is an arrestable offence and it is clear that an offence has been committed. Under PACE, s. 28 the person arrested must be told the reason for his arrest, either at the time, or as soon as practicable thereafter. If the arrest is made by a person who is not a constable, as here, the common law rule is that the arrested person does not have to be informed of the reason for his arrest if the circumstances make the reason obvious (*Christie* v *Leachinsky* [1947] AC 573). Once the arrest is complete, the arrested person must be taken before a magistrate or to a police officer as soon as is reasonably possible (*John Lewis & Co. Ltd* v *Tims* [1952] AC 676). All of these requirements seem to be satisfied with the result that David probably has not committed a tort.

Sarah v *Terry*

Terry's amorous advance raises the issue of hostility. Battery (since there is contact) was defined in *Cole* v *Turner*, above, as the least touching of another in anger. An amorous advance is probably not done 'in anger', but this is not the real issue. The mental element has been defined in terms of hostility (*Wilson* v *Pringle*), above which is taken to mean that the touching should be either something which is not acceptable in the ordinary conduct of daily life (*Collins* v *Wilcock*) or that to which the defendant realises the plaintiff can reasonably object. On either basis, Sarah has a legitimate complaint.

We are told that Terry's acts are carried out in a state of semi-consciousness. Battery depends on intent; therefore, it seems reasonable to suppose that a person who does not appreciate what he is doing cannot be held liable.

Terry v *Dr John*

Whatever Dr John does for Terry, he cannot be sure that Terry would have consented, since Terry is in an unconscious state. Prima facie, Dr John commits a battery within the definition given above, but he has acted in an emergency. One response is to say that his actions are not hostile in the sense that he has done something which is acceptable in the ordinary conduct of daily life (*Collins* v *Wilcock*) and that, on an objective basis, Terry cannot reasonably object to what has been done in order to save his life (*Wilson* v *Pringle* [1986] 2 All ER 440). But the hostility test has been criticised, especially in the context of medical trespass where the courts prefer to approach the issue on the basis of necessity, asking what is in the best interests of the patient (*F* v *West Berkshire Health Authority* [1989] 2 All ER 545). What determines whether the doctor has acted in such a way is general medical practice, i.e., what would other reasonable doctors in the same position have done. Moreover, there is also a presumption in favour of the preservation of life, which justifies the application of the necessity principle in the public interest (*Re T (Adult: refusal of medical treatment)* [1992] 4 All ER 649).

In *F* v *West Berkshire Health Authority*, Lord Goff was of the opinion that if unconsciousness is temporary, a doctor may not proceed contrary to the stated interests of the patient so long as the patient is rationally capable of expressing a wish. Conversely, there may be circumstances in which an operation may be necessary in order to save life, ensure improvement or to prevent physical or mental deterioration. Since the operation on Terry is considered to be essential, given the fact that he has fallen heavily on his head, the medical necessity exception would seem to apply unless Dr John can be taken to have been aware of Terry's objection to receiving blood other than his own. However, on the facts, there is nothing to suggest that Dr John is aware of Terry's religious objections, in which case, his actions will probably be justified and excused.

Bella v Harry

Although Harry probably did not intend to injure Bella, she may still argue that the intent which Harry had towards Gino was such that she may maintain an action for battery. It has been seen above in relation to Gino's blow which inadvertently strikes Terry that it may be the case that there is a doctrine of transferred intent (*Scott* v *Shepherd*; *Livingstone* v *Ministry of Defence*). On this basis, the intent which Harry has towards Gino may be considered to have been transferred to Bella, with the result that her injuries may be regarded as having been caused intentionally by Harry. Moreover, it has always been the law that a person may be guilty of a battery where he intends the act, but does not intend to cause injury (*Wilson* v *Pringle*). On this basis, although Harry may not have intended to strike or injure Bella, the intent he appears to have had towards Gino may suffice for the purposes of any action brought by Bella, subject to whether or not Harry is able to successfully plead that he was acting proportionately in self-defence.

Bella v Dr John

An important consideration in medical battery cases is whether or not the patient consented to the medical procedure about which a complaint may have been made. If the plaintiff consents to the defendant's actions, there can be no battery. The problem which arises so far as Bella is concerned is that she, personally, objects to the X-ray, but her mother, Sophia, does not, and Dr John prefers to override Bella's own wishes. This raises the question of whether, at the age of 15, Bella is capable of consenting or refusing to consent to a medical procedure. If Bella had been aged 16, she would be considered, in law, to have the capacity to give or withhold consent (Family Law Reform Act 1969, s. 8(1)). However, being aged only 15, this provision will provide no assistance and her status remains that of a child. Normally, in the case of child patients, someone else such as a parent, guardian, local authority or court will be able to give or withhold consent on the child's behalf. However, since *Gillick* v *West Norfolk & Wisbech Area Health Authority* [1986] AC 112, the courts have adopted a test based on the understanding of the child patient. In *Gillick* itself, a girl under the age of 16 was given contraceptive advice without the consent of her parents. However, since, at the age of 15, she was considered to have a sufficient maturity and understanding of the nature of the treatment she was to receive, her own wishes could prevail over those of her parents. Under this test, provided Bella was of sufficient maturity to understand what is involved in having an X-ray taken, her refusal to give consent is something which Dr John should have taken account of. In this case, Dr John would have been better advised to ignore Sophia's consent on behalf of Bella. However, where it is in the patient's interests for a doctor to act, it may be possible for a refusal to give consent to be overriden. For example, in *Re R (a minor)* [1991] 4 All ER 177, a 15-year-old girl who suffered phases of disturbed behaviour had refused sedative treatment. Subsequently wardship proceedings were commenced by a local authority. The Court of Appeal considered that a court has wider powers than a parent and can override a withholding of consent if this is in the patient's best interests, thereby seemingly undermining the *Gillick* principle of self-determination. (See also *Re Y (Mental patient: bone marrow donation)* [1997] 2 WLR 556.) However, the injury to Bella might not appear to present a serious threat to Bella's life, in which case the proposed X-ray might not be regarded as a procedure in respect of which a court would choose to override the patient's wishes.

QUESTION 2

Jocky, a keen darts player, was practising his darts' techniques in the Dog and Duck public house. One of his darts strikes the wire on the board, ricochets and penetrates Eric's foot. Eric shouts at Jocky, 'You swine, you did that on purpose, I'll see you outside in two minutes'. Fearing the worst, Sid, the owner of the Dog and Duck, grabs Eric by the shirt collar and frog-marches him to his office. Eric resists violently, aims a punch at Sid, but misses. Sid manages to calm Eric and persuades him to remain in the office in order to avoid further trouble. Having left the office, Sid asks two burly friends, Peter and Phil, to ensure that Eric does not leave the ground floor room. Four hours later, Sid calls the police.

Commentary

This question again covers elements of the three torts amounting to trespass to the person. The principal issues for consideration include:

(a)   the requirement of hostile intention and the relationship between trespass and negligence;

(b)   whether words alone can amount to an assault;

(c)   the requirements for a lawful arrest so as to negative liability for false imprisonment.

Suggested Answer

Eric v *Jocky*

Jocky's dart accidentally penetrates Eric's foot. It would be difficult to say that he has intended to make contact with Eric, in which case an action for battery would be unlikely to succeed. Battery is defined as the unlawful hostile and intentional application of direct force to the person which is undesired by the plaintiff. The element of intention seems to be lacking. What Jocky has done is similar to the unintentional firing of the gun in *Stanley* v *Powell* [1891] 1 QB 86 which was said not to support a right of action in trespass or the unintentional act of driving over the plaintiff's legs in *Letang* v *Cooper* [1965] 1 QB 232.

An alternative action might lie in negligence. Presumably any other reasonably proximate user of the public house can expect Jocky to take reasonable care when throwing his darts. Problems may arise over the issue of breach of duty. The degree of probability that harm might be caused could be said to be small, which would be material in assessing the appropriate standard of care (*Bolton* v *Stone* [1951] AC 850). Moreover, the fact that these events take place in a public house where the game of darts is frequently played might suggest a reduced standard of care similar to that in other cases involving spectators at sporting events (*Wooldridge* v *Sumner* [1963] 2 QB 43; *Murray* v *Harringay Arena* [1951] 2 KB 529). The danger here may not be as obvious as it was in those cases (respectively a photographer on a show jumping course and a spectator at an ice-hockey match). Since darts do not tend to rebound very far, it may be that Eric is standing too close to the board, in which case, any damages he receives may be reduced on the ground of contributory negligence. The relevant tests are whether Eric has taken reasonable care for his own safety and whether his actions contribute to the damage he has suffered (*Jones* v *Livox Quarries* [1952] 2 QB 608).

Jocky v *Eric*

Jocky may decide to sue Eric for assault, but he is unlikely to get very far. An assault is defined as a threat which gives rise to a reasonable apprehension of the impending infliction of a battery. Eric shouts abuse at Jocky, calling him a swine and threatens to see him outside in two minutes. Words alone may not amount to an assault, there being contradictory dicta going both ways (*Meade's case* (1823) 1 Lew CC 184 (no assault); *R* v *Wilson* [1955] 1 WLR 493 (assault)). In any case, the words used by Eric do not disclose an immediate threat as he is indicating that he wishes to speak with Jocky in two minutes time. It is clear that the language used by the threatener will have to be examined to determine whether his words contain an immediate threat of violence. Sometimes the words used may negate the threatening nature of the rest of the defendant's language (*Turbervell* v *Savadge* (1669) 1 Mod Rep 3). Moreover, before anything can be done to carry out the threat, Sid intervenes to prevent any unnecessary violence. A threat, no matter how violent, cannot be an assault if the plaintiff does not fear for his own safety (*Thomas* v *NUM (South Wales Area)* [1986] Ch 20). Accordingly, if Eric is safely in Sid's office there seems little for Jocky to fear.

Sid v *Eric*

In the course of resisting violently, Eric aims a punch at Sid, but misses. The fact that there is no contact means that there cannot be a battery, but there is, once more, the possibility of an assault since a violent punch is likely to cause Sid to fear, quite reasonably, for his own safety.

Eric v *Sid*

In taking hold of Eric and frog-marching him into his office, *prima facie*, Sid commits a battery and by detaining Eric in the office, he commits the tort of false imprisonment. The latter is defined as the unlawful restraint of the person so that the person restrained is not at liberty to go where he pleases (*Meering* v *Grahame-White Aviation* (1919) 122 LT 44).

In order to amount to a false imprisonment, the restraint must be total (*Bird* v *Jones* (1845) 7 QB 742). This raises the question whether there is any means of leaving the office. The question states that the office is on the ground floor, in which case there may be an open window through which Eric can escape. On the other hand, being an office, the window may have been secured. On the facts, Eric does not know that if he tries to leave the office, he will be prevented from doing so by Peter and Phil. It must be considered whether a plaintiff must be aware of the restraint in order for a tort to be committed. On one view, the plaintiff must be aware of the restraint (*Herring* v *Boyle* (1834) 149 ER 1126), but on another view awareness is not relevant to initial liability (*Meering* v *Grahame-White Aviation*) but it is relevant to the quantum of damages in that lack of awareness will normally mean that only nominal damages are awarded (*Murray* v *Minister of Defence* [1988] 1 WLR 692) except in cases of gross unconstitutional misconduct. This analysis suggests that the basic elements of false imprisonment are made out, but the other important element is that the arrest must be unlawful.

Under the Police and Criminal Evidence Act 1984, s. 24(5) anyone can arrest a person where an arrestable offence has been committed and that person has reason to believe the person arrested has committed that offence. It would appear that all of these requirements have been satisfied. However, in the case of a citizen's arrest, the arrestee must be taken before a magistrate or given over to a police officer as soon as is reasonably possible (*John Lewis & Co. Ltd* v *Tims* [1952] AC 676) and the person arrested must be informed of the grounds for his arrest unless this is immediately obvious (*Christie* v *Leachinsky* [1947] AC 573). The four-hour delay before the police are called seems to be excessive and there is no indication that Eric has been informed of the grounds for his arrest. This may well mean that the tort of false imprisonment has been committed.

QUESTION 3

During a party at Fred's house, Barney, a house guest and known prankster, jumped from the doorway in a darkened corridor, with a sheet over his head just as Wilma, another guest, was passing. Wilma fainted through fear. Barney carried her into a room and left her there to recover. Fred saw Barney leave the room and, fearing that someone might tamper with his valuable collection of bowling balls in that room, locked the door.

One hour later, Barney went to see if Wilma had recovered, but found the door locked. Barney asked Fred for the key, having explained what had happened. Fred said he was too busy, but that he would open the door later on.

Thirty minutes later Fred and Barney went to the room to find Wilma asleep. Barney shook her. Wilma awoke and, believing she was being attacked, struck out at Barney. Barney ducked and the blow struck Fred.

Advise Wilma of her rights and liabilities in tort.

Commentary

This question centres on the constituent elements of the intentional torts relating to trespass to the person: the rule in *Wilkinson* v *Downton* [1897] 2 QB 57; assault; battery; and false imprisonment. More particularly, it requires an examination of:

(a)   directly inflicted harm;

(b)   the requisite intent;

(c)   the doctrine of transferred intent;

(d)   self-defence.

Wilma v *Barney*

The general principle is that for the defendant's conduct to amount to trespass to the person, it must have been a direct and intentional act of interference (*Letang* v *Cooper* [1965] 1 QB 232, CA; *Wilson* v *Pringle* [1986] 2 All ER 440, CA). Professor Rogers has expressed the view that the net result of these cases has been the disappearance of actions for unintentional trespass (Rogers, *Winfield and Jolowicz on Tort* (London: Sweet & Maxwell, 1994) at p. 77).

The issue that arises out of Barney's prank of jumping out and scaring Wilma so that she faints is whether this constitutes the direct infliction of damage. Assault has been defined as an act which causes another to apprehend the infliction of immediate, unlawful force on his person, while 'battery' is the actual infliction of force (*Collins* v *Wilcock* [1984] 3 All ER 374). Assuming that there was no physical contact with Wilma so that battery has not been committed by Barney, the question remains whether an action will lie for assault. This is doubtful given that although Barney's act was intentional in so far as he intended to jump out with a sheet over his head, the harm suffered was an indirect consequence of his act (*Reynolds* v *Clarke* (1725) 1 Str 634, at 636). However, if it can be established that Barney's prank was in fact calculated to cause harm to Wilma, an action may lie under the rule in *Wilkinson* v *Downton* [1897] 2 QB 57 even though more harm resulted than was intended (*Janvier* v *Sweeney* [1919] 2 KB 316). At its crux, liability under the rule is contingent upon the intention to cause harm and it may well be the case that Barney was merely engaging in well intentioned horseplay so as to contribute to the party atmosphere.

If, on the other hand, there was some physical contact between them, no matter how trivial, Wilma may have an action for battery. In *Cole* v *Turner* (1704) 6 Mod 149, Holt CJ said that 'the least touching of another in anger is a battery'. The Court of Appeal in *Wilson* v *Pringle* [1986] 2 All ER 440, held that for an action in battery to succeed, the 'touching must be proved to be hostile touching'. The requirement of hostility, and more particularly its meaning, has generated controversy. Professor Jones argues that battery is not limited to overtly hostile acts. He cites by way of example the position of a surgeon who, motivated by concern for a patient's welfare, carries out an operation without the patient's consent. In such a case the surgeon will nevertheless be liable for battery (*Textbook on Torts* (London: Blackstone Press, 1998), p. 456; see *F* v *West Berkshire Health Authority* [1989] 2 All ER 545). Similarly, a person who pushes another into a swimming pool by way of a joke would also be liable for battery (*Williams* v *Humphrey, The Times*, 20 February 1975). Lord Goff has questioned whether there is any requirement that the physical contact must be hostile. In *F* v *West Berkshire Health Authority* he stated that a prank that gets out of hand, or an over-friendly slap on the back, could amount to battery even though they are not hostile acts. On this basis, Barney could be liable unless he is able to show that the prank was 'generally acceptable in the ordinary conduct of daily life' (*Collins* v *Wilcock*).

Wilma v *Fred*

False imprisonment has been defined as the unlawful imposition of constraint on another's freedom of movement from a particular place so that he is not at liberty to go where he pleases (*Collins* v *Wilcock; Meering* v *Grahame-White Aviation Co. Ltd* (1920) 122 LT 44). Any restriction, in the absence of consent, on a person's right to leave a place will amount to false imprisonment. The restraint must be complete so that if there is a reasonable means of egress there is no imprisonment (*Bird* v *Jones* (1845) 7 QB 742). Further, an occupier of premises may impose reasonable conditions with respect to the manner in which those who use the premises exit from them (*Robinson* v *Balmain Ferry Co. Ltd* [1910] AC 295).

When Fred locks the door he appears to be unaware of Wilma's presence in the room and so false imprisonment is not committed at that time. However, upon being informed of the situation by Barney, his refusal to unlock the door amounts to the false imprisonment of Wilma. Her liberty is restrained within an area delimited by Fred. There is no requirement that Wilma should be aware of her detention so that if she in fact slept through it, an action will nevertheless lie. In *Meering* v *Graham-White Aviation Co. Ltd* Atkin LJ stated that the plaintiff's ignorance of his false imprisonment was irrelevant, so a person could be falsely imprisoned while unconscious or insane or otherwise unaware of his position. A plaintiff who is ignorant that she has been falsely imprisoned will receive nominal damages since no harm would have been suffered (*Murray* v *Ministry of Defence* [1988] 2 All ER 521). Accordingly, although Wilma will have an action for false imprisonment provided her restraint was total, she is likely to receive only nominal damages.

Fred v *Wilma*

Fred, who was struck by Wilma when Barney ducked, may have an action for battery against her. Whether or not this is an intentional act which caused direct damage is clearly a material issue. In *Scott* v *Shepherd* (1773) 2 B1 R 892, the defendant threw a lighted firework into a crowded market house. It landed on a stall and the stallholder instinctively picked it up and threw it further which resulted in it exploding in front of the plaintiff. It was held that the defendant was liable for trespass on the basis that the plaintiff's injuries were the direct result of his act of throwing the firework, and the stallholder's instinctive act of throwing it on did not break the chain of causation. The analogy here lies with the criminal law doctrine of transferred intent which has, in fact, been applied in civil proceedings (*James* v *Campbell* (1832) 5 C & P 372; *Livingstone* v *Ministry of Defence* [1984] NI 356). It would therefore seem that Wilma's act does amount to battery. The defence of self-defence may be available to her if she can show that her mistaken belief of being attacked was based on reasonable grounds and her reaction was proportionate (*Albert* v *Lavin* [1981] 1 All ER 628; *Lane* v *Holloway* [1968] 1 QB 379).

4 Negligence

INTRODUCTION

Modern tort law is dominated by the tort of negligence. The principal requirements of the tort are that the defendant should owe the plaintiff a duty of care, that there should be a breach of that duty and that breach of duty should cause actionable damage to the plaintiff which is not too remote. The duty issue is primarily based on the notion of reasonable foresight of harm to the plaintiff. However, since negligence as a tort has strayed from its original objective in compensating negligently inflicted personal injury and property damage other factors have become relevant. In particular, due to attempts to use negligence in relation to economic losses, the courts have had to develop policy driven control devices to ensure that the tort does not run out of control into areas it was never intended to enter.

The breach of duty issue involves an objective consideration of what a reasonable man in the same position as the defendant would have done. Thus it is necessary to ask if the defendant has reached the standards set by a reasonable man.

The defendant who has failed to reach the standard of the reasonable man is not necessarily liable for harm suffered by the plaintiff since his breach of duty must also have caused that harm, both factually and legally. Since the burden of proving all elements in the negligence process, there is every chance of failure at some stage.

In addition to the elements of the tort of negligence, it is also important to consider possible defences which may wholly or partly excuse the defendant. Thus it is relevant to consider whether the plaintiff was contributorily negligent, whether the plaintiff has assented to the risk of injury and whether it would be contrary to public policy to allow the plaintiff to succeed.

PART 1: DUTY OF CARE

(1)   General principles

QUESTION 1

... [T]he only necessary function performed by the duty of care concept in the present law is to deal with those cases where liability is denied not because of a lack of foreseeability, but for reasons of legal policy ...

(Winfield & Jolowicz on Tort.)

Discuss.

Commentary

This question raises the question whether reasonable foresight alone is a satisfactory test for determining when a duty of care is owed or whether policy issues also play a part. Key issues which should be considered are:

(a)   the basis on which *Donoghue* v *Stevenson* was decided;

(b)   the relationship between the elements of reasonable foresight of harm, proximity of relationship, policy and justice;

(c)   the meaning of policy and the range of factors which may influence a decision on the duty issue for reasons of policy;

(d)   how policy considerations affect different types of negligence action in different ways.

Suggested Answer

This question is concerned with the requirements for the establishment of a duty of care in the tort of negligence. In particular, it requires discussion of the extent to which the criteria for the existence of a duty situation have changed since the time prior to *Donoghue* v *Stevenson* [1932] AC 562 when duty situations were identified by reference to the relationship between the parties and were limited in number (e.g., occupier/visitor, doctor/patient, employer/employee). Since that time, the tort of negligence has undergone substantial periods of change and the role of policy has become crucial in identifying when a duty of care is owed. Moreover, the application of *Donoghue* v *Stevenson* principles appears to have become somewhat capricious.

Donoghue v *Stevenson* established the principle that a defendant owes a plaintiff a duty of care if there is a relationship of neighbourhood in the sense that the plaintiff can be reasonably foreseen as likely to be affected by the defendant's act or omission. What this test does is to identify the person to whom a duty of care may be owed, but it says little about when or in what circumstances the duty is owed. A test based on reasonable foresight does not help as it omits essentials and takes into account non-essential issues (*Yuen Kun Yeu* v *Attorney General of Hong Kong* [1988] AC 175). Instead, the modern approach requires an incremental development of the duty issue by reference to or by analogy with established categories of recognised duty situation (*Sutherland Shire Council* v *Hayman* (1985) 60 ALR 1). Although in Australia, where this test was first set out, there appears to have been some degree of departure from the incremental approach, at least regarding the position of builders (see *Bryan* v *Moloney* (1995) 128 ALR 163).

The main considerations in a duty enquiry, following *Yuen Kun Yeu* and *Caparo plc* v *Dickman* [1990] 2 AC 605, are reasonable foresight of harm, proximity of relationship, policy considerations and whether it is just and reasonable to hold that the defendant owes the plaintiff a duty of care. Moreover, in appropriate cases, particularly those which fall within the general scope of the rule in *Hedley Byrne & Co. Ltd* v *Heller & Partners Ltd* [1964] AC 465 concerning economic loss caused as a result of the provision of negligent advice, it has become apparent that an additional consideration is whether the defendant has voluntarily undertaken a responsibility towards the plaintiff for the accuracy of the advice given (see *Spring* v *Guardian Assurance plc* [1994] 3 All ER 129; *Henderson* v *Merrett Syndicates Ltd* [1994] 3 All ER 506; *White* v *Jones* [1995] 1 All ER 691).

These criteria form part of a composite test based on the necessary relationship between the parties (*Yuen Kun Yeu*, above) and it must be appreciated that they all inter-relate. For example, what is foreseeable depends on issues of policy, justice and proximity. But what is a proximate relationship depends on the other criteria and so on. For this reason, Lord Wilberforce in *Anns* v *Merton LBC* [1978] AC 728 was wrong in separating the issues of foresight of harm and policy in his two-stage test.

The question refers to the fact that the existence of a particular relationship alone is not conclusive. This raises the issue of proximity. For example,

Donoghue v *Stevenson* shows that there is a sufficient relationship of proximity between a manufacturer and a consumer in respect of physical harm caused by a negligently produced article. But the fact that such a relationship exists is inconclusive if the consumer suffers economic loss (*Muirhead* v *Industrial Tank Specialties* [1986] QB 507; *Murphy* v *Brentwood DC* [1991] 1 AC 378). This is because the length of the chain of distribution is so long that it would be unreasonable to hold the defendant liable when the plaintiff has a more direct claim against his retail supplier.

In truth, as the question suggests, the real issue is one of policy, namely, is it right that the law should impose a duty of care in the particular circumstances of the case? The main policy issues are, first, the floodgates argument, secondly, should Parliament legislate, thirdly, has Parliament already legislated, fourthly, what practical effects might the imposition of a duty of care have and finally, should the plaintiff do something other than sue the defendant in tort?

The floodgates argument raises two issues. First, would the establishment of a duty situation raise the spectre of a large number of, possibly, unwarranted claims? This was probably at issue in *Alcock* v *Chief Constable of South Yorkshire Police* [1992] 1 AC 310 in relation to psychiatric harm. In respect of this kind of harm there has been a past fear of the 'gold-digging claimant', but this should be met by the requirement that a medically identifiable psychiatric illness has been suffered. But there is also the issue of how many people may recover in respect of negligently inflicted psychiatric damage. This was answered in *Alcock* by allowing any person with a close and caring relationship with the victim of the defendant's negligence to sue, if he/she was present at the scene of the accident or came upon its immediate aftermath (See also *White* v *Chief Constable of South Yorkshire Police* discussed below in question 2). This serves to cut out more remote plaintiffs such as those who read of an accident in a newspaper, or are told of it by friends. But arguably, this goes too far by preventing any person not at the scene of the accident from recovering at all, which could cause injustice in exceptional cases. These cases would have been met by the more flexible reasonable foresight test applied by Lords Bridge and Scarman in *McLoughlin* v *O'Brian* [1983] AC 410. (See also the proposals of the Law Commission, *Liability for Psychiatric Illness* (Law Com No. 249, 1998) which recommends that the requirement of spatial and temporal proximity should be dispensed with.) Apparently, the same issues do not arise in psychiatric damage cases where the plaintiff is a 'primary' victim in the sense that he is personally placed in fear for his own safety as a result of the defendant's negligence (*Page* v *Smith* [1995] 2 All ER 736) as opposed to the situation in *Alcock* and *McLoughlin* in which the defendant's negligence exposed a 'secondary' victim such as a close relative of the plaintiff to the risk of injury. However, it is arguable that there are cases in which the number of 'primary' victims may be substantial.

The floodgates issue is also pertinent in many economic loss claims, especially where negligent advice is concerned, since words spread more widely than actions. Any number of people may hear and act on advice given by the defendant. Accordingly, it is important to consider why the advice was prepared and communicated and who can reasonably be expected to rely on it. Thus in *Caparo* v *Dickman* advice prepared by an auditor could have been relied on by anyone who read the public document in which it was contained. But the advice was only intended for consumption by the company to which the report was directed. It was not intended that potential investors should take account of the contents of the document, even though many such people might choose to consult it. In contrast, the advice prepared in *Morgan Crucible* v *Hill Samuel Bank* [1991] 1 All ER 142 was specifically directed at inducing the plaintiff to make an investment, so that he was owed a duty of care by the advice giver.

The issues of prospective or actual Parliamentary intervention are usually related to matters of consumer protection, which may impinge on the general issue of freedom of contract. Here the court may be disinclined to restrict that freedom by imposing a tortious duty of care. Moreover, if Parliament has already acted, the courts may be disinclined to impose a common law duty which goes further. This seems to have been a motivating factor in *Murphy* v *Brentwood DC* where the Defective Premises Act 1972 was thought to be the appropriate route, despite the fact that it is so narrow in scope as to be almost useless!

There is the question whether the plaintiff should proceed in some way other than via the tort of negligence. Often the plaintiff may sue for a breach of contract or may be expected to insure himself against the risk of loss created by the defendant. If this is so, there should be no duty of care. This may be the case where economic loss is caused by a defective product. Also in cases of negligence by builders, there may be a clear expectation that the building owner should be covered by insurance in respect of risks created by a sub-contractor (*Norwich City Council* v *Harvey* [1989] 1 All ER 1180). In some instances, the plaintiff, himself, may be expected to guard against the risk of harm rather than the defendant. For example, it would be unreasonable to impose a duty of care on the Civil Aviation Authority to ensure that the owner of an aeroplane has properly maintained the aircraft, since the proper role of the CAA is to protect the public rather than to protect individuals from their own failures (*Philcox* v *Civil Aviation Authority, The Times*, 8 June 1995).

A related matter to consider is whether there exists already an alternative remedy, in which case, it might not be appropriate to impose a duty of care. For example, particularly in the case of alleged negligence on the part of a public body or official, there may be an existing remedy in the form of judicial review (*Rowling* v *Takaro Properties Ltd* [1988] 1 All ER 163) or the prescribed means of enforcement of the duty alleged to have been broken may be a complaint to the Secretary of State (*Clunis* v *Camden and Islington Health Authority* [1998] 3 All ER 180). There may also be some other source of compensation such as claim against the Criminal Injuries Compensation Scheme (*Hill* v *Chief Constable of West Yorkshire Police* [1989] AC 53). Similar considerations also apply where there exists an action for breach of contract, even in circumstances where the contractual defendant may not be the same person as the plaintiff could have sued in tort (*Banque Financière de la Cité* v *Westgate Insurance Ltd* [1988] 2 Lloyd's Rep 513).

Policy is also overtly relevant when the courts consider the practical effect of a decision to impose a duty of care. For example, if an advocate were to owe a duty of care in respect of his conduct of litigation, this might result in endless numbers of cases being retried at the instance of dissatisfied litigants (*Rondel* v *Worsley* [1969] 1 AC 191). Similarly, if an advocate's advice culminates in a settlement which requires the approval of the court, otherwise in the absence of the immunity, the judge might be forced to explain what he had said or done (*Kelley* v *Corston* [1997] 4 All ER 466). Likewise if the police were to owe a duty of care in respect of their conduct of an investigation, this might serve to introduce defensive practices which, in the long run, might slow down the investigation process (*Hill* v *Chief Constable of West Yorkshire Police* [1989] AC 53; *W* v *Essex County Council* [1998] 3 All ER 111). Similar considerations also seem to apply to child protection agencies (*X (minors)* v *Bedfordshire County Council* [1995] 3 WLR 152; *W* v *Essex County Council* (above)), the Crown Prosecution Service (*Elguzouli-Daf* v *Metropolitan Police Commissioner* [1995] 1 All ER 833), coastguards (*OLL Ltd* v *Secretary of State for Transport* [1997] 3 All ER 897) and ship classification societies (*Marc Rich & Co.* v *Bishop Rock Marine Co. Ltd* [1995] 3 All ER 307). However, the fear of possible defensive practices by rescue services such as a fire brigade is not sufficiently great to grant them immunity, in circumstances in which a responsible officer has done some act which has the effect of increasing the risk of damage to the plaintiff's premises (*Capital and Counties plc* v *Hampshire County Council* [1997] 2 All ER 865). What sets this last case apart from most of the others is that where there is a public policy immunity it is because some new or different danger has arisen other than that which the protected body is required to guard against. It is sometimes difficult to see why the possibility that a defendant might engage in defensive practices should justify a decision to the effect that no duty of care is owed. For example, in *Spring* v *Guardian Assurance plc* [1994] 3 All ER 129 Lord Woolf appeared to have some difficulty in accepting the argument in the context of an action for negligence arising out of the activity of giving an employment reference.

In summary, policy considerations feature strongly in determining whether a duty of care is owed and the simple fact of a particular type of relationship is not conclusive. This is because regard must be had to the kind of harm suffered and the way it was caused. The use of a criterion of reasonable foresight of harm on its own, in some cases, might create the danger of indeterminate liability. Thus, while it has been said that physical injury is almost always foreseeable (*Alcock* v *Chief Constable of South Yorkshire Police* [1992] 1 AC 310 *per* Lord Ackner), it has also been observed that the relevant considerations such as foreseeability and proximity are merely convenient labels (*Caparo plc* v *Dickman* [1990] 2 AC 605 *per* Lord Oliver) and that what is foreseeable harm may, at times, be a matter prone to manipulation. While the courts may be disinclined to take on the role of legislators, they do have to take steps to keep the tort of negligence within reasonable bounds and it is the use of policy considerations which allows them to do this.

(2)   Psychiatric harm

QUESTION 2

Don, the driver of a stock car, negligently fails to maintain his vehicle. In the course of a race, which is being televised, Don's brakes fail and his car crashes into a crowd of spectators. The car narrowly misses Albert but strikes and kills Bob and his daughter Claire. Bob's son, Eric, is very badly injured, but survives and is taken to hospital. Albert, a person of unusually nervous disposition, develops an anxiety neurosis.

Freda, a friend of Bob and his wife Glenda, is present at the scene of the accident. After tending to Bob, Claire and Eric, but realising that Bob and Claire are dead and that Eric is being dealt with by professionals, she rushes back to tell Glenda what has happened. Some time later, Glenda, who is also Claire's and Eric's stepmother of six months' standing, drives to the hospital, asks to see her deceased husband (Bob) and stepdaughter (Claire). Glenda also sees Eric on a hospital trolley, awaiting treatment and in a badly disfigured state.

Harriet, Bob's mother, sees a live television broadcast of the events, recognises her son in the crowd and realises that Don's car has crashed into the area where her son is standing.

Freda, Glenda and Harriet all feel a sense of revulsion at what has happened. Both Freda and Glenda suffer from reactive depression. Harriet helps to tend to Glenda's and Eric's needs following the accident and becomes a recluse because of her inability to come to terms with the psychological suffering of Glenda and the physical injuries suffered by Eric.

Advise Albert, Freda, Glenda and Harriet.

Commentary

This question involves a discussion of the principles which determine when a person owes a duty of care to another in respect of negligently inflicted psychiatric harm. The major issues for consideration are:

(a)   has the plaintiff suffered legally recognisable psychiatric harm?

(b)   is the relationship between the various plaintiffs and the victims of the defendant's negligent act sufficiently close?

(c)   is the plaintiff proximate in terms of time and space to the scene of the accident?

(d)   how was the psychiatric damage caused?

(e)   What duty, if any, is owed to a rescuer?

The law used to answer this question is that which stood at the beginning of 1998. However, in March 1998, the Law Commission published its final report on *Liability for Psychiatric Illness* (Law Com No. 249) which proposes the abolition of those common law rules which relate to the case where the defendant negligently kills, injures or imperils the primary victim, and the plaintiff (the secondary victim) can establish:

(a)   sufficient proximity in terms of the closeness of the tie of love and affection between the primary and secondary victims;

(b)   the closeness of the secondary victim in time and space to the scene of the accident; and

(c)   that the psychiatric illness suffered is shock induced.

Outside of these cases, common law rules would continue to apply, with the result that there would still be the same requirement that the plaintiff should have suffered an identifiable and reasonably foreseeable psychiatric illness. Existing common law rules which apply where the plaintiff is in the foreseeable area of risk of physical injury or where the plaintiff reasonably fears that he or she is in danger will continue to apply, as will the rules which presently apply to rescuers and mere bystanders.

What is proposed is that, in relation to the category of plaintiffs identified above, the duty of care will be based on the reasonable foreseeability of the psychiatric illness suffered, unaffected by considerations of spatial or temporal proximity. The duty would be restricted to a fixed group of people deemed to have a sufficiently close tie of love and affection to be owed the duty of care. These would include spouse, parents, children, siblings and cohabitants of at least two years' standing. It would also be sufficient if the close tie exists either at the time of the accident or at the time of the onset of the psychiatric illness. Moreover, the Law Commission proposals would also render it unnecessary to consider the manner in which the shock was caused. However, in order to place limits on the scope of the duty, a court would have the power to decide that no duty is owed on the grounds of justice and reasonableness, for example where the plaintiff's conduct is illegal or contrary to public policy, or that the plaintiff has voluntarily accepted the risk created by the defendant's act or omission.

Suggested Answer

Since candidates are informed that Don is negligent in maintaining his vehicle, there is no need to consider the issues of duty and breach of duty in respect of the harm to Bob, Claire and Eric. Assuming the deaths of Bob and Claire and the injuries to Eric are caused by Don's negligence and that harm is not too remote, Don will be liable in damages to both Eric and Glenda, the latter representing the estate of each of the deceased and, being a dependant, thereby being able to recover damages, respectively, under the Law Reform (Miscellaneous Provisions) Act 1934 and the Fatal Accidents Act 1976.

When considering the issue of psychiatric damage, it is important to be able to identify the types of harm which may form the basis of an action for negligence. Not every form of mental suffering will be sufficient to establish a duty situation. It is a requirement of English law that the plaintiff should have suffered an identifiable psychiatric illness. It is now well established that mere grief, sorrow or upset are normal human emotions in respect of which no duty of care is owed (*McLoughlin* v *O'Brian* [1983] AC 410; *Attia* v *British Gas* [1988] QB 304; *Reilly* v *Merseyside Regional Health Authority* [1995] 6 Med LR 246). Moreover, the mere fact that a person actually involved in a road traffic accident feels 'shocked and shaken up' will not be sufficient to reveal a duty situation (*Nicholls* v *Rushton, The Times*, 19 June 1992). It is expected that people should possess sufficient fortitude or 'phlegm' to be able to overcome the normal distress at witnessing an accident (*Bourhill* v *Young* [1943] AC 92). On this basis, it seems likely that the sense of revulsion felt by Freda, Glenda and Harriet will be insufficient to reveal a duty situation.

Actions for negligently caused psychiatric harm fall into one of two groups. First, there are those cases in which the plaintiff fears for his own safety as a result of what the defendant has done, and in consequence suffers psychiatric harm (*Dulieu* v *White* [1901] 2 KB 609). This would appear to cover Albert, although there is the added complication that he is a person of unusually nervous disposition. Albert has suffered an anxiety neurosis, which is a recognised form of psychiatric illness (*Chadwick* v *British Transport Commission* [1967] 2 All ER 945). Moreover, the reason for this is that Don's car has narrowly missed him, and it is reasonable to assume that this neurosis has arisen out of a fear for his own safety. For these purposes, it is not a requirement that Albert should have suffered personal injury himself, so long as it is foreseeable that physical injury might be suffered. Thus in *Page* v *Smith* [1996] AC 155 (applied in *Young* v *Charles Church (Southern) Ltd, The Times*, 1 May 1997 where the plaintiff was some six feet away from a colleague who was killed instantly by falling scaffolding but cf. *Hunter* v *British Coal Corporation* [1998] 2 All ER 97) a primary victim in a road traffic accident was physically unhurt in the collision, but nonetheless developed symptoms of ME (myalgic enencephalomyelitis) from which he had suffered some 20 years earlier, but from which he was in remission at the time of the accident. The relevant test applied in the House of Lords was to ask whether it was foreseeable to the defendant that his conduct would expose the plaintiff to a risk of personal injury, whether physical or psychiatric. If the answer to that question was in the affirmative, it was regarded as irrelevant that the plaintiff did not suffer physical injury or that such injury as there was due to the plaintiff's 'eggshell personality', since the defendant was required to take the plaintiff as he found him. However, where the plaintiff has an 'eggshell skull' personality, the quantum of damages he receives may be reduced to take account of the fact that the plaintiff might have suffered the illness complained of despite the defendant's negligent act (*Page* v *Smith (No. 2)* [1996] 1 WLR 855). Assuming it is reasonably foreseeable that a spectator at a race track might suffer a psychiatric illness as a result of the imminent fear of personal injury, then Albert ought to be regarded as a person to whom Don owes a duty of care. In contrast with the position of secondary victims, considered below, the present state of the law places the primary victim of the defendant's negligence in the same position whether the injury he suffers is physical or psychiatric harm.

The second group of cases involves negligence on the part of the defendant which results in injury to one person with whom the plaintiff, who suffers psychiatric harm, has a caring relationship. As such, this group of plaintiffs may be described as secondary victims of the defendant's negligence and are treated somewhat differently.

Until recently, the leading authority on the question of damages for nervous shock, or psychiatric harm as it is better referred to, was the House of Lords' decision in *McLoughlin* v *O'Brian* [1983] AC 410, but what that case decided was far from clear. Two distinct lines of reasoning were discernible, although, on the facts, they led to the same result. The first of these lines of reasoning, represented by the judgment of Lord Wilberforce, adopted an apparently rigid policy-based approach to the duty issue in respect of negligently inflicted psychiatric harm. The factors considered relevant were, first, the closeness of the relationship between the victim of the defendant's negligent act and the plaintiff who suffered psychiatric damage as a result of witnessing the accident. Secondly, it was considered necessary that the plaintiff should be proximate to the scene of the accident in both time and space, subject to the 'aftermath' exception, on which *McLoughlin* itself was actually decided. The alternative approach, epitomised by the judgment of Lord Bridge, was based on the principle of reasonable foresight of harm, qualified by the policy considerations regarded as relevant by Lord Wilberforce, but not applied quite so rigidly.

Since the decision in *McLoughlin* the whole issue of liability for negligently caused psychiatric harm has been reconsidered by the House of Lords, following the Hillsborough tragedy, in *Alcock* v *Chief Constable of South Yorkshire Police* [1992] 1 AC 310. In *Alcock*, Lord Wilberforce's judgment in *McLoughlin* was taken to represent the ratio of that case, but differences in approach can be identified. While the Wilberforce judgment in *McLoughlin* required, as a starting point, a close relationship of proximity between the victim and the plaintiff, the House of Lords in *Alcock* were prepared to treat the issue of standing to sue as one based on the simple principle of reasonable foresight of harm. Lord Wilberforce's approach in *McLoughlin* seemed to suggest that proximity of relationship was confined to close family ties, primarily, but not exclusively, husband and wife and parent and child. Conversely, in *Alcock* it was admitted that other relationships such as brother/ sister, uncle/nephew, fiancé/fiancée or merely close friends will suffice, provided the plaintiff can prove to the satisfaction of the court that the close, caring bond exists between the two of them.

On this basis, Glenda, as a wife and stepmother of six months' standing may have begun to develop the required bond. Her feelings for Bob are likely to be undeniable and, assuming a close relationship with both Claire and Eric, proximity may be established. Harriet, as Bob's mother, is also likely to be regarded as a foreseeable plaintiff, although the means by which her psychiatric harm is caused may create difficulties. Freda is merely a friend of both Bob and Glenda, and as such she is unlikely to be able to establish the close and caring relationship required by *Alcock* unless her friendship is particularly close. It is more than likely that they will be required to demonstrate 'customary phlegm' and be able to withstand such horrors (*Bourhill* v *Young* [1943] AC 92). Moreover, the Court of Appeal has also held that a mere bystander at the scene of the Piper Alpha disaster, one of the most horrific conflagrations in modern history, was not sufficiently proximate to the defendant to be a foreseeable plaintiff on the basis that he was not in the immediate area of risk, nor was he a rescuer, nor did he reasonably believe that he was in danger and the defendant could not reasonably foresee that he would be in danger (*McFarlane* v *EE Caledonia* [1994] 2 All ER 1). In contrast, there are dicta in *Alcock* which suggest that even a bystander at the scene of a particularly horrific accident may be a foreseeable plaintiff. It seems that the answer to the question whether a mere bystander is owed a duty of care lies in asking whether the plaintiff did genuinely fear that he was in danger, but that if his fear is unreasonable, no duty of care will be owed (*Hegarty* v *EE Caledonia Ltd* [1997] 2 Lloyd's Rep 259).

The fact that Freda has suffered from reactive depression satisfies the requirement of identifiable psychiatric illness and provided a reasonable man of 'ordinary phlegm' would have suffered in the same way, she may be regarded as a person having standing to sue. But the question still remains whether she reasonably entertains a fear for her own safety. The facts of the question state that she is at the scene of the accident, but do not inform whether she is so close as to reasonably fear for her own safety. If she is, then she may be owed a duty of care, but the fact that she escapes unscathed might suggest that any fear of personal danger may be unfounded. Certainly, if a person is not, in fact, in danger, but nonetheless believes that she is, it might not be too difficult to conclude that the fear is an irrational one which the defendant should not have foreseen.

Assuming the proximity of relationship is sufficiently close, both *McLoughlin* and *Alcock* require the witness to be proximate to the accident in terms of both time and space; that is, the witness must be at the scene of the accident when it happens and must witness the events with his or her own senses.

Since Freda also stays to tend to the needs of Bob, Claire and Eric, she may be regarded as a rescuer, to whom a duty of care may be owed. For policy reasons, the courts have developed a more understanding attitude to rescuers than seems to be displayed to members of the family of the deceased on the basis that altruistic acts of rescue should be encouraged. Accordingly, it has been held that a duty of care is owed to a private individual (*Chadwick* v *British Transport Commission* [1967] 1 WLR 912) in respect of psychiatric illnesses suffered as a result of witnessing the consequences of an accident caused by the negligence of the defendant. However, it must be appreciated that *Chadwick* was decided before the control devices introduced by Lord Wilberforce in *McLoughlin* and refined by the House of Lords in *Alcock* had been put in place. The position regarding rescuers generally has to be considered in the light of the decision of the House of Lords in *White* v *Chief Constable of South Yorkshire Police* (as yet unreported, judgments delivered 3 December 1998; See http://www.parliament.the-stationery-office.co.uk/ pa/ld199899/ldjudgmt/jd9) in which the Court of Appeal decision in *Frost* v *Chief Constable of South Yorkshire Police* [1997] 3 WLR 1194 was reversed. In *White* a number of serving police officers who were present at the scene of the 'Hillsborough Tragedy' sought to recover damages in respect of psychiatric illnesses suffered by them as a result of their employer's alleged negligence, but failed. The appeals required consideration of whether the employer owed a duty of care to his employees not to send them to work in an environment which unreasonably exposed them to the risk of psychiatric harm. Alternatively, there was an argument based upon the vicarious liability of the employer for the negligent acts of a senior police officer who allowed a large crowd of spectators to enter an already over-crowded area of the football ground. Finally, it was also asserted by the respondents that they were rescuers and that, as such, they were 'primary' victims of the appellants' negligence and that the question of the appellants' liability for negligently-inflicted psychiatric harm turned on the simple question of whether the damage was reasonably foreseeable, unlimited by the policy considerations which apply to 'secondary' victims such as mere bystanders. In the event, it was decided by a bare majority of the House of Lords that the employers' appeal should be allowed and that the police officers' argument that they were owed a duty of care should fail.

In Freda's case, there is no suggestion that she is suing her employer. Indeed, the question states that she is a friend of the victims of the accident caused by

Don's negligent driving. In this case, the outcome of any action brought by Freda will turn on how the House of Lords in *White* decided the issue on the matter of the duty of care owed to a rescuer. In the first place, it was accepted that professional rescuers could not be regarded as a special category, to which different rules might apply. The basis of the position regarding rescuers, generally, was also considered. Although *Chadwick* v *British Transport Commission* was decided on the basis that Mr Chadwick's state of mind was caused by the 'horror of the whole experience' rather than by virtue of the fact that there was 'an element of personal danger' in what he had done, for a rescuer to succeed, he must have exposed himself to danger or reasonably believe that he had done so. Accordingly, in *White* since there was no evidence that any of the police officers considered themselves to be in any sort of personal danger, no liability would attach. On this analysis Freda comes upon the scene of an accident after it has happened but does not appear to stay long since she realises that two of her friends are dead and that another is being tended to by professionals. This would all seem to suggest that she has not faced any personal danger nor be in a position to reasonably apprehend danger to herself. It would seem to follow from this that unlike *Chadwick* where the plaintiff entered a wrecked railway carriage which might have collapsed upon him, Freda will have no basis upon which to sue as a rescuer. As Lord Steyn observes, without a restrictive rule of this kind, a 'ghoulishly curious spectator who assisted in some peripheral way' might stand to recover. What underlies the majority decision in *White* is that if a rescuer is in danger or reasonably considers himself to be in danger then the justification for holding that a duty of care is owed to him is that he is a primary victim by being in the range of foreseeable physical injury to which the rule in *Page* v *Smith* applies. In other cases, the rescuer becomes a secondary victim, to which the control devices enunciated in *Alcock* v *Chief Constable of South Yorkshire Police* apply.

Glenda was not at the scene of the accident when it happened, but after having been told of the incident she drives to the hospital where she observes the consequences of the accident. Generally, third party communication will not be sufficient to establish the existence of a duty of care (*Hambrook* v *Stokes Bros* [1925] 1 KB 141). This view is further emphasised by the overruling by the Court of Appeal of the lower court decisions in *Hevican* v *Ruane* [1992] 2 All ER 470 (note) and *Ravenscroft* v *Rederiaktiebolaget Transatlantic* [1991] 3 All ER 73 (see now [1992] 2 All ER 470 (note)) in both of which the plaintiff had been informed of the accident by a third party. However, it may be that the person communicating the news has done so in a distressing way, so as to render themselves personally liable rather than the defendant who causes the accident (see *AB* v *Tameside & Glossop Health Authority* [1997] 8 Med LR 91).

However, there is nothing in the facts of the question which suggests that Freda has been particularly insensitive in the way she has communicated the news to Glenda.

In *McLoughlin* v *O'Brian* it was accepted that a person who came upon the immediate aftermath of an accident would be sufficiently proximate to be able to sue. In that case, the plaintiff came upon the aftermath some two hours after the accident had occurred. What constitutes the aftermath is difficult to say. While two hours is a sufficiently short time to be immediate, a time lapse of eight hours in *Alcock* and one of five hours in *Chester* v *Waverley Municipal Council* (1939) 62 CLR 1 was considered too great. In *Alcock* in particular, what was considered relevant was that the relatives had turned up at a mortuary in order to identify the bodies of their loved ones. While Lord Ackner was prepared to regard this as part of the 'aftermath' of the accident, it was not part of the *immediate aftermath*. Moreover, Lord Jauncey opined that if a person is going to identify a body, this is not the same as attendance at the aftermath of an accident for the purpose of providing comfort and care to a person who may still be alive. Provided Glenda arrives at the hospital reasonably soon after the incident at the race track, and does so with a view to providing comfort and care, it would appear that she should be able to recover damages in respect of the reactive depression she suffers. However, it should be observed that there is a world of difference between a person who knows that a loved one is dead and has arrived merely to identify the body and a person who turns up to view bodies in the hope that a loved one is not one of the bodies on show (see Handford, 'Compensation for Psychiatric Injury: The Limits of Liability' (1995) 2 *Psychiatry, Psychology and Law* 37). On the facts, it seems to be the case that Glenda is already aware that Bob is dead, but she is able to provide her stepson, Eric, with care and compassion. It may be that she will be owed no duty of care in respect of the death of her husband, or of Eric, unless it can be shown that she has arrived within a sufficiently short space of time to be included in the 'immediate aftermath' doctrine.

Harriet is not present at the scene of the accident, but she does observe the events at the race track on a live television broadcast. In *Alcock* it was emphasised that it is also necessary to look at the means by which the shock is caused. In that case, it was considered relevant that the police were aware that the football match was being televised, but they were also aware of a code of ethics which forbade the showing of pictures of suffering by identifiable individuals, so that no duty of care was owed to a person who witnessed events through the medium of television. This would seem to suggest that Harriet would not have a claim. Moreover, in the light of the fact that she only feels a sense of revulsion at what she sees, she has not suffered an identifiable psychiatric illness at this stage.

Subsequently, Harriet becomes a recluse as a result of having to tend to the needs of her surviving relatives. This too is unlikely to reveal a cause of action since in *Alcock* it was said that shock involves the sudden appreciation by sight or sound of a horrifying event which violently agitates the mind. Shock does not include psychiatric illness caused by the accumulation over a period of time of more gradual assaults on the nervous system. To date, the general view is that the subsequent witnessing of a distressing condition suffered by a loved one will not be a sufficient ground on which to establish the existence of a duty of care. Thus in *Sion* v *Hampstead Health Authority* [1994] 5 Med LR 170 a claim for damages for psychiatric harm failed where the parents of a boy injured in a motor cycle accident witnessed the boy deteriorating in health, suffering a heart attack, fall into a coma and subsequently die as a result of the alleged negligence of hospital staff. In the event, the claim was struck out on the ground that the psychiatric harm was not 'shock induced'. The only exception to this rule appears to be in cases in which the initial accident and the subsequent suffering can be regarded as a single event (see *Churchill* v *Motor Accidents Insurance Bureau* (unreported, 2 December 1993, Supreme Court of Tasmania)).

QUESTION 3

Andy arranges to meet his girlfriend, Sarah, at the Roxy cinema. While he is daydreaming and thinking of the delights to come that evening, Andy steps into the road and is struck by a car driven at excessive speed by Charlie, a 15-year-old joy rider. Andy is seriously injured.

Sarah visits Andy in hospital as soon as she hears of the accident, six hours after the incident. Sarah is extremely upset and depressed after observing Andy's facial injuries.

Diana, a 9-year-old passenger in the car driven by Charlie, is crushed against the dashboard of the car and is seriously injured. Diana was not wearing a seatbelt at the time of the accident. Advise Charlie of his potential tortious liability.

Commentary

This question raises the issues of duty of care, especially in respect of injuries to other road users and psychiatric damage, breach of duty, contributory negligence and the public policy defence of *ex turpi causa non oritur actio*. In particular, issues which require consideration are:

(a)   what standard of care can be expected of a 15-year-old driver?

(b)   is there evidence of contributory negligence and what rules attach to this defence?

(c)   how do the restrictive rules on who can recover damages for psychiatric harm affect Sarah?

(d)   is Diana's involvement in the joy-riding incident sufficient to disentitle her to an award of damages under the principle *ex turpi causa non oritur actio*, or is the defence of contributory negligence more appropriate?

Regard should also be had to the changes in the law relating to liability for negligently caused psychiatric damage proposed by the Law Commission and referred to in the commentary on question 2 in this chapter. The most important proposal so far as Sarah is concerned is that, assuming there is legislation to give effect to the Law Commission proposals, there would be no need for Sarah to be present at the scene of the accident, providing it is foreseeable that she might suffer clinical depression as a result of seeing Andy's injuries.

Suggested Answer

Andy v *Charlie*

Before considering the question of duty of care, there is the practical problem that Charlie is only 15, and is driving a car stolen from someone else. This raises the problem that Charlie will be uninsured and the owner of the car is unlikely to be liable, since he has not permitted Charlie to drive. In practical terms this means that if Charlie is held to be negligent, he will have to pay out of his own pocket (unless the injuries are covered by the Motor Insurers' Bureau agreement with the Department of Transport, in respect of uninsured drivers) and it is unlikely that a 15-year-old will have the resources to do this.

Charlie as a road user owes a duty of care to anyone who also uses the road (*Nettleship* v *Weston* [1971] 2 QB 691). This includes pedestrians such as Andy. In order to succeed, Andy will have to show that Charlie was in breach of that duty. The test to apply is to ask what a reasonable man would do or would not do in the circumstances (*Blyth* v *Birmingham Waterworks Co.* (1856) 11 Ex

781). The standard to apply is that of the average, reasonable driver (*Nettleship v Weston*) and the fact that he is young and inexperienced will make no difference (*Wilsher v Essex Area Health Authority* [1987] QB 730).

There appear to be no difficult issues in respect of the breach problem since the harm suffered is probable and foreseeable. There are no apparent issues relating to the precautions necessary, the utility of Charlie's actions or the magnitude of harm. But there is the problem of contributory negligence.

Under the Law Reform (Contributory Negligence) Act 1945, contributory negligence is a partial defence where the plaintiff has failed to take reasonable care for his own safety, thereby contributing to the damage suffered, but there is no need for the plaintiff to owe the defendant a duty of care (*Harvey v O'Dell* [1958] 2 QB 78). Contributory negligence requires fault on the part of both Andy and Charlie. Andy's fault requires consideration of two issues. First, is it foreseeable that Andy's actions might increase the risk of injury? The test applied here is the *Blyth* reasonable man test, namely has Andy failed to take reasonable care for his own safety (*Jones v Livox Quarries* [1952] 2 QB 608)? Daydreaming in the middle of the road, for whatever reason, seems to fulfil this requirement.

The second issue is that of causation as to the harm suffered. It must be asked whether, but for the daydreaming, Andy would have been injured (*Jones v Livox Quarries*). Again, there seems little doubt about this, since a person who was not daydreaming would have stayed on the pavement. This, of course, assumes that Andy was in the road and that the car did not mount the pavement. In this latter event, the fact that he is not watching what he is doing in a safe place, will make no difference. Charlie will remain liable as the means of inflicting damage is something against which no reasonable precaution could be taken.

The third issue in contributory negligence cases is the matter of apportionment of damages. This is based on issues of causation of damage and blame-worthiness. The former will normally result in a 50/50 split, but if the blameworthiness of Andy is small, as seems to be the case, even if he is in the road, a much lower deduction of, say 10 per cent is more likely under the Law Reform (Contributory Negligence) Act 1945, s. 1(1).

Sarah v Charlie

Sarah is upset and suffers depression at the sight of Andy's injuries. This raises the issue of psychiatric damage. First, it must be established whether the depression she suffers from is a medically recognisable psychiatric illness (*McLoughlin* v *O'Brian* [1983] AC 410) which does appear to be the case if there is clinical depression. The mere fact that she is upset will not suffice. The second problem concerns her relationship with Andy. In *Alcock* v *Chief Constable of South Yorkshire Police* [1992] 1 AC 310 the House of Lords held that a person may sue provided a close caring relationship between the plaintiff and the victim of the defendant's negligence can be proved or presumed to exist. This may include fiancées.

In *Alcock* it was held that the plaintiff must be at the scene of the accident when it happens or must come upon its immediate aftermath. Since Sarah was not at the scene of the accident, but only visits Andy in hospital the following morning, it must be decided if she is present at the immediate aftermath. In *McLoughlin* v *O'Brian* a period of two hours was short enough to come within the aftermath principle, but in *Chester* v *Waverley Municipal Council* (1939) 62 CLR 1, a six hour delay before the victim's body was found was considered too long. So also in *Alcock*, visits by relatives of the victims of the Hillsborough tragedy to a mortuary, some eight to nine hours after the initial accident, where bodies were known to be present was considered to be too long a period to fall within the definition of the 'immediate aftermath'. The reference in the question to 'the following morning' suggests a very long time, in which Andy has probably been cleaned up and is sitting comfortably in a hospital bed, so that Sarah has probably come too late to fall within the rule.

Diana v *Charlie*

Since Diana is a passenger in the car, she is owed a duty of care in the same way as any other road user (*Nettleship* v *Weston*). Since this is a road traffic accident, the defence of *volenti*, even if its ingredients were satisfied, is ruled out statutorily where the vehicle must be compulsorily insured against third party risks (Road Traffic Act 1988, s. 149(3)).

Diana's involvement in the joy-riding incident may be sufficient to invoke the public policy defence of *ex turpi causa non oritur actio*. In *Pitts* v *Hunt* [1990] 3 All ER 344 the defendant had actively encouraged the defendant to drive in a dangerous manner. On the facts of the problem, there is no similar suggestion that Diana has actively encouraged Charlie — she is simply a passive, but aware, participant. The test applied in *Pitts* v *Hunt* is whether Diana's involvement is such as to prevent the court from being able to identify an appropriate standard of care.

The precise scope of the *ex turpi causa* defence is difficult to ascertain. One view is that the defence amounts to a more or less automatic bar on the recovery of damages where the plaintiff is involved in a joint criminal enterprise with the defendant (*Ashton* v *Turner* [1981] QB 137), but this does seem rather draconian. Alternatively, the less severe test in *Pitts* v *Hunt* requires the court to consider whether it is possible to determine what standard of care should be owed by the defendant to the plaintiff, with the result that if the plaintiff's injuries arise directly, as opposed to incidentally, out of the illegal act, damages should be denied. A third possible approach seems to arise out of the decision in *Tinsley* v *Milligan* [1993] 3 All ER 65 in which emphasis was placed upon the public policy base of the defence and the extent of the court's discretion. According to *Tinsley* it is necessary to weigh the adverse consequences of giving a remedy against the consequences of refusing that remedy. In the circumstances, it may be significant that Diana is only nine years old, since she may be considered too young to appreciate the risks involved and that the *ex turpi causa* defence will not operate against her. Moreover it has been held that in order for the defence to apply, the plaintiff must be aware of the illegality of his or her acts. (See *Chris* v *Camden and Islington Health Authority* [1998] 3 All ER 180). At the age of nine, Diana may not be so aware.

A second issue is whether Diana is contributorily negligent in getting into the car with an unlicensed, uninsured and probably incompetent driver. Diana's age, once again, will be relevant, as the courts are disinclined to hold that a person so young could have foreseen the risk of harm (*Yachuk* v *Oliver Blais* [1949] AC 386). Also, it is relevant to consider causation and foresight of harm. While Diana has not caused the accident by her conduct, she has materially increased the risk of injury by not wearing a seatbelt. A formula stated in *Froome* v *Butcher* [1976] QB 286 suggests a 25 per cent reduction if no injury would have been suffered had the seatbelt been worn, a 15 per cent reduction if the injury would have been less severe had a seatbelt been worn and no reduction at all if the same injury would have been suffered whether or not a seatbelt was worn. Being thrown out of the car suggests at least a 15 per cent if not a 25 per cent reduction in damages, but this is subject to the problem of Diana's age.

(3)   Economic loss

QUESTION 4

Badman Batty, construction contractors, are engaged by Crumbridgeshire County Council to resurface a ten mile stretch of the Crumbridge ring road. Badman Batty hires a surface stripping machine in order to facilitate the work.

Bob, a surveyor engaged by Badman Batty, decides he is capable of using the surface stripping machine but sets the controls in such a way that too deep a cut is made. As a result of this, the machine severs a water main and the road and a nearby power generator are flooded. The following parties claim damages for negligence:

(a) Peter, a businessman, who was driving on the ring road at the time of the incident, claims he has been prevented from attending a meeting at which he had high hopes of securing a £500,000 contract with another business;

(b) Power-Green Ltd, the owners of the generator engulfed in water from the severed main, claim in respect of the cost of repairing their damaged generator and the profit they would have made had the generator been operative during the five days it took to effect repairs;

(c) Plasticraft Ltd, the owners of a factory on an industrial estate supplied with electricity generated by Power-Green's incapacitated generator, also claim. Plasticraft's operations were interrupted for five days. They point to the fact that they had to dispose of a batch of plastic plates in process at the time of the power interruption. These are valued at £10,000. Moreover, the cost of cleaning congealed plastic from their machines is assessed at £2,500. Plasticraft also claim damages for loss of business profit on operations they could have carried on during the remainder of the five day interruption to their power supply.

Advise Badman Batty of their potential liability in tort.

Commentary

This question is concerned with economic loss caused by a negligent act. Generally, the courts have been reluctant to allow an action in this area and have imposed severe restrictions at the duty stage of the enquiry. The question also raises the issue of the vicarious liability of an employer. Relevant considerations are:

(a) who is an employee and who is an independent contractor for the purposes of the doctrine of vicarious liability?

(b) is the employee's act done in the course of his employment?

(c) when is economic loss caused by a negligent act recoverable and what is the relevance of the 'floodgates' argument?

Suggested Answer

Bob's actions result in physical damage to the water main. Generally, the rule in *Donoghue* v *Stevenson* makes it clear that in respect of physical harm, a defendant owes a duty of care to those he can reasonably foresee as likely to be affected by his actions. By using the surface stripping machine to cut too deeply, it seems that Bob has acted in a manner in which the reasonable surveyor would not have acted, thereby establishing a breach of duty, giving rise to liability in negligence so long as the damage suffered by others is not too remote.

Bob acts on behalf of Badman Batty, but it is necessary to decide if he is an employee or an independent contractor. If he is the former, Badman Batty may be vicariously liable for Bob's negligence, if he acts in the course of his employment.

The classic test for determining who is an employee used to be one of control. Thus an employee is a person engaged to obey his employer's orders from time to time, whereas an independent contractor is employed to do work but has a discretion as to the mode and time of doing the relevant work (*Honeywill* v *Stein & Larkin* [1934] 1 KB 191). The difficulty with the control test is that there are now many professional employees whose skill is such that the employer may have little knowledge of how the work is done. This may present a problem so far as Bob is concerned, since the skill of the job of a surveyor may be such that Badman Batty have no detailed knowledge of the type of work he does.

Other distinctions between employees and independent contractors are that employees are engaged under a contract of service whereas an independent contractor is employed under a contract for services. In the former the employer can stipulate not just what has to be done but also the manner in which it is to be done (*Collins* v *Hertfordshire County Council* [1947] KB 598). Moreover, in a contract of service, the employer has a power to select his employees, a power to pay wages and a power to dismiss or suspend. In the case of a contract for services, the contractor is in business on his own account (*Lee Tin Sang* v *Chung Chi-Keung* [1991] 2 WLR 1173). Whether Bob is an employee will depend on the detailed wording of his contract with Badman Batty, which is not revealed in the question. But if Bob's work is done as an integral part of Badman Batty's business it would appear that he is likely to be regarded as an employee (*Stevenson, Jordan & Harrison Ltd* v *MacDonald & Evans* [1952] TLR 101).

On the assumption that Bob is an employee, it must also be asked if he acts in the course of his employment. As a surveyor, he is unlikely to be employed to operate a surface stripping machine. On the other hand, he may have been employed to supervise and give orders to those who do. It would appear that if an employee does an act he is not employed to perform, he may still be held to have acted within the general scope of his employment provided what he does is a method, albeit unauthorised, of performing his ordinary duties (*London County Council* v *Cattermoles (Garages) Ltd* [1953] 1 WLR 997). On the other hand, if Bob is taken to have done an act he was never employed to perform, he might not be acting in the course of his employment (*Iqbal* v *London Transport Executive* (1973) 16 KIR 329). In contrast, there is authority which suggests that acts of employees which benefit the employer's business are acts done in the course of employment even where the act has been prohibited (*Rose* v *Plenty* [1976] 1 WLR 141). Here there is no evidence that Bob has been prohibited from operating the machine and it does appear that he is trying to further his employer's business.

As Peter is unable to secure a lucrative contract he might have hoped to make, he appears to have suffered pure economic loss which is not directly related to the severance of the water main. This raises a serious 'floodgates' problem. In *Ultramares Corporation* v *Touche* (1931) 174 NE 441 it was stated that the law should not guard against liability in an indeterminate amount to an indeterminate class for an indeterminate time. The particular problem with Peter is that any number of other motorists could be affected in the same way, so that there may be an indeterminate class of potential plaintiffs. Because of this the court is likely to conclude that no duty of care is owed to the likes of Peter. To reinforce this view the Court of Appeal in *Spartan Steel & Alloys Ltd* v *Martin & Co. (Contractors) Ltd* [1973] 1 QB 27 has established a 'bright line' rule in respect of pure economic loss caused by the defendant's negligence. While a defendant will be liable for negligently caused physical harm and for economic loss directly consequent on that physical harm, there is no liability for pure economic loss which flows indirectly from a negligent act. The loss of the £500,000 contract must be regarded as falling within this principle and is therefore loss in respect of which no duty of care is owed.

In any event, the loss suffered by Peter is speculative. There is no guarantee that he would have secured the contract, in which case all that can be said is that he has suffered a lost chance. Following the decision of the House of Lords in *Hotson* v *East Berkshire Health Authority* [1987] 2 All ER 909, it remains an open question whether this concept is recognised in the context of a negligence action. In *Hotson* the House of Lords considered that if there was a

75 per cent chance that even with correct diagnosis the plaintiff would have suffered the disability complained of, this was a sufficiently high degree of probability to justify the conclusion that the defendants were not the primary cause of the plaintiff's condition.

In contrast, a slightly different approach was taken in *Maples Group Ltd* v *Simmons & Simmons* [1995] 4 All ER 907 in which the plaintiffs sought to acquire certain businesses belonging to a rival company, but could not do so immediately because of the existence of certain covenants which prevented development of properties owned by those businesses. As a result of the negligence of the defendants, the plaintiffs became liable to the beneficiary of these covenants, but had they been warned of the open-ended nature of the liability to which they had become subject, appropriate warranties might have been given by the vendor. Accordingly, an issue of causation arose which turned upon the hypothetical action of an independent third party. In these circumstances, it was considered that the plaintiff does not have to prove on the balance of probability that the third party would have acted so as to confer the benefit which it is claimed the plaintiff has lost. Instead, it is sufficient to show that he had a substantial chance, as opposed to a purely speculative chance, of being successful. Thus if Peter can show that there was a substantial chance that he would have gained the contract lost because of his late arrival at the meeting, he might be successful. However, this is likely to be very difficult to prove.

Power-Green Ltd have suffered physical damage to their generator. On the assumption that Bob's negligence is something for which Badman Batty are vicariously liable, it is likely that this loss will be regarded as recoverable. The loss of profit arising from the direct damage to the generator also seems to fall within the *Spartan Steel* v *Martin* principle above. It is economic loss which flows directly from physical damage to property owned by Power-Green Ltd and on this basis should be recoverable.

Plasticraft Ltd also suffer physical harm as a result of Bob's negligence in that the plastic plates in process at the time of the interruption to the power supply had to be disposed of. Moreover, the cost of cleaning congealed plastic from their machine will also fall within the general description of physical harm, similar to the additional labour costs incurred in *Muirhead* v *Industrial Tank Specialties Ltd* [1985] 3 All ER 705 when the defendant's negligence caused the failure of a water filtration system used by the plaintiff for storing live lobsters. In addition, any economic loss directly consequent on this physical damage, such as the resale value of the plates in process at the time of the interruption to the electricity supply, will be recoverable (*Spartan Steel & Alloys Ltd* v *Martin (Contractors) Ltd*). However, the loss of general business profits resulting from the inability to continue operations during the total period of interruption to the electricity supply is irrecoverable on the basis that it amounts to indirect economic loss (*Spartan Steel & Alloys Ltd* v *Martin (Contractors) Ltd*). The rule is arbitrary, but does make the limits of the law clear and was said by Lord Denning MR to be based on the policy ground that were such an action to be permitted, there would be no end of claims.

QUESTION 5

In 1979, Constructors Ltd supplied and installed a compression system in a factory owned by Bodgit Ltd A pipe attached to the compressor was damaged by an employee of Constructors Ltd., but the defect was not immediately noticeable as the piping was contained in a protective sleeve. In 1986, Bodgit Ltd sold their factory and stock-in-trade to O'Bottle. At the time of sale, O'Bottle inspected the compressor and noticed cracking in a pipe leading from the equipment, but due to a failure to take care, the cause of the cracking was not identified.

Early in 1990 there was an explosion caused by the rupture of the pipe in which cracking had been discovered in 1986. The explosion totally destroyed the compressor and seriously damaged the rest of the factory. The cost of repairing the factory is assessed at £750,000, but the market value of a similar factory is considered to be £700,000.

At the time of the explosion, the compressor was being used to process a toxic gas, which escaped and severely burned Alice's face. Alice was a production line worker in O'Bottle's factory. Due to inexcusable delay on the part of her solicitors, Doohey, Cheetham & Howe, a writ is not issued until late 1993, when the normal limitation period for personal injury actions has expired. Advise Alice and O'Bottle of any remedies they may have in tort.

Commentary

This question is concerned with the liability of an installer for his defective workmanship, where this results in both economic loss and physical harm. The issue of limitation of actions also requires consideration. The principal issues which need to be dealt with are:

(a)   whether the installation amounts to a defective product under the Consumer Protection Act 1987;

(b)   whether an installer can be a producer for the purposes of the rule in *Donoghue* v *Stevenson*;

(c)   whether the damage is actionable under the rule in *Donoghue* v *Stevenson*;

(d)   how damages in respect of harm to property are assessed;

(e)   how the provisions of the Limitation Act 1980 affect the product liability action, the negligence action in respect of the events leading up to the explosion and whether the court might exercise its discretion to allow the personal injury action to commence out of time.

Suggested Answer

Initially, any defect in the compression system would have been actionable by Bodgit Ltd against Constructors Ltd in accordance with the terms of the contract they made. Failing the presence of any express term, there would have been an implied term to the effect that the goods supplied were merchantable and fit for any purpose made known by the customer to the supplier at the time of contracting. However, the business and stock-in-trade has been sold by Bodgit Ltd to O'Bottle, whose action can lie only in tort, either in an action for common law negligence or, possibly, under the Consumer Protection Act (CPA) 1987.

Under the CPA 1987, s. 2(1), the producer of a defective product is strictly liable for physical harm to the person or to property other than the defective product itself (CPA 1987, s. 5(2)). For the purposes of the Act, a producer does not generally include a mere supplier, unless the user has asked for identification of the producer and the supplier is unable to comply with the request within a reasonable time (CPA 1987, s. 2(3)). This would seem to suggest that Constructors Ltd are not producers for the purposes of the Act. Moreover, the only physical harm to the person and property other than the product itself occurs in 1990, 11 years after the defective product was first put into circulation. Under the Limitation Act 1980, s. 11A(3), no action in respect of a defective product may be brought after the expiry of ten years from the date on which the product was put into circulation. It follows that any action under the CPA will be time barred.

A manufacturer owes a common law duty of care in respect of physical harm to the ultimate user of his product if it reaches the consumer in the form in which it left him and with no reasonable possibility of intermediate examination (*Donoghue* v *Stevenson* [1932] AC 562). For the purposes of the rule, any person who puts a defective product into circulation is a manufacturer and this includes not just suppliers, but also installers of equipment (*Brown* v *Cotterill* (1934) 51 TLR 21) which would cover Constructors Ltd.

The principal difficulty facing O'Bottle in an action for negligence in respect of an alleged defective product is that he will have to show that he has suffered actionable damage. At one stage, it was accepted that if a structure or product was defective so as to create an imminent danger to health, a duty of care might be owed (*Anns* v *Merton London Borough Council* [1978] AC 728). But it has been held subsequently that where a building or product is merely defective, as opposed to being dangerous, the ultimate user suffers only economic loss (*Murphy* v *Brentwood District Council* [1991] 1 AC 378; *D & F Estates Ltd* v *Church Commissioners for England* [1989] AC 177). (But contrast the position in other parts of the common law world after the decision of the Privy Council in *Invercargill City Council* v *Hamlin* [1996] 1 All ER 756.) The decision in *Murphy* in particular makes it clear that economic loss suffered as a result of the mere qualitative defectiveness of a product does not disclose a duty situation. The reasons for this are largely policy based. First, the plaintiff may have an alternative action in contract or may have a legitimate claim against his insurers. In general, English law has set itself against the recovery of pure economic loss through an action for negligence, unless there is evidence of reliance on a negligent misstatement or there is a uniquely close relationship of proximity between the parties. Neither of these exceptions would seem to apply in this case. Since the piping attached to the compressor is defective without, initially, having caused damage elsewhere, relevant damage for the purposes of a negligence action is suffered only when the explosion occurs in early 1990.

In 1990, there is an explosion which damages the factory and the compressor owned by O'Bottle and injures Alice. If the compressor and the defective pipe are treated as a composite single product, the problem of economic loss considered above will arise, and O'Bottle will be unable to pursue Constructors Ltd in an action for negligence. However, it may be possible for the court to regard the pipe and the compressor as separate parts of a complex structure, in which case the damage to the compressor may be regarded as distinct property damage caused by the defective pipe. This complex structure theory was first advanced in *D & F Estates Ltd* v *Church Commissioners for England* [1989] AC 177 as a possible explanation of the decision in *Anns* v *Merton London Borough Council*. However, the theory has proved unworkable, and it is unlikely to be of any assistance to O'Bottle.

The damage to the factory is actionable on proof of a failure to take reasonable care on the part of Constructors Ltd and subject to the operation of rules on contributory negligence and limitation of actions. The defect in the pipe is stated to have been caused by the actions of one of Constructors Ltd's employees. Assuming this amounts to negligence, O'Bottle will be able to recover the loss he has suffered through the damage to his factory. The basic principle which lies behind an award of damages is that of *restitutio in integrum*, that is the plaintiff must be put back into the position he was in before the damage is caused. How damages are assessed may present a problem, since there are two possible rules of assessment. The plaintiff may be able to recover the diminution in market value of the building or he may be able to claim the cost of repairing the damage. Which measure applies is dependent on the plaintiff's intended use. Generally, if the plaintiff uses his land as an economic asset, the appropriate measure of damages will be based on the diminution in its capital value (*Taylor* v *Hepworths Ltd* [1977] 1 WLR 659). However, if the land is required for commercial occupation, as appears to be the case here, the cost of repair or reinstatement is appropriate (*Harbutt's Plasticine Ltd* v *Wayne Tank & Pump Co. Ltd* [1970] 1 QB 447).

Any award of damages which may be made will probably be reduced in accordance with the provisions of the Law Reform (Contributory Negligence) Act 1945 to take into account O'Bottle's contributory negligence in not identifying the cause of the cracking in the pipe attached to the compressor. Contributory negligence consists of a failure, by the plaintiff, to take reasonable care for his own safety (*Jones* v *Livox Quarries Ltd* [1952] 2 QB 608). In determining whether the plaintiff is guilty of contributory negligence it is also necessary to determine the extent to which the plaintiff's failure to take care is a cause of the damage he has suffered (*Jones* v *Livox Quarries Ltd*). In this particular instance, O'Bottle's failure to take care may be more than just causative of the increased damage, but may be, in part, a cause of the accident which results in that damage. In such cases, the courts have been prepared to make substantial reductions in the plaintiff's damages on the basis that his blameworthiness in relation to the harm suffered is substantial. For example, in *Stapeley* v *Gypsum Mines Ltd* [1953] AC 663 the plaintiff's damages were reduced by 80 per cent where he disobeyed safety instructions with the result that the roof of a mine collapsed on him.

Whether O'Bottle's action is defeated by lapse of time depends on the date when damage is said to have been caused since time, for the purposes of a tort action, runs for six years from that date (Limitation Act 1980, s. 2). Since economic loss appears not to be actionable, no damage can be said to have been caused until the date of the explosion (*Nitrigin Eireann Teoranta* v *Inco Alloys Ltd* [1992] 1 All ER 854). This means that if a writ is issued by 1996, the action will be in time. Moreover, it appears not to make any difference that O'Bottle ought to have discovered the cause of the cracking in 1986. This is relevant only to the issue of contributory negligence which applies in relation to the measure of damages awarded rather than in relation to the issue of accrual of a cause of action (*Nitrigin Eireann Teoranta* v *Inco Alloys Ltd*).

Alice is employed by O'Bottle and is injured as a result of the defectiveness of equipment he has acquired via Bodgit Ltd from Constructors Ltd. Her action for damages for personal injuries would lie against Constructors Ltd for their negligence or against O'Bottle under the Employers' Liability (Defective Equipment) Act 1969. If she were to proceed on the latter basis, O'Bottle would be deemed liable for her injuries provided the defect in the equipment is attributable wholly or in part to the fault of a third party (Employers' Liability (Defective Equipment) Act 1969, s. 1(1)). Thus it is still necessary to establish fault on the part of the producer or installer of the equipment.

In the case of personal injury actions, the relevant limitation runs for three years from the date of accrual of the cause of action or for three years from the date when the plaintiff became aware of her injuries or could reasonably have done so (Limitation Act 1980, s. 11(4)). For these purposes, knowledge does not mean that the plaintiff must know with absolute certainty that she has been injured (*Halford* v *Brookes* [1991] 3 All ER 559), but if one is involved in an explosion, it is reasonably certain that one should realise this might be due to the fault of the person who controls the thing which explodes. Alice must also be aware that the injury is attributable to the fault of the defendant (Limitation Act 1980, s. 14(1)(b)) and be aware of the identity of the defendant (Limitation Act 1980, s. 14(1)(c)). Both of these requirements would appear to have been satisfied. However, in any event, it seems likely that the two alternative limitation periods will produce an identical starting date for the running of time, namely, the date of the explosion in 1990. The question states that the normal three year period has expired, but in personal injury cases, the court has a discretion to allow an action for damages to be commenced out of time where it is equitable to do so (Limitation Act 1980, s. 33). A number of guidelines relevant to the exercise of this discretion are given in s. 33(3). These include the degree of prejudice to the plaintiff and the defendant should the discretion be exercised or not, the length of and reasons for the delay, the cogency of the evidence in the light of the delay and the promptness and reasonableness of the plaintiff's action after becoming aware of the cause of action. On the facts, the length of the delay does not appear to be too great, since, on the assumption that Alice's cause of action accrues in 1990, the writ has been issued out of time but still in 1993. Accordingly, the lateness will be a matter of days or weeks rather than years. The sooner the writ is issued the better, but if it is only a matter of days late, this may be a factor which assists the court in exercising its discretion in Alice's favour. (See *Hartley* v *Birmingham City District Council* [1992] 2 All ER 213 — one day late.) This is particularly important since the later the writ is issued, the greater will be the prejudice to the defendant in having to face a stale claim which might be difficult to defend (*Donovan* v *Gwentoys Ltd* [1990] 1 All ER 1018).

The prejudice issue is one which works both ways, since if the court exercises its discretion to allow the action to proceed out of time, there is inevitable prejudice to the defendant since he will be denied a 'windfall' limitation defence. But there is also prejudice to the plaintiff where he is told that he may not proceed with his action because he is out of time. Factors which may be relevant here are the strength or weakness of the plaintiff's case, the size of any possible award of damages and whether the plaintiff has an alternative defendant to sue. This last issue is particularly relevant to Alice since she may have an action for professional negligence against her legal advisor, in which case it may be argued that the court should decline to exercise its discretion under s. 33. But requiring the plaintiff to sue her solicitor can prejudice her if the professional negligence case is not cast iron (*Conry* v *Simpson* [1983] 3 All ER 369). It is also relevant that requiring the plaintiff to sue her legal advisor will result in additional litigation and this is a relevant factor since s. 33 requires the court to have regard to all relevant circumstances (*Ramsden* v *Lee* [1992] 2 All ER 204). Moreover, if the plaintiff is required to sue her solicitor, regard should be had to the fact that she is being forced to give up an action against a tortfeasor who may know little of the weaker aspects of his case, to bringing an action against a person who knows all the finer details of that case by virtue of having represented the plaintiff (*Hartley* v *Birmingham City District Council* [1992] 2 All ER 213). All of this may suggest that the court might be inclined to exercise their discretion in order to allow Alice to sue out of time, so that she does not have to pursue her solicitors, Doohey, Cheetham & Howe.

QUESTION 6

Antonius is an architect. He is also a member of the congregation of a local chapel. About six years ago he gave free advice to the trustees of that chapel about the design of a new sports hall to be built on some vacant land owned by the chapel. He recommended a new type of girder, called the 'plasti-girder', to span and support the main roof. This variety of girder was made from cheap, but very strong plastic. If Antonius had read a circular from the Building Research establishment he would have realised that defects had been discovered in this type of girder and that they were unsuitable for use in projects such as sports centres, assembly halls and similar structures.

Six months ago, the trustees of the chapel sold the sports hall to the local authority. The main roof has now collapsed due to the inadequacy of the girders. No one was in the building at the time, but some valuable sports equipment belonging to Beatrice has been destroyed. Advise Beatrice and the local authority.

Would your answer differ if the building had still been owned by the chapel at the time of the collapse and it was now the trustees who were seeking your advice?

Commentary

The question raises a number of issues relevant to the issue of when a duty of care is owed by professionals involved in the building process. Relevant considerations are:

(a)   did Antonius make a statement or do an act?

(b)   is the loss suffered pure economic loss?

(c)   how does the loss suffered by Beatrice differ from (b) above?

(d)   is there liability under the Occupiers' Liability Act 1957 or for professional negligence?

Suggested Answer

Antonius has not taken on any work 'for or in connection with the provision of a dwelling'. This means that he is not subject to the statutory duty under the Defective Premises Act 1972, s. 1 because that section does not apply to recreational buildings, commercial buildings, churches and the like. The question of Antonius's liability, therefore, falls to be decided according to common law rules.

Did Antonius owe a duty of care?

Since Antonius has received no fee, he will owe no contractual duty, but he may owe a tortious duty of care to the trustees of the chapel. There is no doubt that Antonius was under a duty to take reasonable care to protect the users of the sports hall from personal injury. This duty applies to him whether he designs the structure or supervises the work or both. This principle is not a new one. It pre-dates the decision of the House of Lords in *Donoghue* v *Stevenson* [1932] AC 562; see *Heaven* v *Pender* (1883) 11 QBD 503 (where scaffolding collapsed).

Beatrice will be able to sue the local authority, as owners and occupiers of the premises under the provisions of the Occupiers' Liability Act 1957. She may also have an action against Antonius at common law, provided it can be established that he owed her a duty of care and was in breach of that duty.

Gratuitous bailment and occupiers' liability

If the storage of the equipment was not covered by a bailment for reward, the storage will amount to a gratuitous bailment, or it may not have been a bailment at all. A landowner does not become a bailee of every item of goods left on his land, even if he has no objection to its presence there. A bailment requires a voluntary transfer of possession from the bailor to the bailee, and this is a question of intention as well as a visible act. According to Lord Denning MR in *Morris* v *Martin (C W) & Sons Ltd* [1966] 1 QB 716, the leaving of a coat with a servant in a friend's house amounts to a gratuitous bailment of the coat (the friend becoming the gratuitous bailee of it). At common law, the duty of a gratuitous bailee was regarded as not particularly onerous, in the sense that he was required to do no more than treat the goods as if they were his own (*Coggs* v *Barnard* (1703) 2 Ld Raym, 909). However, more recently, it has been accepted that there is little difference between the position of a bailee for reward and a gratuitous bailee in so far as each of them will owe a duty to take reasonable care of the bailor's property while in his possession. Thus it has been held that if the gratuitous bailment arises in the course of a commercial relationship between the parties, the burden of proof will rest on the bailee to show that he was not negligent in his care of the goods. So in *Houghland* v *Low (R R) (Luxury Coaches) Ltd* [1962] 1 QB 694 a coach tour operator who had stored luggage belonging to a paying passenger was required to prove absence of fault on his part when the luggage went missing. On the assumption that the local authority has voluntarily taken possession of Beatrice's sports equipment and allowed her to leave it at the sports centre, it will be necessary for the authority to show that they have taken reasonable care of the equipment and that it was not their fault that it came to be damaged. This they may be able to do by proving fault on the part of Antonius.

Whether or not the storage of Beatrice's equipment in the sports hall amounts to a bailment, the local authority will also owe Beatrice the common duty of care under the Occupiers' Liability Act 1957. This requires the occupier to take reasonable care to see that a lawful visitor is reasonably safe in using the premises for the purposes for which she is invited to be there. The duty also extends to protect the lawful visitor's property (*AMF International Ltd v Magnet Bowling Ltd* [1968] 2 All ER 789). Accordingly, the local authority will be required to take reasonable care of Beatrice's sports equipment. Indeed, the duty even extends to property which the visitor does not own, for example hired goods (*Drive Yourself Lessey's Pty Ltd v Burnside* (1959) SR (NSW) 390). However, the duty under the 1957 Act is no more than a duty to take reasonable care, and in order for Beatrice to succeed in an action against the local authority, it will be necessary for her to satisfy the burden of proving fault on the part of the local authority in taking care of her possessions. Given that the primary fault appears to lie in the manner of construction of the building, it will be necessary for Beatrice to establish that a responsible officer of the local authority was aware of the dangerous method of construction.

Antonius's duty to Beatrice

Having regard to the fact that Beatrice's loss is not a form of pure economic loss, there appears to be no reason why her position should be adversely affected by the decision of the House of Lords in *Murphy v Brentwood District Council* [1991] 1 AC 378, to the effect that a builder who has negligently constructed a building owes no duty of care to a subsequent owner in respect of the diminution in value of the building itself. Nothing in *Murphy* affects the ability of a plaintiff to maintain an action for negligence against a builder who has caused personal injuries or damage to property other than the defective building itself. For example, in *Dove v Banham's Patent Locks* [1983] 2 All ER 833 goods belonging to the plaintiff were stolen from a building as a result of the defendant's negligence in installing a defective security gate. Although there were problems in terms of the issue of limitation of actions in this case, it is clear from the decision that a duty of care was owed by the defendant in respect of the loss of the plaintiff's property.

To the extent that Beatrice will have to prove fault on the part of Antonius, it was held in *Greaves & Co. (Contractors) Ltd v Baynham Meikle & Partners* [1975] 3 All ER 99 that a professional person, such as an architect or engineer, may be considered to be guilty of negligence if he ignores relevant circulars and other publications made available to members of the profession. Thus the fact that Antonius has ignored the advice proffered by the Building Research establishment to the effect that the plasti-girder is inappropriate for use in structures such as sports halls may be sufficient evidence of fault on the part of Antonius.

Can the local authority sue Antonius?

At the time the Latent Damage Act 1986 was passed, it seemed to be the intention of Parliament that the owners of a building, the value of which was diminished due to negligently caused latent damage, should have a right of suit against the negligent builder, architect or engineer, etc., provided the time limits set down in the 1986 Act had not expired. However, the duty issue in this area is now subject to the decision of the House of Lords in *Murphy* v *Brentwood District Council* [1991] 1 AC 378 which did not consider the provisions of the Latent Damage Act 1986 but concluded that where the loss suffered by the plaintiff building owner is pure economic loss, in the form of diminution in the value of the building itself, no duty of care is owed by the builder, etc. According to the House of Lords, it is the duty of the building owner to seek contractual guarantees or obtain insurance in respect of the cost of future repair. The problem with latent damage is that while it remains latent, it is clearly not discoverable. However, the present position under the rule in *Pirelli General Cable Works Ltd* v *Oscar Faber & Partners* [1983] 2 AC 1 is that although undiscoverable, latent damage is nonetheless actionable damage with the result that the plaintiff's cause of action will accrue on the date damage is caused. In the case of a subsequent purchaser of damaged property, since damage has already been caused, it seems highly unlikely that an insurance company would insure against a risk which, in legal terms, has already manifested itself. Accordingly, the position of the subsequent purchaser seems to be that his primary cause of action will lie in contract if he has secured a contractual guarantee of the fitness of the property.

The only practical exception to the *Murphy* principle appears to be that relating to negligent misstatements under the rule in *Hedley Byrne & Co. Ltd* v *Heller & Partners Ltd* [1964] AC 465 which requires proof of a special relationship under which advice is given and reasonably relied upon by the person to whom it is given, with the result that the recipient of the advice suffers pure economic loss.

The problem from the point of view of the local authority is that under the law prior to *Murphy* builders, architects and engineers, etc. were taken to have done an act in the form of engaging in the building process (*Pirelli General Cable Works Ltd* v *Oscar Faber & Partners*). However, in the light of *Murphy*, it seems that these cases must now be reinterpreted on the basis that advice has been given. While this may be the position according to English law, it is clear that other common law jurisdictions have moved in a different direction and that an action in tort may avail the purchaser of a defective building if there has been an assumption of responsibility by the builder, etc. and there is evidence of reasonable purchaser-reliance (see *Invercargill City Council* v *Hamlin* [1996] 1 All ER 756).

The problem facing the local authority is that they do not appear to have relied on Antonius's advice. Any advice given was to the trustees of the chapel, and since the rule in *Hedley Byrne* v *Heller* places such considerable emphasis on the requirement of a special relationship between the giver of the advice and the person who relies upn it, it seems unlikely that such a relationship will exist. *Caparo Industries plc* v *Dickman* [1990] 2 AC 605 considered that an auditor of company accounts was entitled to take account of the limited number of people for whose benefit his advice was prepared. Thus in that case the auditor had prepared accounts for the benefit of the company concerned, so that no duty of care would be owed to individual shareholders in the company or to potential investors. On the facts revealed in the problem, since Antonius's advice was prepared for the benefit of the trustees, it would seem to follow that no duty is owed to a subsequent purchaser such as the local authority, unless it was known that the advice would be passed on to an interested party, as in *Morgan Crucible plc* v *Hill Samuel Bank Ltd* [1991] 1 All ER 142.

As an alternative to the *Hedley Byrne* exception, Lord Bridge in *D & F Estates Ltd* v *Church Commissioners for England* [1988] 2 All ER 992 suggested that there might be a further exception to the general restriction on the recovery of pure economic loss in tort in cases where there is a 'complex stucture', part of which causes damage to another part of the same structure. However, this 'complex structure theory' is conceptually very difficult to define, if only because it is almost impossible to make a proper distinction between something which is an integral part of an overall structure and an item incorporated into a structure but which is distinct from the rest of that structure. However, in *Jacobs* v *Morton* (1994) 72 BLR 92, Mr Recorder Jackson QC considered that the exception could apply, so that damage could be regarded as physical harm rather than economic loss if certain conditions were complied with. These were held to include: (1) the fact that the defective item was constructed by a person other than the main building contractor; (2) the defective item retained a separate identity; (3) the defective item positively inflicted damage on the rest of the structure; and (4) the defective item was constructed at a different time to the rest of the structure. Since the sports hall is a new structure, it would seem to follow that the last of these requirements is not met in Antonius's case, so that the complex structure theory cannot apply.

The trustees of the chapel

The maxim *caveat emptor* still continues to apply with some force in the field of property sales so that it is unlikely that they will be liable for the collapse of the sports hall unless they had given some sort of a contractual guarantee to the local authority. Although it is the trustees to whom Antonius has given his advice, by the time it is realised that any loss has been suffered, the building has changed hands. Assuming the trustees have been paid a reasonable market price for the sports hall, it is unlikely that they will be able to point to any loss suffered by them as a result of relying on the advice given by Antonius.

QUESTION 7

Punter, a partly qualified accountant, has recently been left a substantial sum of money by his late aunt which he now wishes to invest. He is told by Spiv, a stockbroker client of his employers, that Flybinight plc is currently enjoying considerable success and that since the company's shares are underpriced Punter should buy now. He offers to undertake the purchase for Punter when given the go-ahead by him. Punter meets Hackett, an old friend of his, for a drink in a pub. Hackett has recently been appointed under-manager at Eastminster Bank and Punter asks him about the wisdom of buying the shares. Hackett says that although he does not have much experience in financial advising as yet, he is interested in business matters and always reads the relevant papers. He says that *Whizz Weekly*, one of the more respected financial papers, predicts that Flybinight is undervalued since the company seems poised to declare record profits. Hackett therefore concludes that on the basis of this report and his general overview of business affairs, Punter should go ahead and buy.

Following the advice he received, Punter invests heavily in the company. After two months the company is put into liquidation by its creditors and Punter loses his investment.

Advise Punter as to whether he has any legal redress to recover his losses against Spiv, Hackett and *Whizz Weekly*.

Commentary

This question requires consideration of the rules governing economic loss caused by negligent statements. In particular an examination of the principles governing the imposition of a duty of care is required and the following matters need to be considered:

(a) is the advice both prepared and communicated?

(b) is advice given on a social occasion actionable?

(c) is there a distinction between those who merely transmit information and those who produce it?

Suggested Answer

Liability for economic loss caused by negligent misstatement is not determined by the *Donoghue* v *Stevenson* [1932] AC 562 neighbour principle alone, but in accordance with more restrictive tests which govern the imposition of a duty of care for such statements. This is because the potential liability of the representor is far wider than that where the issue involves a negligent act since a statement can affect a large indeterminate class of plaintiffs. Claims for negligent misstatement can often involve potentially huge sums of money because unlike physical harm, where events tend to rest where they fall, advice can be relied upon by any number of people who come into contact with it. In formulating the rules governing liability, the courts have long been mindful of the so-called floodgates argument which is encapsulated by Cardozo CJ's warning delivered in *Ultramares Corporation* v *Touche* (1931) 174 NE 441, of opening 'liability in an indeterminate amount for an indeterminate time to an indeterminate class'.

To determine whether Spiv owes a duty of care to Punter for the advice given to buy the shares, the criteria laid down in *Hedley Byrne & Co.* v *Heller & Partners* [1964] AC 465 must be satisfied. Basically, the House of Lords stated that a 'special relationship' must exist between the representor and representee so that reasonable reliance which was known, or ought to have been known, to the representor was placed on the statement by the representee. Lord Morris stated that a 'special relationship' will arise where someone possessed of a special skill undertakes, irrespective of contract, to apply that skill for the assistance of another person.

These requirements have been refined and explained in subsequent cases. Thus in *Caparo Industries* v *Dickman* [1990] 2 AC 605, Caparo, a shareholder in Fidelity plc, bought further shares in the company prior to making a successful takeover bid. Caparo alleged that they had relied on the accounts for 1984 which had been prepared by the defendant auditors which showed a pre-tax profit of £1.3 million when in fact they should have recorded a loss of some £400,000. Had they known the true state of affairs they would not have bid for the company. Lord Bridge formulated a tripartite test for determining liability in negligence. First, there must be foreseeability. Secondly, there must be proximity between the plaintiff and defendant; and finally, it must be just, fair and reasonable in all the circumstances of the case to impose a duty of care. In finding that on the particular facts of the case the defendant auditors did not owe a duty of care, the House of Lords stated that the following criteria must be satisfied to found liability for negligent misstatement:

(a)   the representor must be fully aware of the nature of the transaction which the recipient of the advice had in contemplation;

(b)   he must know that the information would be communicated to him directly or indirectly;

(c)   he must know that it was very likely that the plaintiff would rely on the information when deciding whether or not to engage in the transaction in question;

(d)   the purpose for which the plaintiff does rely on that information must be a purpose connected with interests which it is proper to expect the representor to protect.

In *Smith* v *Bush (Eric S.)* [1990] AC 831, the plaintiff suffered loss as a result of the defendants' negligence in surveying a house which she intended to purchase through a mortgage supplied by the instructing building society. It was held to be reasonable for the purchaser to rely on the survey carried out by the lender's surveyor. The defendants knew the identity of the plaintiff and knew that she would rely on their advice. Further, the nature of the transaction depending upon their advice was clear. The requirement laid down in *Hedley Byrne* that liability depends upon the existence of voluntary assumption of responsibility was discredited by Lord Griffiths as being unrealistic, while in *James McNaughton Paper Group* v *Hicks Anderson* [1991] 1 All ER 134, the Court of Appeal stressed that the plaintiff's 'reliance' upon the information must be reasonable. Accordingly, the skill of the advisor is an influential factor when imposing a duty of care.

In applying the rules laid down in *Hedley Byrne* (as interpreted by the House of Lords in *Caparo*), to Spiv, it is suggested that a 'special relationship' may be found to exist given that Spiv, as a stockbroker, must know that his advice would be relied upon for investment purposes, it was communicated directly to Punter and he is advised to 'buy now.' As a professional he obviously has skill and it is reasonable and proper to expect Spiv to have due regard to the interests of those who receive his advice and information. The meaning of 'special skill' has been held to include special knowledge (*Henderson* v *Merrett Syndicates Ltd* [1995] 2 AC 145, *per* Lord Goff). Further, as a stockbroker, Spiv may be held to be in a fiduciary relationship with Punter. In *White* v *Jones* [1995] 2 AC 207, which concerned an action by two intended beneficiaries against a solicitor who negligently failed to amend a will before the testator's death, Lord Browne-Wilkinson extended the *Hedley Byrne* principle by holding that there is no requirement on the plaintiff to prove foreseeable reliance where a fiduciary duty is owed to him or her by the defendant. His Lordship observed that in the case of a fiduciary, it was sufficient that the defendant was aware that the plaintiff's financial welfare was dependent upon the exercise of proper care by him and, as such, a 'special relationship' arises. The decision clearly broadens the ambit of *Hedley Byrne* given that on its facts, there was no reliance on the solicitor's skill by the plaintiffs but rather it was the deceased testator who had placed reliance on him. This dilution of the reliance requirement is also discernible in *Henderson* v *Merrett Syndicates Ltd* and *Spring* v *Guardian Assurance plc* [1995] 2 AC 296. The essential issue identified in all three of these recent House of Lords' cases was the question of finding a sufficient degree of proximity so as to accord with the second limb of the tripartite test promulgated in *Caparo*. It is suggested that such proximity can be said to exist between Spiv and Punter because, in the language of Lord Atkin in *Donoghue* v *Stevenson* [1932] AC 562, Punter was clearly 'closely and directed affected' by Spiv's negligent advice.

With respect to Hackett, the circumstances in which the advice is given and the nature of the relationship between him and Punter are material. It was stated by Lord Reid in *Hedley Byrne* that when opinions are expressed on social occasions, they are often made without the care that would normally be accorded if asked for professionally. Hackett's status at the bank as under-manager is also significant given that his degree of expertise must be open to question. In *Chaudry* v *Prabhakar* [1989] 1 WLR 29, the defendant, who was a friend of the plaintiff, offered to help her find and purchase a car. Although not a mechanic, he told her that he had a good knowledge of cars. The plaintiff specifically requested that he help her find a car which had not been crashed. The defendant found a low mileage vehicle which he knew had had its bonnet repaired or replaced. It was unroadworthy, a fact not discovered before the sale because of the defendant's advice not to have the car inspected by a professional mechanic. The Court of Appeal held the defendant liable on the ground that this was not a purely social relationship given the plaintiff's reliance upon the defendant's skill and his knowledge of that reliance.

Since Hackett had informed Punter that he lacked relevant experience and did not profess to be an expert, coupled with the fact that the advice appears to be tendered on a social occasion, the court is unlikely to impose a duty of care in these circumstances. Further, in *Royal Bank Trust (Trinidad)* v *Pampellonne* [1987] 1 Lloyds Rep. 218, the Privy Council drew a line between those who merely transmit information and those who produce it. A duty of care would only arise with respect to the latter. On this view, Hackett's advice would seem to fall into the former category. However, more recently the distinction between advice and information has been limited to the issue of determining the scope of the duty of care, so that the mere provision of information may now fall within the *Hedley Byrne* principle (see *South Australia Asset Management Corporation* v *York Montague Ltd* [1996] 3 All ER 365). Nevertheless, taking all the circumstances into account, it is unlikely that the court would consider it just, fair or reasonable to impose a duty of care on Hackett.

The imposition of a duty of care on *Whizz Weekly* is also unlikely. In *Hedley Byrne* the House of Lords recognised the danger of formulating rules which could result in the maker of a careless statement being liable to a wide, indeterminate class of plaintiffs. For this reason, Lord Bridge in *Caparo* stressed the necessity of 'proximity' between the plaintiff and defendant and warned against the dangers of holding a defendant liable 'to all and sundry' for any purpose for which they may choose to rely on it. The statement that the shares of Flybinight are 'undervalued' does not amount to an unequivocal recommendation that the company's shares should be bought.

(4) Omissions

QUESTION 8

David, a painter and decorator, lived across the road from a block of flats in which Haley lived. He saw her trying to paint her window frames and offered to do the job for her at the weekend saying that it would be no trouble and that if he ever needed a return favour he would know where to come.

On the Saturday when David did the job, Haley spent the afternoon sun-bathing in her garden which lay to the rear of her ground-floor flat. In view of the nice weather and in order to let the premises 'air' he left the front door open.

While David was painting the kitchen window, Tommy Leaf, a local petty criminal, crept in and stole many valuable antiques from Haley's apartment. In addition he took the opportunity of being inside the main door to the block of flats to break into and burgle Pam's third-floor apartment as he knew her to be away on holiday in Greece.

Tommy Leaf has not been caught.

Advise David, Haley and Pam as to their respective rights and duties.

Commentary

This question requires consideration of the general rule that tortious liability is not ordinarily imposed for the failure to act to prevent harm (nonfeasance). Particular regard should be had to:

(a)   the nature of David's undertaking to Haley;

(b)   the limited circumstances in which occupiers of property may be placed under a duty to take reasonable precautions against the wrongdoing of third parties to determine whether Haley owes a duty of care to Pam.

Suggested Answer

The essential issue which arises from the given facts revolves around the failure of David and Haley, the occupier of the flat, to prevent the infliction of damage by the act of a third party. The general rule is that there is no duty at common law to prevent persons harming others by their deliberate wrongdoing, however foreseeable such harm may be in the absence of steps being taken to prevent it. This proposition arises from the notion that ordinarily liability is not imposed for pure omissions (see *Stovin* v *Wise* [1996] AC 923). In *Smith* v *Littlewoods Organisation Ltd* [1987] AC 241, the defendants bought a disused cinema which they left unoccupied for a period of time pending its demolition. During that period vandals broke into the empty premises and lit a fire which spread to neighbouring properties causing serious damage. Littlewoods were unaware of the general reputation for vandalism which the particular locality possessed. The owners of those damaged properties sued the supermarket chain. It was held by the House of Lords, in rejecting the claim, that the duty of care did not extend to a duty to take 'exceptional' care. Of primary concern to their Lordships was the issue that if a duty of care were to be imposed on occupiers of property in such circumstances, it could not be discharged short of placing an intolerable burden on the occupiers to mount 24 hour guards on empty premises.

In examining David's duty to Haley, it is of crucial importance to determine the nature of the undertaking he makes to her since an affirmative duty to prevent harm may arise therefrom. It is clear that if there is a contractual relationship between them, liability for the theft of the antiques may be borne by him. In *Stansbie* v *Troman* [1948] 2 KB 48, the defendant, a decorator, was employed in the plaintiff's house and was instructed to lock the door if he went out. He went out leaving the door on the latch whereby a thief entered the house and stole the plaintiff's jewellery. The defendant was held liable for the loss. The decision has been explained on the basis of an implied term of the contract that in decorating the house the defendant would exercise reasonable care in respect of its contents *(Perl (P) (Exporters) Ltd* v *Camden London Borough Council* [1984] QB 342, *per* Oliver and Goff LJJ). Further, in *Home Office* v *Dorset Yacht Co. Ltd* [1970] AC 1004, a group of borstal boys who were under the supervision and control of three borstal officers, escaped while the officers were asleep in breach of their instructions not to leave the boys unsupervised. The boys boarded a nearby yacht and caused it to collide with a yacht owned by the plaintiff. The Home Office was held vicariously liable for the negligence of the officers. The House of Lords held that a duty of care arose out of the special relationship between the boys and their custodians since the boys were under the control of the officers and 'control' imports responsibility. Lord Diplock stressed that liability should be restricted to the harm caused in the course of the escape to those in close physical proximity.

Applying these authorities to the facts of the problem, it seems unlikely that David will be considered to owe a duty of care to Haley. Carrying out the job on the loose understanding that if he 'ever needed a return favour he would know where to come' does not of itself suggest a contract between them from which a term can be implied to keep the door locked. Also, since Haley is in her garden he does not appear to have the requisite 'control' of the premises under which he may bear responsibility for Tommy Leaf's entrance into the flat. He is not therefore under a legal obligation to control the activities of the thief.

Pam is in an analogous position to the neighbouring property owners in *Smith* v *Littlewoods Organisation Ltd*. In considering the situation where a thief gains access to property through the failure of an adjacent neighbour to keep his property lockfast, Lord Goff opined that liability cannot be imposed on the neighbour for the burglary since every occupier must take such steps as he thinks fit for the protection of his own property. His Lordship stated that when considering what precautions should be taken, an occupier should take into account the fact that from time to time his neighbours may leave their properties unlocked. Such a proposition follows from the general rule that there is no general duty to prevent third parties causing damage to others. As Lord Keith observed in *Yuen Kun Yeu* v *Attorney-General of Hong Kong* [1988] AC 175, there is no liability in negligence on one who sees another about to walk over a cliff with his head in the air, and fails to shout a warning. Lord Goff went on to explain that exceptionally liability for the activities of others may arise in two situations. First, where a landowner has knowledge, or means of knowledge, that trespassers have created a risk of fire on his property, and then fails to abate the risk of that fire from damaging neighbouring property. It is clear that the given facts do not fall within this exception. Secondly, where a landowner creates, or allows to be created, an unusual source of danger on his land and it is reasonably foreseeable that a third party may interfere with it thereby causing damage to another (*Haynes* v *Harwood* [1935] 1 KB 146). Lord Goff stressed that liability under this principle should only be imposed where a defendant has negligently caused or permitted a source of danger and it is foreseeable that a third party may 'spark it off'. Haley's failure to ensure that her decorator keeps the apartment block locked is not of itself likely to result in theft to a resident, and therefore cannot be described as creating a source of danger which was foreseeably 'sparked off' by Tommy Leaf.

The decision of the Court of Appeal in *Perl (P) (Exporters) Ltd* v *Camden London Borough Council*, is also of particular significance to Pam's legal position. Briefly, the facts were that a local authority which owned a block of flats failed to secure a basement flat which was unoccupied. Burglars entered this flat and knocked an 18 inch hole through the party wall and burgled the plaintiff's property. It was held that the relationship of neighbouring property owners was not of itself sufficient to impose on one owner the duty to guard the other against the foreseeable risk of burglary through unsecured property. The court pointed out that to impose such a duty would place an unreasonable burden on ordinary householders and an unreasonable curb on the ordinary enjoyment of their property.

In *Smith* v *Littlewoods* Lord Goff was of the view that *Perl* was correctly decided and pointed out that the law has to accommodate 'the untidy complexity of life' and therefore there are situations where considerations of practical justice will pre-empt the imposition of a duty of care. This approach was followed in *Topp* v *London Country Bus Ltd* [1993] 1 WLR 976, where the defendant had left a minibus unattended outside a pub at a bus stop for some nine hours with its door unlocked and with its key still in the ignition. A thief stole the bus and knocked over and killed the plaintiff's wife. The thief was never detected and the plaintiff sued the defendants as owners of the bus. Both

May J at first instance and the Court of Appeal found that there was a relationship of proximity between the defendants and the deceased. However, applying the language of *Caparo Industries plc* v *Dickman* [1990] 2 AC 605, it was held that it would not be 'fair, just and reasonable' to recognise a duty of care on the facts since any affirmative duty to prevent deliberate wrongdoing by third parties, if recognised by English law, is likely to be strictly limited. Accordingly, it is submitted that Pam is not owed a duty of care by Haley to prevent the thief, Tommy Leaf, gaining access to the building by her failure to ensure that her decorator kept the building lockfast during the repainting. Given that this factual situation does not fall within the exceptional circumstances outlined by Lord Goff, it would not be just and reasonable to subject Haley to such a duty. As such, the facts fall squarely within the principle formulated by Lord Sumner in *Weld-Blundell* v *Stephens* [1920] AC 956, that in general, 'even though A is at fault, he is not responsible for injury to C which B, a stranger to him, deliberately chose to do'.

PART 2: BREACH OF DUTY

QUESTION 9

> In general the relevant circumstances [occasioning variations in the standard of care] will be the physical conditions in which the act takes place ... and should exclude those factors which describe the actor rather than the act. (Kidner)

To what extent is this, and should it be, the case?

Commentary

This question requires consideration of the factors which, in English law, are relevant to the process of determining whether the defendant is in breach of a duty of care in a negligence action. These include:

(a)   special characteristics of the tortfeasor;

(b)   the circumstances in which the alleged negligence took place.

The question also requires an intelligent critique of whether factors which are germane to the actor should ever be relevant to the setting of a standard of care which purports to be objective in nature.

Suggested Answer

For the most part, it is true to assert that the idiosyncrasies of the tortfeasor are irrelevant to ascertaining the requisite standard of care in a negligence action. However, see *Mansfield* v *Weetabix Ltd* [1997] PIQR P526, where the Court of Appeal held that a driver who was unaware of a disabling condition could not be in breach of his duty of care. This is because, according to received wisdom, the standard of care is an objective one (*Blyth* v *Birmingham Waterworks* (1856) 11 Ex 781 per Alderson B) and, as such, a question of law to be determined by the courts (*Nettleship* v *Weston* [1971] 2 QB 691). Even so, as will be explained, there are factors which relate to the defendant as *a member of a particular class* of persons which can equally affect the level of care that must be shown in order to avoid liability in negligence. It is not, however, all classes of person that seem to attract 'special treatment' under the law. This fact no doubt forms the basis of the generalisation comprising the essay title. But it remains, none the less, a generalisation. As such, it is necessarily destined to be least helpful where specificity and precision are most needed.

A sophisticated analysis of the law relating to the standard of care might seek to argue that the (seeming) inconsistency in the decided case law stems from the several, sometimes conflicting, objectives which the law of tort strives to achieve. Thus, briefly to supply an example to which we will return, the desire to ensure that a 'worthy' plaintiff receives compensation might conflict, for example, with the aim of the tort system to do justice. Accordingly, in *Nettleship* v *Weston* [1971] 2 QB 691 the price of compensating the injured party was holding a learner driver liable for failure to meet the driving standard one would expect of a qualified driver (which, on one conception of justice, seems mightily unfair).

For present purposes, appropriate scrutiny of the hypothesis put forward in the title entails a two-step approach. First, it is necessary to assess whether the standard of care is indeed more responsive to changes in the physical conditions in which the act takes place than the particular characteristics of the defendant. Secondly, it is necessary to explain why the law should take this approach.

To begin with, it is clear that the standard of care is fixed very much with the circumstances in which the accident takes place very much in mind. No more stark example of this may be supplied than the case of *Watt* v *Hertfordshire County Council* [1954] 2 All ER 368. There, because of an accident, a woman found herself trapped under a lorry. In a hurry to release her, a truck ill-suited to transporting a heavy jack was used for just that purpose. In braking suddenly, the jack was propelled forwards and it injured the plaintiff, one of the firemen, on his way to releasing the trapped woman. In finding the defendants not negligent, Denning LJ stated that:

> If this accident had occurred in a commercial enterprise without any emergency, there can be no doubt that the servant would succeed. But the commercial end to make profit is very different from the human end to save life or limb. The saving of life or limb justifies considerable risk.

It is also clear that other circumstantial factors may affect the level of care demanded of the plaintiff, such as the relative cost of precautionary measures (e.g., *Latimer* v *AEC* [1953] AC 653); the likelihood of harm occurring (*Bolton* v *Stone* [1951] AC 850); the social utility of the defendant's conduct (*Daborn* v *Bath Tramways* [1946] 2 All ER 333). In short, in respect of the first limb of Kidner's proposition, it would be incorrect to assert that the scenario in which the accident occurs is unimportant. But that is, in truth, only part of the matter. There are equally as many factors which relate to the characteristics of the defendant (albeit as a member of an identifiable class) that affect the level of care expected at law.

The first factor which the courts would seem able to take into account in ascertaining the appropriate standard of care is the minority of the defendant. In *McHale* v *Watson* (1965) 111 CLR 384, for example, a decision of the High Court of Australia, the fact of the defendant's minority (he was a 12-year-old boy) was held relevant to the standard of care issue. This case has been followed in England in comparatively recent times in *Staley* v *Suffolk CC* (unreported). However, since that case is only one at first instance, it is, technically, not binding on any subsequent court. Even so, in relation to the defence of contributory negligence, it has been held at Court of Appeal level that minority is a relevant criterion when the court assesses the degree of care that that child can be expected to take for his or her own safety (*Gough* v *Thorne* [1966] 3 All ER 398). It seems reasonable, therefore, to suggest that English law does take account of minority in setting the standard of care.

A second factor which the courts may take into account is the degree of skill or professionalism that can be expected of the particular defendant. Thus, in *Philips* v *William Whiteley Ltd* [1938] 1 All ER 566, for example, it was held that a jeweller performing an ear-piercing was not expected to adhere to the same standards of hygiene as a surgeon performing a comparable 'operation'. But the point must be stressed that the standard of care expected of the jeweller in that case is the standard to which *all* jewellers must aspire. The standard was set by reference to the jeweller, not as an individual, but as a member of a particular class. It is clear that there will not be variations of the standard of care within a class. Thus, a junior and overworked houseman is expected to demonstrate the same standard of care as a more experienced doctor (*Wilsher* v *Essex Area Health Authority* [1987] QB 730). To allow a lower standard would be to:

> ... subordinate the legitimate expectation of the patient that he will receive from each person concerned with his care a degree of skill appropriate to the task that [the doctor] undertakes to an understandable wish to minimise the psychological and financial pressures on hard pressed young doctors.

A final factor that describes the actor more than the act, and which is again relevant to setting the standard of care, is the fact that the defendant was, at the time of the accident, engaged in a sporting pursuit. Here the standard of care will be lowered to take account of the fact that the sporting arena is one which naturally gives rise to the need to take spur-of-the-moment decisions (*Wooldridge* v *Sumner* [1963] 2 QB 43). But even here, outright recklessness on the part of a sportsperson will not be tolerated (*Condon* v *Basi* [1985] 2 All ER 453).

Thus far, we have seen that English law takes account of many factors in setting the relevant standard of care. Some such factors do relate to the characteristics of the defendant, perhaps more than Kidner's suggestion that this is not generally the case would imply. However, those factors which describe the actor, and which are relevant in this context, do so *only* so far as they take account of the defendant as a member of a defined class of persons. But this does not derogate from the importance of asking whether such factors ought to be relevant in the first place. Simply to identify that certain characteristics of the defendant are taken into account by the courts is not also to justify them.

It can certainly be argued that no variations in the standard of care should properly be founded on the idiosyncrasies of the defendant. To do so would be to drive a sledgehammer through the principle that the standard of care is an objective one, intended to promote certainty both as to when a defendant will be held negligent and as to the level of safety a plaintiff may legitimately expect. The same objection — that is, the loss of objectivity — arises when the standard is set with a class of persons in mind as it is ultimately the judiciary who are final arbiters of when class status is made out. This is important since the standard of care may only be adjusted if such class status is recognised. Such determinations may be policy-driven so that in order that an insurance company ultimately bears the loss rather than an individual citizen, the standard can be artificially kept high by refusing to recognise class status. Thus, learner drivers, an ostensibly distinct class of road users, are simply bracketed with qualified drivers and the fact of compulsory insurance means that such a driver can be held liable in negligence to ensure that anyone injured by the mishap will receive compensation (*Nettleship* v *Weston* [1971] 2 QB 691). Equally, policy might be said to underpin the approach taken in *Wilsher* where Mustill J was clearly of the view that patients must be able to have confidence in the quality of their health care regardless of the absence of seniority in the doctor in attendance. The fact is that flexibility promotes justice, while harsh objectivity promotes certainty. Certainty is something which may be valuable in relation to any set of legal rules, but at what price it should be bought is a matter for debate. Ultimately, taking characteristics of the defendant into account militates against the principle that the standard of care is an objective one. This can promote justice. But if the courts refuse to take a consistent approach to the matter of identifying a class of persons that deserve individual treatment, as seems to be the case in English law, then neither objective prevails and the law looks hopelessly inconsistent and flawed.

QUESTION 10

Advise the litigants in each of the following cases:

(a)   Clarence, who was walking along the street, was hit by a milk bottle which fell from one of the upper windows of the local primary school. The local education authority claims that there were no children in the school at the time because lessons had ended 45 minutes earlier and all the children had gone home. Clarence wishes to sue the local education authority in negligence.

(b)   Vera, on her last visit to her manicurist, was cut when, on hearing an explosion in the street outside, Liz momentarily took her eyes off Vera's hand. At the time, Liz simply gave her a sticking plaster for the cut, but since then the cut has turned septic causing Vera considerable pain and preventing her from doing her work as a typist. Vera seeks your advice as regards suing Liz in negligence.

(c)   Leslie, a keen amateur sailor, was injured last week when he was rescued by the air-sea rescue team after the weather had suddenly changed and caused his boat to capsize. Leslie tells you that he has received several cracked ribs which have prevented him working as a labourer, as he usually does. He says that the rescue team used only a rope, tied round his chest, to hoist him into the helicopter instead of a proper, padded harness of the kind that the rescue team further along the coast use. He seeks your advice in relation to a potential negligence action against his rescuers.

Commentary

This question raises three different, but related, kinds of problems associated with breach of duty in the tort of negligence:

(a)   The problem of proving fault and the role of the doctrine of *res ipsa loquitur*.

(b)   The problem of assessing the standard of care demanded of the defendant in the light of characteristics particular to the defendant.

(c)   The problem of assessing the standard of care demanded of the defendant in the light of the particular circumstances in which the allegedly negligent act took place and the relative cost of ensuring injury avoidance.

Suggested Answer

(a)   Since Clarence was oblivious to the milk bottle above him, and because there is no obvious explanation as to why the milk bottle should have fallen, Clarence faces a problem of proving negligence on the part of the local education authority. However, as the accident is of a kind that does not normally occur in everyday life, Clarence may invoke the doctrine of *res ipsa loquitur* which raises a rebuttable presumption of negligence on the part of the defendant. More specifically, in order to invoke this doctrine, Clarence must, on the authority of Erle CJ in *Scott* v *London and St Katherine Docks Co.* (1865) 33 H & C 596, show three things. He must show first that the accident was of a kind that does not normally occur in the absence of a want of care. He must show, secondly, that the defendant had exclusive control over the thing which has occasioned him harm and he must show, finally, that the defendant has no plausible alternative (innocent) explanation of what caused the accident to occur.

In respect of the first of these, there is ample authority to suggest that falling objects are within the class of things that do not normally occur without negligence (*Byrne* v *Boadle* (1863) 2 H & C 722; *Scott* v *London and St Katherine Docks Co.* (1865) 33 H & C 596).

In respect of the second limb, it is clear that the bottle fell from the premises of the defendants and was thus under their exclusive control since the school had closed some 45 minutes earlier and the bottle, like the underwear in *Grant v Australian Knitting Mills* [1936] AC 85, could not have been interfered with by an intermediary. In relation to the third hurdle, the local education authority, on the facts that we are given, does not appear able to disprove negligence. Nor does it appear able to supply evidence of a plausible alternative explanation of how the bottle fell (which is all it need do to rebut the presumption of negligence raised by the *res ipsa loquitur* doctrine: *Ng Chun Pui* v *Lee Chuen Tat* [1988] RTR 298).

(**b**)   With respect to Vera's injury two potentially negligent occurrences need to be discussed. First, there is the question whether the cut caused by Liz's momentary inattention was negligent and secondly, there is the issue of whether Liz's treatment of Vera's cut — that is, simply putting a sticking plaster on it — amounted to negligence. Finally, a question arises as to whether Liz was negligent in failing to keep her manicuring equipment in a suitably hygienic state.

As regards the infliction of the cut, the starting point is to note that the law of negligence distinguishes between (actionable) negligence and (non-actionable) errors. The law does not demand that a defendant, on pain of suit for negligence, should act to the maximum attainable standard of which human beings are capable. Instead, it requires only that the defendant should have behaved in a manner consistent with the actions of a reasonable man (*Blyth* v *Birmingham Waterworks Co.* (1856) 11 Exch 781; *Glasgow Corporation* v *Muir* [1943] AC 448). Moreover, the standard demanded will vary according to circumstances and certain types of defendant. In our case, it is arguably material that Liz's slip stemmed from the 'heat of the moment' in which the explosion took place. For in *Marshall* v *Osmond* [1983] QB 1034, it was held that errors of judgment in the heat of the moment should be regarded as errors that the reasonable man might make and that they should, therefore, not be actionable. In relation to the second point — the mere (and insufficient) application of a sticking plaster to Vera's injury — there can be little doubt that Liz owed a duty to Vera on the basis of her assumption of responsibility towards Vera (*White* v *Jones* [1995] 1 All ER 691). In this case, then, it is relevant to ask whether her 'treatment' of Vera was negligent. Here, it is to be noted that the standard demanded of Liz will not, on the authority of *Philips* v *William Whitely* [1938] 1 All ER 566, be the same as that demanded of a doctor, had a doctor been summoned to treat Vera. In the *Philips* case, which is clearly analogous, a jeweller was held not to be liable in respect of an infection in the plaintiff's ears caused by the jeweller's ear-piercing. The court in that case held that the standard of care in respect of hygiene, etc. was that of a jeweller doing such work, not that of a doctor. In our case, then, Liz will be required to meet the standard of care of the reasonable manicurist, not that of the reasonable doctor. Arguably, she has met this standard in supplying her client with a sticking plaster.

A final argument that Vera may make is that Liz's negligence lay in respect of her failure to keep her manicuring tools sufficiently hygienic. Here, evidence would have to be adduced as to two things, about neither of which are we told anything. First, and most obviously, we would need evidence on the actual cleanliness of Liz's tools. Secondly, we would also need evidence on the frequency with which clients received cuts of this kind. For the more often they occurred, the greater the precautionary measures the law would demand of Liz (*Bolton* v *Stone* [1951] AC 850).

(c) The standard of care demanded by the law of negligence of the (presumably professional) rescue team is that of any such persons possessed of the skills required to do that job, namely 'the standard of an ordinary skilled man exercising and professing to have that special skill' (*Bolam* v *Friern Hospital* [1957] 1 WLR 582, 586). The fact that we know of another air-sea rescue team that uses different, safer equipment begs the question whether the team were negligent in using merely a rope. The answer to this lies in two stages. First, it is clear that so long as a significant body of professional opinion, gleaned from other rescue teams, backs the use of a rope alone that, prima facie, will exculpate the team in our case. As Lord Scarman put it in *Maynard* v *West Midlands Regional Health Authority* [1984] 1 WLR 634: '[A] judge's preference for one body of distinguished professional opinion to another also professionally distinguished is not sufficient to establish negligence'. However, and this is the second point, if the decision to use a rope alone could be shown to be so unreasonable a choice that no reasonable rescue team could have made it, an action for negligence might still lie (see *Bolitho* v *City and Hackney Health Authority* [1997] 4 All ER 771). As regards the reasonableness of using a cheap rope rather than an expensive harness, the court would be entitled to consider whether the cost of preventing an injury outweighed the risk of the injury (both in terms of the magnitude and likelihood of that injury occurring: *Bolton* v *Stone* [1951] AC 850; *Latimer* v *AEC Ltd* [1953] AC 643).

On the assumption that all other rescue teams would not use merely a rope (for the contrary assumption stymies further discussion) it remains to be asked whether the rescue team may nonetheless escape liability on other grounds. Two suggest themselves: the fact that it was an emergency situation (the weather had changed suddenly) and the potential frailty of the plaintiff.

In respect of the former, the rescue team might argue that, had they had more time, they could have procured a harness to use in the operation but, since it was a life and death situation, they were forced to act swiftly with whatever (non-ideal) tools they had to hand. Such an argument would clearly be premised on the analogous case of *Watt* v *Hertfordshire County Council* [1954] 1 All ER 835. In respect of the latter — the plaintiff's possible frailty — the rescue team may legitimately deny any duty of care in respect of damaged ribs if such an injury was unforeseeable in a plaintiff of ordinary strength (*Brice* v *Brown* [1984] 1 All ER 997).

PART 3: CAUSATION AND REMOTENESS OF DAMAGE

QUESTION 11

Algernon is crossing a pedestrian crossing when he is struck by a car driven by Beatrice. Algernon is knocked to the ground and staggers to his feet, but is concussed and blinded by blood from a head wound. He is then hit by a car driven by Cassandra, and knocked to the ground again. While lying on the ground, Algernon is kicked by Desdemona, who steals his wallet containing £500 in cash which he is taking to the bank on behalf of his employers.

Beatrice and Cassandra have both been breath-tested by the police, and have been found to be significantly affected by alcohol.

Algernon is found to have serious injuries which will make it impossible for him to work again, but his doctors are not able to say which car caused those injuries.

Advise Algernon, and his employers, whether they have any remedy against Beatrice and/or Cassandra.

Commentary

The question is about the tort of negligence. The following issues arise:

(a)   Beatrice and Cassandra are joint tortfeasors;

(b)   whether the law of negligence requires particular damage to be ascribed to particular defendants;

(c)   whether the criminal act of a third party amounts to a *novus actus interveniens*;

(d)   whether a motorist owes a duty of care to persons not present at the scene of an accident, particularly if they only suffer economic loss.

Suggested Answer

Assuming Algernon's injuries have been caused by the traffic accident, it is necessary to consider the liability of Cassandra and Beatrice. There will be no dispute about the duty of care which Beatrice and Cassandra, as motorists, owe to Algernon, another road user (*Nettleship* v *Weston* [1971] 2 QB 691). If Beatrice is convicted of a criminal offence relating to her driving, or her fitness to drive, the conviction will be admissible evidence against her in any relevant civil proceedings brought by Algernon (Civil Evidence Act 1968, s. 11). A heavy burden of proof will lie upon Beatrice if she contends that the criminal court made a mistake (*Stupple* v *Royal Insurance Co. Ltd* [1971] 1 QB 50).

There is little to choose between Beatrice and Cassandra so far as their breach of duty is concerned. Nevertheless, it is possible that Cassandra may argue that she was not to blame (or not solely to blame) for the second collision with Algernon because he stumbled unpredictably into her path. This will be an allegation of negligence against Beatrice because Algernon was still suffering from the effects of the first collision at the time. However, it is more likely that Beatrice and Cassandra will both be regarded as causes of the harm suffered by Algernon and that the issue of contribution between joint tortfeasors will arise. Such argument is permissible under the Civil Liability (Contribution) Act 1978, s. 1 (*Pride of Derby and Derbyshire Angling Association Ltd* v *British Celanese Ltd* [1952] 1 All ER 1326).

So far as the Civil Liability (Contribution) Act 1978 is concerned, it will make no difference whether Beatrice acted deliberately and Cassandra only negligently, since they will both be regarded as joint tortfeasors. Both may be required to make a contribution under the terms of the Act, and it will not be a defence for the merely negligent to argue that the degree of fault of the other tortfeasor was greater. Thus it has been held that the defence of *ex turpi causa non oritur actio* will not apply as between joint tortfeasors (*K* v *P (J third party)* [1993] 1 All ER 521). However, the greater degree of fault of one joint tortfeasor will clearly be a relevant consideration in determining what share of responsibility should be allocated to each defendant.

Algernon's injuries

If Beatrice tries to put all the blame for Algernon's injuries on to Cassandra, she faces two problems. First, the medical evidence does not support such an allegation since we are told that Algernon's doctors cannot say which car was the cause of his serious impairment. Secondly, she cannot reasonably expect to escape being brought in as a joint tortfeasor, even if it could be shown that Cassandra's car caused the greater amount of the injuries to Algernon.

This is a case in which it is known that Beatrice caused at least some of the injuries suffered by Algernon and the only question to be resolved is whether Cassandra added to those injuries or not. Since the second collision has rendered Algernon unconscious when, previously, he was in a concussed state, this would suggest that the added damage would be attributable to Cassandra under the 'but for' test (*Barnett* v *Chelsea & Kensington Hospital Management Committee* [1969] 1 QB 428). This case is not to be likened to *Baker* v *Willoughby* [1967] AC 467, where there was a pre-existing disability caused by one tortfeasor and a subsequent worsening of that disability by another tortfeasor, there being no connection between the two tortfeasors or between the two incidents giving rise to the successive disabilities. Moreover, in *Baker* there were also important policy considerations since the later injury was caused by a criminal who shot the plaintiff in the leg, causing that leg to be amputated. This later act was held not to affect the plaintiff's existing claim for damages against his former employer for injuries caused to the same leg in an accident at work. Ignoring the 'but for' test, the defendant employer was held liable for the loss resulting from the original accident, the additional damage caused by the criminal being discounted. Had the plaintiff sought to bring an action in respect of the later injuries caused by the criminal, it was considered that the pre-existing injuries to the leg would have had to have been taken into account, thereby reducing the plaintiff's quantum of damages. However, it remains the case that the criminal would not have been insured in respect of the damage he had caused and there was probably little likelihood of the criminal being able to pay the damages even if the plaintiff had chosen to sue him. As an alternative to the *Baker* v *Willoughby* approach, it was held in *Jobling* v *Associated Dairies Ltd* [1982] AC 794 that a court should take account of the vicissitudes of life, such as in that case the subsequent development of the disease myelopathy, thereby reducing the plaintiff's overall claim for damages against the defendant in respect of a negligently caused work injury. However, it may be argued that the second road accident is not a 'vicissitude of life' but a separate tortious act which is a cause of the harm suffered by Algernon.

The present case should also be distinguished from the situation which arises when the plaintiff *must* have been injured by one of two defendants, but it cannot be determined which of the two is responsible. In such a case the court will have to give judgment in favour of both parties, unless it can be shown that they are acting as joint tortfeasors. In *Cook* v *Lewis* [1952] 1 DLR 1, however, a Canadian Court held that it was the responsibility of each defendant to exculpate himself in such a case, so that judgment could be given against both defendants if they both failed to call exculpatory evidence. However, this proposition may be limited to cases where there is some common venture between the defendants (e.g., a hunting trip). On the evidence in the present case, it would be difficult to say that Beatrice and Cassandra were engaged on a joint venture.

Desdemona's intervention

The question arises whether Algernon's employers can successfully sue Beatrice or Cassandra for the loss of their money which had been entrusted to Algernon. Such a claim would face three possible problems. First, a negligent motorist may not owe a duty of care to the employers of a pedestrian who is injured as a result of the motorist's negligent driving. Secondly, the employers have suffered pure economic loss and thirdly, the intervention of Desdemona may be regarded as a *novus actus interveniens*, which breaks the chain of causation between the original negligence and the loss of the money.

If Desdemona's kick caused significant injuries to Algernon, this would justify an argument by Beatrice and Cassandra to the effect that they should not be liable in damages in respect of those injuries. They could only be treated as joint tortfeasors with Desdemona if Desdemona's criminal assault had been a sufficiently related consequence of the original accident. If Desdemona's conduct amounted to a *novus actus interveniens* this will release Beatrice and Cassandra from any liability for any additional damage which Desdemona caused. Generally, a third party act will not be a *novus actus interveniens* if it is a reasonably foreseeable consequence of the original defendant's conduct (*Stansbie* v *Troman* [1948] 2 KB 48), but it would be difficult to argue that Desdemona's intervention could have been foreseen, with the result that it may be put forward as a break in the chain of causation. Thus, as in *Baker* v *Willoughby*, the defendants (Beatrice and Cassandra) may not be responsible for the additional loss caused by Desdemona's criminal act following their original negligence.

The House of Lords has held that, in cases where damage might have been caused by one tortfeasor or by natural causes, the tortfeasor cannot be held responsible unless it can be shown that the tortfeasor's negligence is the most likely cause of the damage (*Wilsher* v *Essex Area Health Authority* [1988] AC

1074). When there is doubt as to whether a particular defendant caused certain damage to the plaintiff, or whether it was caused by a *novus actus interveniens*, English law seems to dictate that there is no substitute for proof.

QUESTION 12

Sixteen-year-old Danny suffers from anorexia nervosa, an obsessional psychological disorder which results in excessive weight loss. He is referred to Dr Hook, a psychiatrist who correctly diagnoses Danny's complaint and prescribes a course of treatment involving the use of 'Adeposa', a drug recently developed by Billick Pharmaceuticals.

Dr Hook is aware that there is a small risk that patients treated with 'Adeposa' may develop kidney disease, but decides not to tell Danny on the ground that this might unduly worry his patient.

After three weeks of treatment, Danny develops a blood disorder and no progress appears to have been made in defeating Danny's weight problem. Dr Hook decides that it is necessary to feed Danny through the use of a drip-feed. Danny refuses to give his consent to this procedure. Believing that this is in Danny's best interests, Dr Hook orders the use of the drip-feed despite Danny's unwillingness to consent.

Dr Hook is subsequently informed by a colleague that, two months ago, an article published in a specialist medical journal concerned with blood disorders, suggested that patients treated with 'Adeposa' might develop blood disorders. Danny subsequently dies as a result of the blood disorder he has developed. Advise Horace, Danny's father.

Commentary

This question raises the issues of breach of duty and causation in the context of medical negligence. There is also the question of whether the drug is a defective product under the Consumer Protection Act 1987 and it also has to be considered whether the appropriate tort is that of negligence or trespass with particular reference to the issue of informed consent. Particular issues which require consideration are:

(a) the difference between damages awarded under the Fatal Accidents Act 1976 and the Law Reform (Miscellaneous Provisions) Act 1934;

(b)   whether the doctrine of informed consent is applicable in English law and if not what alternative test is used;

(c)   whether there is a breach of duty;

(d)   whether such breach of duty as there is causes the harm complained of;

(e)   whether 'Adeposa' is a defective product.

Suggested Answer

Since Danny is now dead, the effect of his death on the claim brought by his surviving relative, Horace, must be considered.

The fact of death does not prevent a person representing the estate of the deceased from bringing an action in tort. The Law Reform (Miscellaneous Provisions) Act 1934, s. 1(1) preserves an action in favour of the estate, provided the deceased would have been able to sue had he survived. The damages awarded to the estate cover the period between the date of breach of duty and death, but not into the future. Under the Fatal Accidents Act 1976 death also creates a new cause of action in favour of a dependant. The list of dependants in s. 1(3) of the 1976 Act include parents. Essentially, the action under the 1976 Act is one for the loss of a breadwinner and at the age of 16 Danny may not have been earning anything at all. The 1976 Act also permits an action for bereavement in favour of spouses or the parents of an unmarried child. At the age of 16 Danny is still a child and on the assumption that he is unmarried, Horace will be entitled to the fixed amount of bereavement damages of £7,500.

In Horace's action representing Danny's estate, it must be established that had Danny lived, Dr Hook would have owed him a duty of care, was in breach of that duty and that the breach of duty was the cause of the harm complained of. The duty issue will present no problems given the close proximity of the doctor/patient relationship and the fact that the damage seems foreseeable. However, there is the question whether Dr Hook was under a duty to warn Danny of the risks involved in the proposed course of treatment.

It is clear that such a duty does exist in some circumstances. For example, in *Thake* v *Maurice* [1986] 1 All ER 497 there was a duty to warn a patient about to undergo a vasectomy (male sterilisation) operation of the small risk that the operation might reverse itself. But Danny's position is different since there is a risk that telling him the truth might unduly worry him. This raises the issue of informed consent. In English law it is clear that the doctrine of informed consent has been rejected in relation to matters of disclosure of information (*Sidaway* v *Board of Governors of the Bethlem Royal Hospital and the Maudsley Hospital* [1985] AC 871), although there was an illuminating dissent on the part of Lord Scarman. But even he would admit to the existence of a therapeutic privilege in favour of a doctor where telling the whole truth might be injurious to the health of the patient. The majority in *Sidaway* based their decision on principles of negligence, requiring two questions to be answered. First, it must be asked whether a reasonable body of medical opinion would have gone along with the actions of the doctor under consideration, although in rare cases it is possible that general professional opinion is not capable of withstanding logical analysis, in which case, the court may hold that the body of opinion is not reasonable or responsible (*Bolitho* v *City and Hackney Health Authority* [1997] 4 All ER 771). For example, it has been held that the prevalent practice of ships' masters in allowing a roll-on roll-off ferry to sail before its bow doors were closed was unreasonable (*Re Herald of Free Enterprise, The Independent*, 18 December 1987).

If a body of responsible medical opinion would not have acted in the same way as Dr Hook, it should follow that the doctor is guilty of negligence. But if other reasonable doctors would have acted in the same way, it becomes necessary to enquire whether that practice is acceptable by asking if there is a substantial risk involving grave and adverse consequences which requires disclosure. What is grave and adverse will require consideration of the percentage risk. Thus in *Sidaway* a risk of spinal cord injury of less than 1 per cent was too small, but a 10 per cent risk of suffering a stroke was sufficient to invoke a duty to take care in *Reibl* v *Hughes* (1980) 114 DLR (3d) 1.

The risk of which Dr Hook is aware does not develop, but a risk of which he is unaware does. Since in *Sidaway* it was held that the doctor's duty is to exercise skill and judgment to improve the patient's health, there is little he can do to guard against a risk of which he is unaware, in which case, a duty may not be owed.

Even if a duty of care is owed, there is still the issue of breach of that duty. The standard set is that of the reasonable doctor (*Bolam* v *Friern Hospital Management Committee* [1957] 2 All ER 118). Under this test, current knowledge must be considered (*Roe* v *Minister of Health* [1954] 2 QB 66) and the basis of the test is whether Dr Hook has acted as other doctors would have acted in the circumstances, provided their general practice is acceptable

(*Whitehouse* v *Jordan* [1981] 1 All ER 267). However, this test has been criticised by Lord Scarman in *Sidaway* on the ground that it means doctors actually set their own standard of care in their expert medical evidence. Other members of the House of Lords in the same case were prepared to regard a general practice as unacceptable if no reasonable or prudent doctor would adopt it, and this extended to include non-disclosure.

The problem is whether a psychiatrist should be aware of an article in a purely medical journal. *Roe* v *Minister of Health* is distinguishable here as the risk in that case was one of which no doctor could have been aware. But here awareness prior to the alleged breach of duty is a possibility, in which case there may be a breach of duty. Conversely, an important issue in medical negligence cases is the utility of the defendant's conduct. It has been observed that the risk of medical negligence has to be weighed against the undoubted benefits to society provided by doctors (*Roe* v *Minister of Health*) so that some risks may have to be accepted. In any case, it seems that a doctor is not to be regarded as negligent simply because he fails to take account of an article in a medical journal such as *The Lancet*. What is required, instead, is that he should have failed to adopt a practice which has become accepted in the profession (*Crawford* v *Board of Governors of Charing Cross Hospital, The Times*, 8 December 1953). Thus it has been said that a gynaecologist ought to be aware of developments in mainstream practice but would not have to be aware of the content of more obscure journals (*Gascoine* v *Ian Sheridan & Co.* [1994] 5 Med LR 437).

Even if a breach of duty is established, the issue of causation also has to be considered. It must be asked whether a prescription followed by a failure to disclose facts is the cause of the blood disorder. Prima facie, the blood disorder would not have occurred 'but for' the prescription (*Barnett* v *Chelsea & Kensington HMC* [1969] 1 QB 428), but there is also the problem that the defendant must take the plaintiff as he finds him (*Smith* v *Leech Brain & Co.* [1962] 2 QB 405) which raises the issue of remoteness of damage. Conversely, if there are dual causes of the harm, it must be proved that Dr Hook's breach has materially increased the risk of harm (*McGhee* v *National Coal Board* [1973] 1 WLR 1). Alternatively, where there are multiple causes, it must be proved that it was Dr Hook's breach which caused the harm (*Wilsher* v *Essex Area Health Authority* [1988] AC 1074).

There is also the possibility of an action for medical trespass. An action for battery is appropriate where invasive treatment is given without the consent of the patient. In this case, Danny has quite clearly refused to consent to the use of a drip-feed, but Dr Hook claims to have acted out of necessity. A child cannot give a valid consent below the age of 16 (Children and Young Persons Act 1969, s. 8(1)). Since Danny is a minor, Horace, his father, is likely to have been consulted over the question of medical treatment. At common law and by statute, the parent is presumed to have a power to give a proxy consent (Children and Young Persons Act 1969, s. 8(3)). However, if a child under the age of 16 is competent to decide for itself, parents cannot give proxy consent unless there is authorisation to speak on the child's behalf. If a child is competent in the sense that he has a significant understanding and intelligence to fully understand the proposed medical procedure (*Gillick* v *West Norfolk and Wisbech AHA* [1985] 3 All ER 402) and does not give his consent the doctor may decide whether to treat or not. The child's refusal should be an important factor in that decision. If the child is not '*Gillick* competent', the doctor must use his professional judgment. When the doctor takes his decision it must be decided what is in Danny's best interests. Thus if the invasive medical procedure is carried out in order to save Danny's life, the court, acting under its inherent wardship jurisdiction may provide a valid consent in the face of the minor's objections (*Re W (a minor)* [1992] 4 All ER 627).

Finally, there is the question whether the drug, 'Adeposa', is a defective product under the Consumer Protection Act 1987. Section 2(2) of the Act imposes primary liability on the producer rather than the supplier. Dr Hook is not the producer, but the producer, whoever he is, has supplied a product which has caused damage of the kind covered by the Act. However, the facts of the problem suggest that the possible defect has only recently been revealed to the medical world. Under s. 4(1)(e) the producer has a defence if he can show that the state of scientific knowledge at the time the product was put into circulation was not such as to allow the defect to be discovered. The wording of s. 4(1)(e) might appear to introduce subjective considerations such as whether the defendant could afford to keep up with the pace of change in pharmaceutical and medical research, which may mean that the defence protects the producer. However, that view has been denied in the European Court of Justice in *EC Commission* v *United Kingdom (Re The Product Liability Directive)* (Case C-300/951) [1997] 3 CMLR 923, it being held that the unusual wording of the defence as stated in s. 4(1)(e) is in accordance with the language used in the EC Product Liability Directive. It must therefore be assumed that a court should now apply an objective standard in determining whether the development risks defence is applicable or not. If a purely objective test is applied and the research had revealed the defect before the drug was first put on the market, the producer will be liable under the Act provided the relevant research was discoverable at the time 'Adeposa' was first put into circulation. But what is 'discoverable' was regarded by the ECJ as a matter to be decided by the court of first instance, as a matter of fact. However, some advice was given in the ECJ on the matter of discoverability. For example, it was observed that a brilliant piece of scientific research by a Chinese academic which had been published only in the Cantonese language in a little-heard-of scientific publication would not be regarded as discoverable knowledge in the United Kingdom. Conversely, a piece of research published in a major United States publication in the English language might have to be treated differently. These observations would seem to raise the question whether a psychiatrist such as Dr. Hook would be expected to be aware of developments pertaining to blood disorders. Assuming the relevant publication was generally available in the United Kingdom, it might be regarded as a publication of which Dr. Hook should have been aware.

QUESTION 13

Graham, a professional cricketer, had been making his way by car to a cricket match in Chelmsford when he noticed that a lorry, owned and operated by Nationwide Carriers Ltd, had run out of fuel and come to a halt in the middle lane of the motorway along which he was driving. Graham decelerated but was struck by a car that was being driven by Tom, which had crossed the central reservation from the other side of the motorway. The reason for the crash was that Tom had been paying too much attention to what had been happening on the other side of the road.

Graham's leg was badly injured in the collision, and while he was awaiting medical treatment at the roadside, Nick, a thief, stole his wallet and made off with it. In the course of his treatment, Graham's doctor told Graham that if he is to stand any chance of continuing his career as a professional cricketer, he will need an operation to remove an excess of fluid on his knee. The build up of the fluid may have been caused by the accident with Tom, or by natural causes.

Later, while Graham was being transferred from the hospital to an ambulance to take him home, his injured leg was struck by a projectile thrown by a person protesting about cuts in National Health Service expenditure. It soon became clear that Graham would never play cricket again and that he would lose earnings of £60,000 per year for the next two years.

Advise Nationwide Carriers Ltd, Tom and the protester as to their respective potential liabilities in tort.

Commentary

The issues arising out of the above facts are numerous and include the following:

(a)   What is the cause of the crash? Is there a *novus actus interveniens*?

(b)   Is the theft a *novus actus interveniens*?

(c)   Is the build up of fluid on the knee caused by the accident or is there a natural cause?

(d)   What is the relevance of the vicissitudes of life?

(e)   Is the throwing of the projectile a *novus actus interveniens*?

(f)   How far is the extent of damage suffered a relevant consideration? Is there an eggshell skull plaintiff?

The first problem with which Graham is faced is that of identifying just whom to sue in respect of the injuries sustained in the car crash. There is *prima facie* evidence of negligence on the part of both Nationwide Carriers Ltd (in their failure to ensure that the lorry was fit for motorway driving) and Tom (who failed to drive with sufficient attention). This, however, does not resolve the difficult causation question of who, for the purposes of the tort of negligence, may be held responsible for the several losses that have been suffered by Graham. For the purposes of clarity of analysis, it is best to treat each head of loss separately.

In respect of the initial injuries occasioned by the crash between Tom and Graham, it is clear that the usual determinant of causation — the 'but for' test propounded in *Barnett* v *Chelsea and Kensington HMC* [1969] 1 QB 428 — is of no use, as this applies only to situations in which there is clearly only one factor that has caused the plaintiff's loss. In the present situation, by contrast, there are the two possible causes already alluded to. The relevant law in this context is that contained in *Rouse* v *Squires* [1973] QB 889. There, Cairns LJ said that:

> If a driver so negligently manages his vehicle as to cause it to obstruct the highway and constitute a danger to other road users, including those who are driving too fast, or not keeping a proper look-out, but not those who

deliberately or recklessly drive into the obstruction, then the first driver's negligence may be held to have contributed to the causation of an accident of which the immediate cause was the negligent driving of the vehicle which because of the presence of the obstruction collides with it or with some other vehicle or some other person.

In applying that speech to the present facts it is apparent that if Tom's driving was merely negligent, then both he and Nationwide Carriers would be liable for the injuries suffered by Graham. If, however, Tom's driving was reckless — and the fact that he was oblivious to what was happening in his own carriageway suggests this — then Tom's act will constitute a *novus actus interveniens* rendering him solely liable for the injuries suffered by Graham (*Wright* v *Lodge* [1994] 4 All ER 299).

Since there is no evidence to suggest any contributory negligence on Graham's part it can be stated with some measure of confidence that (at least) Tom (if not Tom and Nationwide Carriers jointly) may be held liable for the full extent of those losses flowing from the original accident. The key question thus becomes (which of the losses may be treated, in law, as having been caused by the original accident? As regards the loss of Graham's wallet, it is likely that the courts would take the view that it was too unforeseeable an event to be regarded as flowing from the initial accident. Accordingly, it would mark a break in the chain of causation and hence be something for which neither Tom nor Nationwide Carriers could be held liable.

In respect of the fluid on Graham's knee, we are not sure whether it was caused by the accident, by natural causes or by a combination of the two. If it can be proved that it was attributable to natural causes then it will be regarded as a vicissitude of life for which the defendant(s) will not be held responsible (*Jobling* v *Associated Dairies* [1982] AC 794). If, however, Graham can show that, on the balance of probabilities, the accident did cause the accumulation of fluid on Graham's knee, then the defendant(s) may be held liable for whatever losses he suffered as a consequence (*Hotson* v *East Berkshire AHA* [1987] 3 WLR 232). Indeed, liability will attach even if the accident made only a 'material contribution' to the accumulation of fluid on his knee so long as the loss he suffered thereafter was attributable to his knee condition (*McGhee* v *NCB* [1973] 1 WLR 1).

It should not be assumed, however, that Graham's loss of a professional cricketing career is attributable to any unitary cause. It could be due to the fluid on his knee that an operation would not be able to cure. It could equally be due to the projectile that struck his leg. In these circumstances, since the onus of proving causation lies on Graham, if an alternative explanation remains a possibility, Graham may not have discharged the burden of proof which lies on him. (See *Pickford* v *Imperial Chemical Industries* [1998] 3 All ER 462.) Finally, it could, as noted above, be a product of both of these causes. There is certainly a strong case for arguing that the unreasonable act of the protester amounted to a *novus actus interveniens* so long as the act was also unforeseeable (see *The Oropesa* [1943] P 32). On the other hand, it was held in *Baker* v *Willoughby* [1970] AC 467 that the deliberate act of a third party that merely 'exacerbates' the plaintiff's initial injury (which latter was caused by the defendant) is insufficient to exonerate the defendant from liability for the loss of amenity that can still be attributed to the initial injury. On this authority, then, if it could be shown that on the balance of probabilities the defendant(s) in our case made a material contribution to Graham's loss, he (or they) might still be liable in damages. Similarly, if it could be shown that the loss of Graham's career was wholly attributable to the injury caused by the projectile, then it would be the person who threw it who would be liable for Graham's loss of earnings (but not loss in terms of pain and suffering that was caused by the original accident (*Baker* v *Willoughby* [1970] AC 467).

The likelihood, given the complex facts, is that Graham would sue them all as joint defendants. This would be advisable since it would help to ensure the recovery of compensation by way of damages subject to his loss of earnings being caused by fluid on the knee which had occurred by natural causes. Even if he had had a chance of recovery before the throwing of the projectile, if it is more likely than not that the fluid on his knee would have put a stop to his career, then no action would lie (*Hotson* v *East Berkshire AHA* [1987] 3 WLR 232). Assuming, however, that a remedy could be awarded, with respect to the quantum of damages it could be argued that the 'eggshell skull' principle could be invoked to allow Graham to recover the full amount of lost earnings (*Vacwell Engineering Ltd* v *BDH Chemicals Ltd* [1971] 1 QB 111). These would not, however, be calculated on the usual multiplier basis because of the short-term nature of sports careers. We are told that Graham only had a very limited number of years to go and this would figure in the assessment of damages.

5 Employers' Liability

INTRODUCTION

The collection of tort-based duties which form the basis of an employer's liability all raise different issues. The personal, non-delegable duty of care owed by an employer to his employees is fault-based and can be discharged by the exercise of reasonable care. Where the duty applies, it is one to take reasonable care to provide a competent staff, a safe place of work and a safe system of work. Moreover, since the duty is non-delegable, it is no defence for the employer to claim that he expected another person to ensure that the duty was complied with.

Where an employee commits a tort in the workplace so that a fellow employee or a stranger suffers actionable damage, the employer may be held vicariously liable. Since there is no fault on the part of the employer, this is a variety of strict liability and is justified on the basis that an employer is in a unique position to be able to spread the cost of accidents by way of insurance. The key issues here are whether the person who commits the tort is an employee or servant and whether the tort is committed in the course of employment.

A further basis for the liability of an employer is that he may be in breach of a statutory duty giving rise to a civil cause of action in damages. It is frequently the case that industrial safety legislation creates penalties for a failure to keep a safe place of work, but it must also be decided whether the statutory provision also confers an action in tort. Generally, it is said that the test to apply involves ascertaining the intention of Parliament, but this may not always be easy since what Parliament intended may not be immediately apparent. Having established that a cause of action exists, it then has to be determined whether the duty is owed to the plaintiff, whether it has been broken and whether the breach is the cause of the harm complained of by the plaintiff.

Although the following questions appear together under the heading 'employers' liability', it should be appreciated that the relevant rules of law do not exist in a vacuum and must be considered to form part of the wider picture of the law of tort. Thus an employee cannot claim to be able to sue his employer in circumstances where others would fail, for example, in a common law negligence action (see *White* v *Chief Constable of South Yorkshire* discussed in **Chapter 4**).

QUESTION 1

The (fictious) Safety at Work (Miscellaneous Provisions) Regulations 1994 provide, inter alia, that:

(1)   Employers shall ensure, so far as is reasonably practicable, that all abrasive wheels are safe to use.

(2)   It shall be the responsibility of both employer and employee to ensure that safety harnesses are worn when work is carried out more than six metres from ground level.

(3)   Where inflammable materials are stored in the workplace, it shall be the responsibility of the employer to ensure that, for the protection of employees and the community at large, all fire appliances are adequately maintained.

The Regulations state that breach of the above provisions constitutes the commission of a criminal offence punishable by the payment of a fine. No provision is made for civil law remedies.

Eric and Roland are employed to clean the windows in a factory owned and operated by Plasticraft Ltd. Neither employee is wearing a safety harness. Roland is working on windows five metres from ground level and Eric is cleaning a window seven metres from ground level. Eric slips and falls on to Roland. Both men are injured. The noise caused by the fall causes Norman to look away while he is sharpening a chisel on an abrasive wheel. Norman's finger is badly injured when it makes contact with the rotating wheel. Evidence shows that a device could have been fitted to the wheel which would cause it to stop as soon as a chisel ceases to make contact. Plasticraft Ltd claim not to have the resources to be able to fit such a device.

As a result of his injury, Norman drops a burning cigarette, which ignites a quantity of rag on the floor. Because fire extinguishers have not been properly maintained, the fire spreads and damages a car owned by Percy, a visitor to the factory.

Advise Plasticraft Ltd of their tortious liability for breach of the provisions of the Safety at Work (Miscellaneous Provisions) Regulations 1994.

Commentary

The principal issues to consider are:

(a)   Does the statutory provision confer an action in tort? What tests help to give the answer?

(b)   Assuming such an action does exist, is the standard of liability strict or fault-based?

(c)   Is there a breach of the duty imposed by the statute?

(d)   Is that breach, if proved, the cause of the harm complained of?

Suggested Answer

Two principal issues arise when it comes to be decided whether the breach of a statutory regulation gives rise to an action for damages. First, it must be asked whether the regulation confers an action in tort and the second question is whether there is an actionable tort.

Whether or not a statutory provision creates a civil cause of action (known as an action for breach of statutory duty 'simpliciter' by Lord Browne-Wilkinson in *X (minors)* v *Bedfordshire County Council* [1995] 3 WLR 152) turns on an interpretation of the intention of Parliament (*Hague* v *Deputy Governor of Parkhurst Prison* [1991] 3 All ER 733). There is a primary assumption that where a statute creates an obligation and provides for its enforcement in a particular manner, it does not confer a civil cause of action unless it is intended to protect an identified class of persons (*Lonrho Ltd* v *Shell Petroleum Co.* [1981] 2 All ER 456).

The regulations in this question impose a fine in the event of breach, which might result in a decision to the effect that this is the only intended consequence of breach (*Atkinson* v *Newcastle Waterworks Co.* (1877) 2 Ex D 441). Indeed, if the statutory provision does provide an adequate remedy, there is a presumption that there will be no civil action for damages (*Wentworth* v *Wiltshire County Council* [1993] 2 WLR 175). However, the emphasis here is upon the adequacy of the statutory remedy. Thus there may be cases in which a remedy is provided for which a civil court may not regard as adequate recompense for an injured plaintiff. For example, in *Read* v *Croydon Corporation* [1938] 4 All ER 631 a penalty was provided for by the Waterworks

Clauses Act 1847, but this did not affect the decision to confer a civil right of action for failure to provide a wholesome water supply, although in this case there was also evidence of negligence on the part of the defendants (see also *Reffell* v *Surrey County Council* [1964] 1 All ER 743).

Even if the presumption against a civil cause of action were not to apply, it would also have to be established by the various potential plaintiffs that they formed part of an identifiable class of persons who Parliament intended to protect. For these purposes, it is generally assumed that employees are a sufficiently identifiable class to warrant protection (*Groves* v *Lord Wimborne* [1898] 2 QB 402). Moreover, a visitor to premises which are not safe because of a breach of fire safety regulations may also be treated as falling within an identifiable class of persons (*Solomons* v *Gertzenstein Ltd* [1954] 2 QB 243). Conversely, a statutory provision which purports to protect the whole community, such as highway users (*Phillips* v *Britannia Laundry Ltd* [1923] 2 KB 832) or the water consuming public (*Atkinson* v *Newcastle Waterworks Co.*) is considered not to confer an action in tort. Generally, the rule based on the class protected has not proved helpful since it may be invoked or ruled out depending on what the court, on a particular occasion, regards as a class of people protected by the statutory provision (see *Richardson* v *Pitt-Stanley* [1995] ICR 303). These rules might be taken to indicate that regulations (1) and (2) which are intended for the benefit of employees will confer an action in tort, but that regulation (3) may be construed so as not to give rise to an action in tort. It is worth emphasising that fire safety regulations are likely to be aimed at the protection of individuals rather than their property. This would seem to suggest that Percy may have no cause of action under the 1994 Regulations in respect of the damage to his car.

Norman is likely to bring an action for damages based on the breach of regulation (1) which requires employers to ensure, so far as is practicable, that all abrasive wheels are safe to use. The duty clearly rests on the employer, but it must be asked whether the reference to reasonable practicability imposes a fault-based or a strict standard of liability. The use of the phrase 'so far as is reasonably practicable' might suggest a standard of reasonable care on the part of the employer, although the phrase has been held to impose a stricter standard (*Edwards* v *National Coal Board* [1949] 1 All ER 743). In *Larner* v *British Steel plc* [1993] 4 All ER 102 the Court of Appeal held that for the purposes of the Factories Act 1961, s. 29(1), which uses similar language, it was for the employee to prove that the workplace was unsafe and that this lack of safety was the cause of his injury, but that it was for the employer to prove that reasonably practicable precautions could not have been taken to guard against the harm caused (see also *Nimmo v Alexander Cowan & Sons Ltd* [1968] AC 107). Moreover, it is for the defendant to plead and prove that it was not reasonably practicable to keep the workplace safe, which will involve an assessment of the degree of risk and the time and cost involved in averting the risk (*Mains v Uniroyal Engelbert Tyres Ltd, The Times*, 29 September 1995).

The question states that a safety device could have been fitted, but that Plasticraft Ltd could not afford to install such a device. On the assumption that the cost of fitting the safety device is not exorbitantly expensive, this may seem to suggest that reasonably practicable precautions have not been taken by Plasticraft Ltd and that they may be liable for the injury suffered by Norman.

Paragraph (2) of the Regulations places a joint responsibility on the employer and his employees to ensure that safety harnesses are used when work is carried out at a height greater than six metres from ground level. The wording of regulation (2) is so specific that it seems unlikely that anyone working at a height lower than six metres will be owed a duty (*Chipchase v British Titan Products Ltd* [1956] 1 QB 545). On this basis, regulation (2) will provide no remedy in favour of Roland since he is working only five metres from ground level. Conversely, Eric was working at the specified height when he fell, with the result that it must be considered whether Plasticraft's alleged breach of the duty is the cause of the harm suffered by Eric. Matters are complicated by the fact that Eric is also in breach of the duty which rests on him to ensure that a safety harness is used. Which breach is the cause of the harm complained of will often turn on whether there were further precautions which could have been taken by the employer to ensure compliance with the safety regulation. Thus in *Ginty v Belmont Building Supplies Ltd* [1959] 1 All ER 414 the employer could not have done more than he had to explain to employees the importance of using crawling boards when working on an unsafe roof. Accordingly, the employee's deliberate breach of the instructions given to him was regarded as the cause of the harm complained of. In contrast, in *Boyle v Kodak Ltd* [1969] 2 All ER 439, the employer had failed to give adequate instructions on how to use a ladder, with the result that his breach of duty was regarded as the cause of the injury. The question does not state what precautions have been taken by Plasticraft Ltd, but if there is more they could have done, this would seem to suggest that their failure to ensure that a safety harness is used by Eric is the cause of the injury.

QUESTION 2

Douglas drives a petrol tanker for British Diesel Fuels Ltd (BDF) and wears an overall which bears the BDF logo. He is also paid a higher than average wage for a tanker operator on a weekly basis, but is required by the terms of his contract to assume financial responsibility for the cost of maintaining his vehicle.

Douglas has been told not to offer lifts to anyone. In breach of this instruction, he takes his 17-year-old son, Eric, on a delivery round. Douglas fails to apply the brake to his tanker while he goes to a shop to buy a packet of chewing gum. While he is away, he asks Eric to guard the vehicle. The tanker begins to roll forward and strikes a petrol pump owned by Petrol Dispensers Ltd, causing a fire in which Eric is badly burned.

A term in Douglas's contract of employment provides that his wages are to be paid in respect of all journeys undertaken on BDF's behalf, whether or not the tanker is under Douglas's control. Subsequently, Douglas is asked by BDF to undertake work for another company, English Petroleum Ltd (EP). While Douglas is waiting for his brand new tanker to be filled up at EP's depot, he slips on a patch of oil which has been deliberately spilled by Alphonse, a known practical joker. The spillage had not been cleaned up despite the fact that Brian, a supervisor, had known of it for some 30 minutes. Douglas cuts his leg when he falls to the ground, but nonetheless takes the tanker out on a delivery round. Because the new tanker has defective brakes, Douglas is unable to stop it and he crashes into a lamp-post. Douglas's arm is broken in the collision. As a result of this Douglas suffers depression at the thought of being absent from work.

Advise British Diesel Fuels Ltd and English Petroleum Ltd of their tortious liability for these incidents.

Commentary

Factors to consider include:

(a)   has Douglas committed a tort?

(b)   is Douglas an employee under the control, integration and commercial risk tests?

(c)   does Douglas act in the course of his employment?

(d)   does English Petroleum or British Diesel Fuels owe a duty of care to Douglas in respect of the unsafe place he is asked to work in and the equipment he is asked to use and does that duty, if any, extend to cover mental harm?

Suggested Answer

A preliminary, but essential, consideration is whether Douglas's failure to apply the brake to his vehicle amounts to the commission of a tort. While omissions to act can cause problems in terms of establishing the existence of a duty of care, it is clear that an omission in the course of conduct, such as a failure by a driver to apply his brakes, does reveal the existence of a duty to take care (*Kelly* v *Metropolitan Railway* [1895] 1 QB 944). Moreover, it is accepted that a driver owes a duty of care to other road users (*Nettleship* v *Weston* [1971] 2 QB 691) and that in not applying his brakes, Douglas falls below the standard expected of a reasonable man.

While Douglas may be personally liable, it may be in the interests of Petrol Dispensers and Eric to show that Douglas is an employee acting in the course of his employment so that BDF may be held vicariously liable for Douglas's tort.

Whether Douglas is an employee will depend on a number of considerations. Generally, an employee is a person who is subject to the control of his employer in the sense that the employer can tell him what to do and how to do it (*Collins* v *Hertfordshire County Council* [1947] KB 598). This test has given rise to difficulties of application in that many employees are highly skilled and often the employer has little knowledge of precisely how the work is to be done. As a result, a number of other tests have been employed by the courts in determining who is an employee. It may be relevant to consider whether Douglas has been integrated into BDF's business (*Stevenson, Jordan & Harrison Ltd* v *MacDonald & Evans* [1952] 1 TLR 101). Since Douglas wears a BDF uniform and is paid weekly wages, this would appear to be the case, although there is the difficulty that Douglas bears a responsibility to maintain his vehicle. In this last respect, it has been suggested that it is important to have regard to the incidence of the commercial risk in relation to the work done by the alleged employee (*Ready Mixed Concrete (South East) Ltd* v *Minister of Pensions & National Insurance* [1968] 2 QB 497). Here, Douglas does appear to undertake some risk in respect of the operation of his vehicle, but the fact that he is paid an enhanced wage might be taken to suggest that BDF have covered most of this risk themselves. On this basis, it may be assumed that Douglas is an employee. Another relevant factor to consider is the intention of the parties. This may be derived from evidence such as a description of somebody as an employee, but special care may need to be taken to ensure that the description of somebody as an employee or an independent contractor is not a mere sham (*Ferguson* v *Dawson Partners (Contractors) Ltd* [1976]

1 WLR 1213 — the description 'labour only sub-contractor' was used to avoid tax and national insurance liability).

Whether Douglas acts in the course of his employment raises a number of issues. Generally, an employer will be vicariously liable if an employee wrongfully performs a function he is employed to carry out (*Century Insurance Ltd* v *Northern Ireland Road Transport Board* [1942] AC 509), but the employer will not be vicariously liable if the employee is engaged on a 'frolic of his own' (*Joel* v *Morrison* (1834) 6 C & P 501) or does an act he was never employed to do.

The question informs us that Douglas has been expressly forbidden to offer lifts to another person. The mere fact that there has been an express prohibition does not necessarily mean that the forbidden act is not done in the course of employment. In *Twine* v *Bean's Express* (1946) 62 TLR 458, a prohibition on giving lifts to others was held to exclude the possibility of vicarious liability where a hitchhiker was injured in a collision caused by the employee's negligence. However, in *Rose* v *Plenty* [1976] 1 WLR 141 regard was had to the purpose for which the prohibited act was done. It followed that an express prohibition against giving lifts to others had no effect where a milkman had asked the plaintiff to help him on his milk round. The prohibited act had been done for the benefit of the employer. The difference between the two cases appears to be that the plaintiff in *Rose* was assisting the employer's business. This view seems to be borne out by the decision in *Vasey* v *Surrey Free Inns Ltd* [1995] 10 CL 641 where two 'bouncers' attacked the plaintiff after he had kicked a door on the defendant's premises. The Court of Appeal held the defendant vicariously liable on the basis that the bouncers had acted unlawfully but for the protection of their employer's property. In the present question Eric appears to be closer to the plaintiff in *Rose* than the hitchhiker in *Twine* which might suggest that Douglas's act is done in the course of his employment.

A further consideration is whether the plaintiff is aware of the prohibition, since this will allow him to avoid injury due to the prohibited act (*Stone* v *Taffe* [1974] 3 All ER 1016). This may be the case since Eric and Douglas are father and son and Douglas might have mentioned the prohibition, but it seems odd that the knowledge of the plaintiff should turn what is an act done in the course of employment into one which is not.

Apart from the problem of prohibited acts, the question states that Douglas is in a shop at the time the accident occurs. It has been held that an employee who takes a meal break no longer acts in the course of his employment if he is the cause of an accident while on the break (*Crook* v *Derbyshire Stone* [1956] 1 WLR 432). However, in the question, Douglas does go to a shop, but the cause of the accident is the failure to apply the brake, which happened while he was in charge of the vehicle. On this basis, he is still likely to be acting in the course of his employment. Moreover, Douglas's contract of employment provides that he is to be paid in respect of all journeys whether or not he is in control of the vehicle. In *Smith* v *Stages* [1989] 2 WLR 528 the House of Lords held that an appropriately worded provision in a contract of employment could mean that an employee is on duty even when not engaged in the particular task he is employed to do. It may be that the term as to payment in Douglas's contract means that he is acting in the course of his employment so that BDF is liable for the damage to the petrol pump and for the injury to Eric.

Douglas is later asked to work for another employer. In these circumstances, BDF does not cease to be an employer and will owe Douglas a personal duty of care by virtue of the rule in *Wilsons and Clyde Coal Co. Ltd* v *English* [1938] AC 57. This non-delegable duty is to provide a safe place of work and requires the provision of a competent staff, adequate plant and equipment and a safe system of work. The fact that the accident occurs at the English Petroleum depot makes no difference since it is for the first employer to ensure that the duty is complied with (*McDermid* v *Nash Dredging & Reclamation Co. Ltd* [1987] 2 All ER 878).

The duty to provide a safe place of work extends not just to the bodily safety of an employee but also to his mental well-being (*Petch* v *Customs and Excise Commissioners* [1993] ICR 789). However, if an employee is to succeed in an action for stress-induced illness, it must be shown that the mental breakdown is foreseeable. This may be the case where an employee has suffered more than one nervous breakdown (*Walker* v *Northumberland County Council* [1995] 1 All ER 737), but perhaps not where it occurs for the first time. On this basis, the depression suffered by Douglas may not be regarded as foreseeable loss. However, the injury must be caused by the job the employee is asked to perform and must not be merely incidental to it. (See *White* v *Chief Constable of South Yorkshire*, discussed in **Chapter 4**.)

The question informs us that Douglas slips because he has slipped on a patch of oil deliberately left by a known practical joker. This would seem to suggest that a competent staff has not been employed, in which case it is the duty of the employer, if he is aware of Alphonse's propensity to play practical jokes, to protect other employees (*Hudson* v *Ridge Manufacturing Co. Ltd* [1957] 2 QB 348). This protection might be achieved by not employing Alphonse or by placing him in a job where he cannot pose a threat to others. Apart from the practical joke, there is a failure to clear up the spillage despite the fact that a supervisory employee has been aware of the danger for 30 minutes. This might suggest that there is not a safe system of work, in that inadequate instruction appears to have been given to Brian, or if it has the system has not been put into operation. In either event, whether the failure is that of the employer or an independent contractor to whom an employee has been lent, the first employer remains liable (*McDermid* v *Nash Dredging & Reclamation Co. Ltd* [1987] 2 All ER 878).

The tanker supplied to Douglas for use while he is working for EP might also infringe the requirement that proper plant and equipment be given to carry out the job. The duty owed by the employer in this respect is now provided for in the Employers' Liability (Defective Equipment) Act 1969 which holds the employer liable for defects in equipment given to an employee provided fault on the part of a third party can be proved. The term equipment is construed widely to include anything supplied to an employee for the purpose of carrying out the job he is employed to do (*Knowles* v *Liverpool City Council* [1993] 4 All ER 321). This would seem to include the petrol tanker in the present case. Moreover, it should not be too difficult to prove fault on the part of the manufacturer of a new petrol tanker. In these circumstances, it would seem that the equipment provided for Douglas's use is not of the required standard and that there is a further breach of the personal duty owed by his employer, BDF.

Since both English Petroleum Ltd and British Diesel Fuels Ltd may be responsible for the injury suffered by Douglas, they may be regarded as joint tortfeasors, in which case BDF may be able to seek a contribution from EP under the Civil Liability (Contribution) Act 1978, which has been held to apply to the situation in which an employer lends an employee to another employer (*Nelhams* v *Sandells Maintenance Ltd* [1996] PIQR P52).

6 Occupiers' Liability

INTRODUCTION

Although the two Occupiers' Liability Acts are based on previously existing common law rules, they do appear to differ somewhat from the common law rules they replaced. As such, the action is one for breach of a statutory duty, but the duty bears a very close resemblance to the fault-based rules of the tort of negligence. The duty owed to a lawful visitor is broader than that owed to a non-visitor, perhaps the most frequent example of which is a trespassing child, but the rules on breach of duty are identical to those which apply at common law. Often it is necessary to consider the effect of a warning identifying a particular danger or a disclaimer notice which seeks to exclude or restrict the liability of the occupier. In this last case, the provisions of the Unfair Contract Terms Act 1977 become particularly relevant.

QUESTION 1

Shambles Ltd are contracted by Multimillion plc to construct a block of flats. Shambles Ltd are responsible for the security of the site and they leave it unattended on Sundays when work is not in progress. The site is protected by a perimeter fence.

During working hours, Jack, an electrician under contract with Shambles Ltd, arrives hoping to repair a defective generator. He is told by a security guard that he must report to the site office in order to be provided with protective headgear to guard against the risks present on a building site, especially the possibility of debris falling from overhead operations which are in progress.

Jack sees the defective generator and decides to make a preliminary inspection before reporting to the site office. During this time, Jack stumbles over a drainage pipe left on the ground and is struck by rubble which falls from a crane. As a result of these incidents Jack suffers head and leg injuries. Some time after the event, Shambles Ltd put up a notice near the site office which states clearly that visitors should keep their eyes on the ground to avoid tripping over articles left temporarily on the site.

The following Sunday, Mark, aged 10, and his brother, Billy, aged 5, discover that if Mark pulls at the wire fence, Billy can crawl through a small gap. While crawling under the fence, Billy badly gashes his leg.

Harriet, a district nurse who is on call, sees what has happened and stops to give first aid. She treats Billy's wound and takes Mark and Billy to their home. Harriet fails to advise Billy's parents, Vanessa and Tarquin, that Billy should be taken to hospital. Billy's wound becomes infected with the result that his leg has to be amputated some weeks later.

Advise Jack and Billy.

Commentary

This question raises the issue of occupiers' liability to lawful visitors, child trespassers and rescuers as well as medical professional negligence and the question of causation.

The key issues to consider are:

(a)   who is an occupier?

(b)   when is an occupier liable for the acts of an independent contractor?

(c)   in order to effectively discharge the common duty of care, what must a warning do?

(d)   what is the nature of the duty owed to a non-visitor and in what circumstances is the duty broken?

(e)   is the intervention of the nurse a *novus actus interveniens* and if so does the nurse owe a duty of care?

Suggested Answer

Jack v *Shambles Ltd and Multimillion plc*

A duty is owed by an occupier who has *control* over the premises on which a child trespasser is injured (*Wheat* v *Lacon (E.) & Co.* [1966] AC 552), construing the Occupiers' Liability Act 1957, s. 1(2)(a). It is possible for there to be more than one occupier, since control of different parts of the same premises is a possibility. Multimillion plc, as owners, may be regarded as occupiers, but whether they are responsible for the acts of their contractors is a matter which requires consideration. The Occupiers' Liability Act (OLA) 1957, s. 2(4)(b) provides that an occupier is not to be treated as answerable for damage caused by any work of construction, maintenance or repair by an independent contractor if in the circumstances of the case it was reasonable to entrust the work to an independent contractor and that such steps as are reasonable have been taken to ascertain that the contractor was competent and the work was properly done. If the work done by the contractor is technical, which the occupier cannot be expected to check, it will be sufficient that the occupier has ascertained that the contractor is competent before employing him (*Haseldine* v *Daw & Sons Ltd* [1941] 2 KB 343). Building work seems to be sufficiently complex to justify the view that Multimillion will not be responsible for Shambles' acts, provided Shambles are reputable building contractors.

Since Shambles Ltd carry out building work for which they are responsible and that they are in charge of the security of the site, it is to be assumed that they have control of the premises and are occupiers for the purposes of both OLA 1957 and 1984 (*AMF International Ltd* v *Magnet Bowling Ltd* [1968] 2 All ER 789).

As a visiting contractor, Jack is owed the common duty of care (OLA 1957, s. 5(1)). Under OLA 1957, s. 2(2) the common duty of care is one to take such care as is necessary to see that the visitor is reasonably safe in using the premises for the purposes for which he is invited by the occupier to be there. Jack is invited on to the site to repair a generator, but he is injured when he trips over a pipe and when rubble falls on him from an overhead crane. But these events occur after he has been told to report to the site office in order to be provided with protective headgear.

As a preliminary issue, it is necessary to consider the circumstances in which the common duty of care is owed to a visitor. Prior to the enactment of the 1957 legislation, the common law rule was that an occupier only owed a special duty to lawful visitors in respect of the state of the premises and that if harm was caused by an activity carried out on land, ordinary negligence principles would apply. However, there are apparently conflicting provisions in the 1957 Act on this matter. In the first place, OLA 1957, s. 1(1) states that the occupier's duty applies in respect of dangers due to the state of the premises or to things done or omitted to be done on them. Taken at face value this would seem to suggest that activities on land, such as the operation of a crane, might be covered by the Act. In contrast, OLA 1957, s. 1(2) provides that the duty regulated is that imposed in consequence of a person's occupation or control of premises, which may be interpreted to mean that the duty only applies to the state of the land and does not apply to the activity duty. OLA 1984 also contains very similar language, and in *Revill v Newbury* [1996] 1 All ER 291 the Court of Appeal has held that for the purposes of the 1984 Act, alleged negligence on the part of an occupier in carrying out an activity on his land is to be considered under ordinary common law principles rather than under the special statutory rules which apply to occupiers. On this basis, the accident resulting from a pipe being left on the land may be regarded as a matter relating to the state of the premises, but the accident caused by the operation of the crane will have to be dealt with according to ordinary common law rules.

It is therefore necessary to ask whether, on *Donoghue v Stevenson* principles, Multimillion plc owe Jack a duty of care, whether there is a breach of that duty and whether that breach of duty is the cause of damage which is not too remote. It would be reasonable to assume that the occupier of a building site owes a duty of care to someone entering the premises as a contractual visitor and that, assuming there is some element of fault which leads to the rubble falling on Jack, there is a breach of duty. However, the fact that Jack ignores instructions given to him by a security guard which are specific to the particular risk which causes injury might lead to the conclusion that, at the very least, he is contributorily negligent, having failed to take reasonable care for his own safety (*Jones* v *Livox Quarries Ltd* [1952] 2 QB 608) and that his injuries are more serious than would otherwise have been the case had he heeded the warning given to him by the security guard (*Froome* v *Butcher* [1976] QB 286). Moreover, under the 'but for' test established in *Barnett* v *Chelsea & Kensington HMC* [1969] 1 QB 428, it might be argued that but for Jack's failure to heed the request to pick up a safety helmet, the accident might not have happened, although it seems more likely that in the circumstances outlined in the question, the accident would have happened anyway, whether Jack was wearing a hat or not and that the wearing of a hat would not have prevented all of the injury suffered by Jack. On this basis, it is probably more likely that Jack's damages will be apportioned in line with his degree of responsibility for the damage under the provisions of the Law Reform (Contributory Negligence) Act 1945, s. 1(1).

The duty under OLA 1957, s. 2(2) is to ensure that the visitor is reasonably safe, not absolutely safe. It might be argued that the warning given to Jack concerning the risks present on a building site serves to discharge the duty owed by Shambles Ltd to Jack. However, in relation to the risk of tripping over a pipe, the warning is non-specific. Warning of a risk can discharge the duty owed by an occupier, but it must enable the visitor to be safe (OLA 1957, s. 2(4)(a)). If Jack had gone to the site office, he would have been provided with a hat, which might have protected him from falling rubble, but it would have little effect in relation to the risk of harm resulting from tripping over a pipe. Although the occupier can expect a skilled person to guard against risks ordinarily incident to the job he does (OLA 1957, s. 2(3)(b) as explained in *Roles* v *Nathan* [1963] 2 All ER 908), this might be regarded as a general risk rather than one specific to the job undertaken by Jack, which according to the decision in *Roles* v *Nathan* is a risk in respect of which the warning will have no effect. Moreover, it has been held that there is no need to warn in respect of obvious dangers, such as the presence of slippery algae on a sea wall (*Staples* v *West Dorset DC* (1995) 93 LGR 536). It might be argued that the presence of a pipe on the ground on a building site is such an obvious possibility that no warning needs to be given, although it has been observed, in another context, that pedestrians in the street cannot be expected to walk around all day with their eyes to the ground (*Haley* v *London Electricity Board* [1965] AC 778). Jack might argue that the subsequent erection of a notice warning of the danger which has resulted in his injury is some admission of liability. However, there is authority to suggest that this is not the case, provided the danger is one which was obvious at the time of the accident (*Staples* v *West Dorset DC*).

Billy v *Shambles Ltd and Multimillion plc*

The same rules on who is an occupier apply whether the plaintiff is a lawful visitor or a non-visitor. Although at one time children were often regarded as implied visitors, it is probable that since the enactment of the 1984 legislation, the courts will recognise them as non-visitors to whom a limited duty is owed under OLA 1984. Moreover, since *Edwards* v *Railway Executive* [1952] AC 737 repeated trespass has been held not to be sufficient to create an implied licence.

OLA 1984, s. 1(3) lays down three criteria for the existence of a duty of care owed by an occupier to a trespasser. First, Shambles Ltd must be aware of the danger or have reasonable grounds for believing that it exists (OLA 1984, s. 1(3)(a)). Here there is no suggestion that Shambles Ltd knew the fence could be lifted, since force has to be applied. But the fact that young boys can lift it suggests that a reasonable occupier might have known otherwise.

Secondly, Shambles Ltd must have known or must have had reasonable grounds to believe that a child might come into the vicinity of the danger presented by their land or their fence (OLA 1984, s. 1(3)(b)). Building sites have been regularly regarded as allurements to children, e.g., *Pannett* v *McGuinness* [1972] 2 QB 599, therefore it is probably reasonable to assume this second requirement is satisfied.

The third requirement is that Shambles Ltd must be aware that the risk is one against which they could reasonably be expected to offer Billy some protection (OLA 1984, s. 1(3)(c)). This may require consideration of the practicality of taking greater precautions. But the fact that children have managed to lift the fence would suggest that a stronger structure might have been desirable.

Assuming there is a duty of care, breach of that duty must also be established. For these purposes, OLA 1984, s. 1(4) provides that Shambles Ltd must take reasonable care to ensure that Billy does not suffer personal injury or death due to the danger created on their premises. Thus it will be necessary to consider the magnitude of risk, precautions necessary to guard against that risk and the cost of taking such precautions, the objective to be attained by Shambles Ltd, the age of Billy and the nature of the premises.

Shambles Ltd may argue that under OLA 1984, s. 1(5) they have discharged their duty by taking sufficient steps to discourage Billy from taking the risk in the first place. They have erected a fence, but it is defective since children can lift it, which suggests that the steps taken are not sufficient.

Alternatively, it could be argued that Billy is contributorily negligent, having failed to take reasonable precautions for his own safety and having been in part a cause of the harm he suffers (*Jones* v *Livox Quarries* [1952] 2 QB 608). Indeed, Billy is in part a cause of the accident which results in his injuries, which may justify a high percentage reduction in his damages, based on the degree of his blameworthiness (*Stapeley* v *Gypsum Mines* [1953] AC 663). However, the courts are reluctant to hold a child to be guilty of contributory negligence, judging children by the standards expected of a reasonable child of the same age (*Gough* v *Thorne* [1966] 1 WLR 1387). Here Billy and Mark are aged 5 and 10 respectively, and it may not be reasonable to expect them to understand the risk.

Shambles Ltd may also be liable in damages for the events which follow the initial accident. Whether they are liable for the amputation depends on whether Harriet's intervention is a *novus actus interveniens*.

The act of a third party is capable of breaking the chain of causation if it is unreasonable (*The Oropesa* [1943] P 32). It must be asked if Harriet's failure to advise Billy to consult the hospital is sufficiently unreasonable to have the same effect. If Harriet has acted reasonably, which may be the natural assumption to make about a person who has engaged in an act of rescue, it is unlikely to break the chain of causation (*Haynes* v *Harwood* [1935] 1 KB 146).

Billy v *Harriet*

As a person with some medical knowledge, Harriet might have been expected to appreciate the risks associated with a deep gash and perhaps should have advised Billy and his parents of the need for a further consultation. If this is seen as an unreasonable and improbable omission, it may break the chain of causation (*Knightley* v *Johns* [1982] 1 All ER 851).

This raises the question whether Harriet owes Billy and his parents a duty of care in respect of the later damage (amputation). Having decided to act, she will owe a duty of care if she makes Billy's position worse and she will be required to act as would a reasonable professional person in the same position (*Bolam* v *Friern Hospital Management Committee* [1957] 2 All ER 118; *Wilsher* v *Essex Area Health Authority* [1988] AC 1074). Generally, this will require the defendant to show that he has acted in the same way as a responsible body of similar professionals would have acted, but where the practice adopted by such a body is shown to have been unreasonable, the court does have the power to determine that acting in the same way amounts to a breach of duty (*Bolitho* v *City and Hackney Health Authority* [1997] 2 All ER 771).

The duty owed by Harriet seems to have been satisfied up to and including the point of bandaging the wound, but possibly not thereafter. It is clear that a medical professional's duty extends not just to treatment, but also to advice (*Sidaway* v *Board of Governors of the Bethlem Royal Hospital and the Maudsley Hospital* [1985] AC 871).

If this duty is broken, Harriet will be liable for the damage she has caused to an already damaged leg. Moreover, as she is a district nurse, Harriet's employers may be vicariously liable for her actions, if she is acting in the course of her employment. The question tells us she is on her rounds and applying the analogy of *Rose* v *Plenty* [1976] 1 All ER 97 it can be said she was furthering the general objectives of her employer's business.

QUESTION 2

Pleasureland is an entertainment park owned and operated by Kidkicks Ltd. One of the attractions offered is a ride on 'the Serpent', a notoriously frightening car ride which for part of its route travels underground. At the entrance to the Serpent ride there is a notice which states ('All possible precautions are taken in the interests of safety. However, people taller than 6 feet 3 inches should not join this ride'.

Adam who is 6 feet 4 inches tall decides that the discrepancy of one inch will make little difference and bends his knees as he passes under the height checking device provided by Kidkicks Ltd as he enters the ride. During the ride, the Serpent dips sharply into an underground cavern and Adam, who is sitting high up in his seat, suffers a glancing blow to the head on the entrance to the cavern when the car leaps sharply from the track.

First aid work at Pleasureland has been sub-contracted to Guardian Angels Ltd. Two of their employees, Waldorf and Stadtler, tend to Adam, and carry him to the surface from where he is taken by ambulance to St Brian's Hospital. Adam is found to have a broken neck and has suffered irreversible brain damage which may have been the result of the blow to his head or may have been caused by the way in which he was treated by Waldorf and Stadtler at the scene of the accident. Kidkicks Ltd has been unable to explain why the car jumped sharply from the track as it entered the cavern.

Advise Adam whose medical advisors have suggested that there is a possibility that his condition may worsen in years to come.

Commentary

This question is concerned with the liability of an occupier to a lawful visitor. The principal issues are:

(a)   who is an occupier?

(b)   does the occupier's duty extend to activities on land?

(c)   how does a warning of danger affect liability?

(d)   is there a breach of duty and, if there is, does it cause the harm suffered?

(e)   what damages may be recovered if liability is established?

Suggested Answer

Kidkicks Ltd both own and operate Pleasureland. It seems likely that they will be treated as occupiers under the Occupiers' Liability Act (OLA) 1957 on the basis that they are in control of the premises (*Wheat* v *Lacon (E.) & Co. Ltd* [1966] AC 552).

For the purposes of the 1957 Act, the common duty of care is owed to any person who would have been treated as an invitee or a licensee at common law (OLA 1957, s. 1(2)). On the assumption that Adam has paid to enter Pleasureland, he will be a lawful, contractual visitor to whom the common duty of care is owed under OLA 1957, s. 2(2). Moreover, he can chose whether to sue in tort or under his contract with Kidkicks Ltd but, in either case, the same common duty of care will be owed (OLA 1957, s. 5(1)). The common duty of care is one to take such care as in all the circumstances of the case is reasonable to see that the visitor is reasonably safe in using the premises for the purposes for which he is invited or permitted by the occupier to be there.

A point of controversy, in the past, has been whether the 1957 Act applies only to the state of the occupier's premises or whether it also applies to activities on the land. Prior to the enactment of the 1957 legislation, the common law approach was that the special rules applicable to occupiers did not apply to activities on land and that such activities had to be dealt with on ordinary negligence principles. The language used in the 1957 Act did not seem to be entirely clear, since s. 1(1) refers to both the state of the land and to things done or omitted to be done on the land. However, in contrast, the language of s. 1(2) states that the Act applies only to the consequences of occupation or control, which suggests that the legislation is concerned merely with the state of the occupier's premises. The matter has now been made clear for the purposes of the Occupiers' Liability Act 1984 in relation to persons other than lawful visitors, since in *Revill* v *Newbury* [1996] 1 All ER 291 it was held that activities on land, such as the act of shooting a trespasser, have to be dealt with in accordance with common law principles. On the basis that the relevant wording in the 1984 and 1957 Acts is very similar, it would seem to follow that the 1957 Act applies only to the state of the land. On the facts in this question, the activity of operating a car ride is closely associated with a defect in the state of the land, in which case, it is suggested that the 1957 Act will still apply to the events detailed in the question. In contrast, the injuries caused by Waldorf and Stadtler clearly involve an activity on land and will be governed by common law principles.

The notice displayed at the entrance to the ride does not purport to limit or restrict the liability of Kidkicks Ltd. Instead, it seeks to warn tall people of a possible danger. The duty under OLA 1957, s. 2(2) is one to see that the visitor is reasonably safe. The occupier is not an insurer against all risks. Moreover, a suitably worded warning can enable a person to be safe, provided he heeds that warning. OLA 1957, s. 2(4)(a) provides that a warning on its own is not sufficient to discharge the duty unless in all the circumstances of the case it is sufficient to enable the visitor to be reasonably safe. Relevant factors here are that Adam is an adult (or a very tall young person) who has read the notice and understood its content. Despite this, he goes ahead and ignores the advice given by Kidkicks Ltd. In *Roles* v *Nathan* [1963] 2 All ER 908 two industrial chimney sweeps had been warned by an engineer that they should not work on certain boiler flues if the fire in the boiler was lit. They ignored these instructions and were overcome by carbon monoxide fumes which was a danger to which they had been alerted. It was held by the Court of Appeal that the warning was sufficient to discharge the occupier's duty of care. A possible distinction between this and Adam's case is that in *Roles* there was specific reference to the particular danger which caused the death, whereas Kidkicks Ltd have been a little less specific. In these circumstances, the warning, as worded, might not be sufficient to discharge the duty.

Assuming the duty is owed by Kidkicks Ltd, it must be established that there is a breach of that duty. The question raises the issue of proof of negligence in that it is stated that Kidkicks Ltd can give no explanation why the car jumped sharply from the track. This may attract an application of the principle *res ipsa loquitur*. This principle applies where there is no explanation of the accident in circumstances in which the thing which causes the harm complained of is under the exclusive control of the defendant and where the common experience of mankind suggests that events such as those which have occurred do not happen in the absence of negligence (*Scott* v *London and St Katherine Docks Co.* (1853) 3 H & C 596). The problem here is that there may be a number of reasons why the car has left the track, for example the car itself might be defective, the track might be defective or there might have been inadequate maintenance. If there are a number of possible explanations of the accident, the onus will fall on Adam to prove negligence in the normal way. However, provided one of the explanations of the accident is that there has been fault on the part of the defendant, it is a matter of common sense for the court to decide whether or not the defendant is to blame. In this regard, it is not necessary for the plaintiff to show that any particular individual has been guilty of an act or omission which gives rise to the breach of duty. Moreover, if the defendant's operations had worked as they were intended to work, this may be sufficient evidence of negligence (*Grant* v *Australian Knitting Mills Ltd* [1936] AC 85 and see also *Carroll* v *Fearon, The Times*, 26 January 1998, Court of Appeal).

Adam's knowledge of the risk might be sufficient to allow Kidkicks Ltd to raise the defences of *volenti non fit injuria* or contributory negligence. *Volenti* is a defence based on agreement to accept the legal risk of injury and is not to be equated with mere knowledge of the risk (*Smith* v *Charles Baker & Sons* [1891] AC 325). Here the notice merely informs visitors that if they are more than as certain height they should not join the ride. This might be so for a number of reasons. Since the particular risk which causes injury has not been made clear, the defence of *volenti* might not be available.

What is more likely is that Adam will be treated as having failed to take reasonable care for his own safety and may be guilty of contributory negligence, so that any damages awarded may be reduced under the provisions of the Law Reform (Contributory Negligence) Act 1945.

While Adam is lying injured in the underground chamber, he is tended to by two employees of Guardian Angels Ltd. It is more than likely that Guardian Angels Ltd, as independent contractors, will be responsible for their own torts. Generally an occupier will not be liable for the acts of an independent contractor unless there is evidence that he has failed to take reasonable steps to ensure that the independent contractor is competent (OLA 1957, s. 2(4)(b)). Moreover, s. 2(4)(b) applies only where the independent contractor is employed to carry out work of construction, maintenance or repair, which is clearly not the case so far as Guardian Angels Ltd are concerned. Furthermore, it seems unlikely that Kidkicks Ltd, as occupiers of Pleasureland, will be liable for the acts or omissions of Waldorf and Stadtler, since they are employed by Guardian Angels Ltd rather than Kidkicks Ltd.

The injuries suffered by Adam include a broken neck and irreversible brain damage, but the question states that it is not clear whether these injuries were caused by the blow to the head or by the treatment provided by Waldorf and Stadtler. On the facts, it is presumably the case that Adam must have suffered injuries as a result of the blow to the head and that mistreatment by Waldorf and Stadtler can only have made matters worse. On this basis, Kidkicks Ltd are the primary cause of the harm suffered by Adam, although the actions of Waldorf and Stadtler might be regarded as a *novus actus interveniens* if they are unreasonable and improbable. While it seems both reasonable and probable that in the event of an accident, two trained first-aiders will go to the scene of the accident, if the manner in which they give first aid is such that Adam is harmed to an even greater extent, this might be regarded as an unreasonable act which breaks the chain of causation (*Knightley* v *Johns* [1982] 1 All ER 851).

Finally, Adam's medical advisors state that there is a possibility that his condition may worsen in the future. Generally, an award of damages is made on a once-and-for-all basis at the date of trial and must cover future eventualities in the form of a lump sum payment. However, the Supreme Court Act 1981, s. 32A allows the court to award provisional damages where there is a chance that as a result of the defendant's tort the plaintiff will, inter alia, suffer some serious deterioration in his condition. For these purposes, it has been held that there must be more than just a general deterioration in the plaintiff's condition and that there must be some causal connection between the serious future deterioration and the defendant's tort (*Willson* v *Ministry of Defence* [1991] 1 All ER 638).

QUESTION 3

The Grotbag Trust, a charitable organisation, owns a 50 acre estate consisting of gardens and country walks, which are open to the public on the payment of a small charge to defray the expenses of the charity. Day-to-day management of the estate is entrusted to Dastardly Ltd, which charges the Grotbag Trust a management fee.

At the public entrance to the estate, there is a prominently displayed notice which states:

Dastardly Ltd and the Grotbag Trust ask you to take care on these premises. Children must be accompanied by responsible adults. No responsibility can be accepted for injury or damage suffered while on these premises.

Tom and his wife Harriet take their children, Danny, aged seven, and Violet, aged four, for a day trip to the Grotbag estate. Tom and Harriet wish to visit the gardens, but Danny and Violet become bored and wander off. The two children come upon a bush bearing bright red berries. In front of the tree there is a notice which states that the berries are poisonous and should not be eaten. There is also a small fence around the bush which Violet is able to step over. Violet eats some of the berries and feels very ill. Danny decides to look for Tom and Harriet because he is worried about his sister. He passes through a door marked 'Private — no public access'. Inside Danny discovers a quantity of weedkiller and a number of garden tools. Momentarily forgetting that his sister is ill, Danny stops to play with a lawn-edging tool with which he cuts himself and his trousers. Thinking that the weedkiller might be an antiseptic solution, he dabs some on his bleeding leg, subsequently licks his fingers and becomes violently ill.

Advise the Grotbag Trust Ltd and Dastardly Ltd.

Commentary

The question concerns the liability of an occupier of premises to both lawful visitors and possibly trespassers. The principal issues which require consideration are:

(a)   who is an occupier?

(b)   who is a lawful visitor and who is a trespasser and are the children implied licensees?

(c)   is any duty owed by the parents of the children to the occupier?

(d)   are exclusions or restrictions on liability permitted and in what circumstances do the restrictions on the use of disclaimers of liability imposed by the Unfair Contract Terms Act 1977 come into play?

(e)   what is the effect of the Occupiers' Liability Act 1984?

Suggested Answer

The person who owes the common duty of care under the Occupiers' Liability Act (OLA) 1957, or the duty to non-lawful visitors under OLA 1984, is one who has control over the relevant premises. It is clear that since the test is based on control rather than ownership, it is possible to have more than one occupier. For example, in *Wheat* v *Lacon (E.) & Co. Ltd* [1966] AC 522 both the owner, a brewery company, and the manager of a public house were considered to be in control of different parts of the same premises and because the accident in that case occurred in a part of the building which was under joint control, the defendant brewery could be regarded as an occupier. Here either the Grotbag Trust or Dastardly Ltd could be occupiers of the Grotbag estate. Since day-to-day management of the estate has been entrusted to Dastardly Ltd, this would seem to suggest that they have primary control of the premises and it could be that the Grotbag Trust are merely sleeping partners with little overall control. However, the fact that the notice at the entrance to the estate refers to both the owner and the manager of the estate could be taken as an indication that both organisations have some element of control and that both may be regarded as occupiers.

OLA 1957, s. 2(2) provides that the occupier owes a common duty of care to all lawful visitors. This is a duty to take such care as in all the circumstances of the case is reasonable to see that the visitor is reasonably safe in using the premises for the purposes for which he is invited or permitted by the occupier to be there.

There is nothing to suggest that any harm is suffered by Tom and Harriet, but before they wander into a prohibited area, the children, Danny and Violet, come across a bush bearing brightly coloured berries. The fact that the children are only seven and four is a relevant consideration since OLA 1957, s. 2(3)(a) provides that an occupier can expect children to be less careful than adults. However, the notice outside the estate states that the Grotbag Trust and Dastardly Ltd expect children to be accompanied by responsible adults. Generally, if an occupier has something on his land which might be regarded as an allurement or attraction to children, but which is in fact dangerous, such as a bush or tree with poisonous berries, extra care will need to be taken to guard against injury to a child plaintiff. For example, in *Glasgow Corporation* v *Taylor* [1922] All ER 1 a 7-year-old child became ill as a result of eating poisonous berries from a bush in the defendants' public park. Unlike in the present case, there was no fence around the bush and the occupiers were held liable on the basis that the bush amounted to a trap or allurement to the child.

On the facts of the present case, there are differences from the position in *Glasgow Corporation* v *Taylor*. In the first place, there is a notice which warns that the berries on the bush are poisonous and should not be eaten, secondly there is a small fence around the bush and thirdly, the injured child (Violet) is only four years old. So far as the notice and the fence are concerned, neither may be sufficient to discharge the duty owed to a child visitor, since it is possible that a 4-year-old child cannot read, and even if Violet can read, being a child, she may take no notice of the warning. Accordingly, due to the provisions of s. 2(3)(a), the occupier may need to take extra precautions to guard against injury to child plaintiffs. Moreover, the fence cannot serve as much of an impediment if it can be scaled by a 4-year-old child. All of this would seem to point towards a breach of the duty owed to the children, in so far as they are lawful visitors. However, a counter-argument is that the children should not have been allowed by their parents to wander off on their own, especially in the light of the warning that children should be accompanied by a responsible adult. If a very young child is allowed to wander off by its parents there have been instances in which it has been held that an occupier will not be liable for injuries suffered by the child because the child should have been under the care and control of its parents (*Phipps* v *Rochester Corporation* [1955] 1 QB 540 (5-year-old child)). Furthermore, since Violet's parents have allowed her to wander off on her own, it may be that they do not regard the estate to be a dangerous place, in which case, the occupiers may also be able to argue that the estate is not dangerous (*Simkiss* v *Rhondda BC* (1983) 81 LGR 640). However, more recent case law under OLA 1984 seems to suggest that in more modern times, the fact that a child is not accompanied by its parents will not prevent a duty of care being owed to that child.

Even where there is an allurement or trap, it does not automatically follow that an occupier will be liable for injuries suffered by a child when misusing the allurement, since any injury suffered by the child must be a foreseeable consequence of the presence of the allurement. Thus in *Jolley* v *Sutton London Borough Council* [1998] 3 All ER 559 the local authority had left a boat on public amenity land which the plaintiff and a friend decided to restore. They raised the boat using a car jack and blocks of wood and the plaintiff was injured when the boat fell on him. Although the boat was considered to be an allurement and the defendants were in breach of their duty of care by not removing it, the injury suffered by the plaintiff was taken to be of an unforeseeable kind, for which the defendants' could not be held responsible. In the present case, however, the illness caused by poisonous berries and weedkiller would appear to be highly foreseeable varieties of harm in the circumstances outlined.

The duty is owed to all lawful visitors who include those who have been invited or licensed to be there. This will certainly cover contractual visitors such as Tom, Harriet and their children, provided they stay within the areas set aside for lawful visitors. In this regard, it is clear that an occupier is free to limit the scope of the permission given to visitors, since s. 2(2) states that the duty only extends to the purposes for which the visitor is invited or permitted to be on the land. Thus a visitor may become a trespasser if he accidentally enters an area he has been warned not to enter (*Mersey Docks & Harbour Board* v *Proctor* [1923] AC 253). However, the occupier must clearly specify that there are limits to the permission to be present on the land (*Pearson* v *Coleman Bros Ltd* [1948] 2 KB 359).

After the injury to Violet, Danny proceeds to find assistance, but in so doing, he passes through a door marked 'private'. This might suggest that from this point onwards, he becomes a trespasser, since he has passed into an area which is not open to the public. However, as has been observed above in relation to Violet, an occupier can expect a child to be less careful than an adult (OLA 1957, s. 2(3)(a)) and it may be that Danny, at the age of seven, either did not see the notice, or if he did, did not appreciate what it meant. In any case, it is possible that an object which presents no danger to an adult may be dangerous if a child were to encounter it. Furthermore, dangers which are obvious to adults may not be so to children. Precautions should be taken to guard against the fact that children are naturally inquisitive and may be attracted to objects which would not interest an adult. For example, in *Latham* v *Johnson (R) & Nephew Ltd* [1913] 1 KB 398, a pile of stones, while not considered to be an allurement, was regarded as something which could attract children. What is important is that the occupier should have taken reasonable and sufficient precautions to guard against the risk posed to a child visitor. In this regard, posting a notice to the effect that a certain area is private may not suffice, especially since Danny appears to have encountered no difficulty in passing through the door into an area where dangerous substances and objects are stored. An obvious precaution which appears not to have been taken is that the door should have been locked. Moreover, there is no warning, except in the area marked as private, to alert visitors to the fact that certain parts of the estate are not open to the public. All of this would seem to suggest that a duty of care may still be owed to Danny, even though he is in an area he is not supposed to be in.

The duty owed to lawful visitors may be restricted, modified or excluded by agreement or otherwise, so far as this is permitted by law (OLA 1957, s. 2(1)). The word 'or otherwise' will be sufficient to cover a general notice modifying the common duty of care, even though it does not form part of a contractual arrangement (*Ashdown* v *Samuel Williams & Sons Ltd* [1957] 1 QB 409). However, all the notice says is that parents should accompany young children. It does not specify the particular dangers which cause harm to the children. The notice, whether contractual or not, will also be subject to the provisions of the Unfair Contract Terms Act (UCTA) 1977, provided the occupiers fall within the intended scope of that Act. It is clear that in order for the 1977 Act to apply, the premises must be occupied in a business capacity (UCTA 1977, s. 1(3)). We are told that the Grotbag Trust makes a charge for entry, but that this is merely to defray their expenses as a charity. It is quite possible that a purely charitable organisation is not a business, with the result that the Trust will not be affected by the provisions of the 1977 Act, since they do not act with a view to making a profit, which is probably the clearest indication of business activity. In contrast, Dastardly Ltd charge a management fee, which might be taken to suggest that they are in business with a view to profit, in which case the provisions of UCTA 1977 will affect their ability to exclude or limit their liability to lawful visitors.

By virtue of UCTA 1977, s. 2(1), any attempt to exclude or limit liability for death or bodily injury caused by negligence is void (UCTA 1977, s. 2(1)). For these purposes, negligence is defined as including a breach of the common duty of care under OLA 1957 (UCTA 1977, s. 1(1)(c)). Accordingly, Dastardly Ltd will not be able to exclude liability for the injury caused to Violet or Danny, provided he is regarded as a lawful visitor when he strays into the area marked private. On the assumption that the Grotbag Trust do not act in the course of a business, the provisions of the 1977 Act will have no application to their operations, and it would seem that the exclusion, in so far as it relates to their liability, will be operative. UCTA 1977, s. 2(2) further provides that any attempt to exclude or limit business liability for loss other than death or bodily injury caused by negligence will be permitted only in so far as it satisfies the test of reasonableness set out in UCTA 1977, s. 11. This will cover negligently caused property damage, such as the damage to Danny's clothing caused by contact with the lawn-edging tool.

Should Danny be regarded as a trespasser when he passes into the area marked private, OLA 1984 will apply. Section 1(3) of this Act provides that a duty of care is owed to a non-visitor, including a trespasser, if the occupier is aware of the danger or has reasonable grounds to believe that it exists; and that he knows or has reasonable grounds to believe that Danny is in the vicinity of the danger or may come into that vicinity; and that the risk is one against which the occupier may reasonably be expected to offer some protection. It seems reasonable to assume that the danger presented to a child by sharp gardening tools and toxic substances such as weedkiller is obvious to the person who owns such articles. Moreover, since the Grotbag Estate is open to the public, it seems reasonable to assume that children will be brought there by their parents. Finally, the protection which could have been offered to Danny is fairly obvious, namely that precautions could have been taken to lock away securely any article which is capable of causing injury to children. The implication in the facts of the question is that Danny has simply walked through an unlocked door. Assuming that a duty is owed under s. 1(3), it has to be considered whether there is a breach of that duty. In this respect, s. 1(4) provides that the occupier must take such care as is reasonable in all the circumstances of the case. This creates an objective standard which will require consideration of, *inter alia*, the magnitude of risk, the precautions which could have been taken to guard against the risk and the age of Danny. Generally, more care is necessary where young children are concerned (*Yachuk* v *Oliver Blais Co. Ltd* [1949] AC 386). In these circumstances, it seems likely that the duty owed to Danny will have been broken.

The duty owed under the 1984 Act applies only to death or bodily injury (OLA 1984, s. 1(8)), with the result that if Danny is treated as a trespasser, he will be unable to claim in respect of the damage to his clothing. Moreover, if Danny did understand fully what he was doing when he passed into the area marked private, Dastardly Ltd may be able to argue that the defence of *volenti non fit injuria* applies (OLA 1984, s. 1(6)). However, it may be argued that children rarely read notices or, if they do, they may not understand their import. Furthermore, since the defence of *volenti* is based on willing acceptance of a known risk, it may be argued that until Danny encounters the weedkiller and consumes it, he is not likely to be aware of the risk involved.

While *volenti* is a possible defence, there is nothing in the 1984 Act which sanctions the use of disclaimer notices. If the duty imposed by the 1984 Act is akin to the duty of common humanity created in *British Railways Board* v *Herrington* [1972] AC 877, this might suggest that it is a basic human right which cannot be excluded by way of a notice or a disclaimer of liability. Accordingly, if Danny is a trespasser then the exclusion of liability will have no effect in relation to his illness resulting from the consumption of the weedkiller and the personal injury caused by the lawn-edging tool.

7 Product Liability and Liability for Animals

This chapter contains questions on both liability for defective products and on the liability of a person who keeps animals. The principal linkage between the two areas of tort law is that both are capable of imposing a form of strict liability, although closer examination will reveal that the notion of fault is still very much alive in both areas. If a person produces a defective product, the traditional common law response is that he will be liable in damages only if it can be proved by the plaintiff that there has been a failure to exercise reasonable care on the part of the manufacturer of that product. However, since the introduction of the Consumer Protection Act 1987, the potential for strict liability has emerged, but closer examination of the defences available under the Act and the definition of defectiveness suggest that there are still elements of fault-based liability present in the statutory regime.

Liability for damage caused by an animal depends largely on the type of animal concerned. The Animals Act 1971 distinguishes between those animals which belong to a dangerous species, in respect of which a strict liability regime prevails, and those animals which are effectively domesticated and therefore considered not to be dangerous, in respect of which liability is substantially fault-based. Candidates should have close regard to the range of defences available under the Animals Act 1971, s. 5.

(1)   Product liability

QUESTION 1

Albert is a fruit and vegetable farmer who grows a large quantity of apples. Some of these he processes into cider, others he supplies to local retailers.

Jane purchases five bottles of Albert's cider and ten pounds of Albert's apples from George, a local retailer who has since gone out of business. Jane eats one of the apples, but becomes ill due to the presence of insecticide traces on the skin.

The bottles of cider all bear the warning that it has a very high alcohol content and that no more than two pints should be consumed in any period of 24 hours. Albert is also aware that he has used a preservative in the cider which possesses hallucinogenic qualities.

When she arrives home, Jane opens a bottle of cider, but as she does so a plastic plug suddenly flies off the bottle top and part of the contents of the bottle splash into the face of Susan, Jane's daily help. Susan licks the cider and suffers from a delusion that she can walk on water. She then jumps into Jane's swimming pool and drowns. Jane consumes three pints of the cider as a means of coping with Susan's death. Subsequently she feels violently sick. It transpires that her sickness is due partly to a chemical reaction between the contents of the cider and traces of curry she had recently eaten and partly due to excessive alcohol consumption. An obscure article in the *Journal of Apple Science* has recently identified the possibility of a chemical reaction between certain varieties of curry and strong cider.

Advise Albert of his potential liability.

Commentary

This question concerns the liability of a manufacturer of a product for the physical harm suffered by a consumer of his product. The principal issues for consideration are:

(a)   what is the narrow rule in *Donoghue* v *Stevenson*?

(b)   how is fault established?

(c)   is the manufacturer the cause of the harm suffered?

(d)   does the Consumer Protection Act 1987 apply to agricultural produce?

(e)   what is a defective product under the Consumer Protection Act 1987?

(f)   what defences to liability are available?

Suggested Answer

The 'narrow' rule in *Donoghue* v *Stevenson* [1932] AC 562 states that a manufacturer of products, which he sells in such a form as to show that he intends them to reach the ultimate consumer in the form in which they left him with no reasonable possibility of intermediate examination, and with the knowledge that the absence of reasonable care in the preparation or putting up of the product will result in an injury to the consumer's life or property, owes a duty to the consumer to take reasonable care.

Being a variety of negligence, the narrow rule creates a form of fault-based liability on the part of the manufacturer. Although the word manufacturer is used to describe the potential defendant, it is better to think in terms of a person who has put a product into circulation, so that anyone in the chain of distribution is capable of owing the duty of care. Accordingly, a farmer who puts agricultural produce into circulation is capable of being a producer, provided fault on his part can be proved.

Fault on the part of a manufacturer may be established in a number of ways. First, there may be a breakdown in the production process whereby there is one or more 'rogue' products which are capable of causing harm to the consumer. For example, in *Grant* v *Australian Knitting Mills* [1936] AC 85 the manufacturer failed to wash clothing adequately after it had been bleached in a sulphur-based solution, with the result that the consumer contracted dermatitis. Had adequate precautions been taken, the excess sulphites would not have contaminated the clothing. By analogy, the failure by Albert to wash his apples so as to rid them of traces of insecticide before putting them into circulation may amount to a breach of his duty to take care, especially if he ought reasonably to have foreseen that the presence of traces of the insecticide would be harmful to a consumer of the apples. Moreover, the use of inadequate materials in the product or its packaging is also capable of constituting a breach of duty. Thus if a bung comes out of a bottle so that the contents injure the user (*Fisher* v *Harrods Ltd* [1966] 1 Lloyd's Rep 500), or if the packaging used is generally unsafe (*Hill* v *James Crowe (Cases) Ltd* [1978] 1 All ER 812), there is a potential breach of duty.

A further possible breach of duty arises where the manufacturer fails to give an adequate warning of a known risk. The question informs us that Albert has warned of the danger of over-consumption, but he has not warned of the possible hallucinogenic qualities of his cider. It is clear that a warning can be inadequate for what it does not say. Thus in *Vacwell Engineering Ltd* v *BDH Chemicals Ltd* [1971] QB 88 a warning that a chemical gave off noxious fumes was not sufficient when the warning failed to refer to a probable violent reaction if the chemical were to come into contact with water. It may follow from this that the failure to warn of the hallucinogenic effect of the preservative used by Albert constitutes a breach of duty, especially since this indirectly results in Susan's death.

There is also the possibility of a breach of duty where a range of products suffers from a design fault. The question indicates that the cider may chemically react with certain varieties of curry so as to cause illness. Since this possibility has only been referred to in an obscure scientific journal, this may not be a fact of which Albert can reasonably have been aware. It is important that in a fault-based enquiry the defendant is judged only by reference to information available to him at the time of the alleged breach of duty (*Roe* v *Minister of Health* [1954] 2 QB 66).

The mere fact that there is a potential breach of duty does not settle the matter since it must also be shown that the breach of duty is the cause of the harm suffered by the plaintiff. In this regard, it is important to consider the possibility of intermediate examination and of possible consumer misuse.

If the manufacturer can reasonably expect another person to inspect or do something to the product before it reaches the ultimate consumer, this possibility of intermediate examination may exonerate the manufacturer on the basis that his fault is no longer the cause of the harm suffered. In *Grant* v *Australian Knitting Mills* it was unsuccessfully argued that the consumer ought to have washed the underwear he had purchased. This shows that the mere opportunity for intermediate examination is not sufficient to point to a cause other than defective manufacture and that the manufacturer must reasonably expect someone else to take up the opportunity to examine the goods. This reasonable expectation will arise where the manufacturer has issued an appropriately worded warning (*Kubach* v *Hollands* [1937] 3 All ER 907), but there appears to be no warning given by Albert which requires any sort of examination. However, there is a warning which pertains to consumer misuse. Albert has warned that no more than two pints of his cider should be consumed in a period of 24 hours, and Jane fails to heed this warning. If it transpires that her misuse of the product in the face of the warning is the cause of the illness she suffers, it seems reasonable to assume that Albert will not be liable (*Farr* v *Butters Bros Ltd* [1932] 2 KB 606).

The burden of proving the causal link between Albert's breach of duty and the harm suffered by Jane lies on Jane herself. She will have to prove that it is the chemical reaction rather than her own misuse of the cider which is the cause of the harm she has suffered. If she cannot satisfy the burden of proof on this matter, she will fail in her action (*Evans* v *Triplex Safety Glass Ltd* [1936] 1 All ER 283). In any case, even if she does prove this link, it has been observed already that Albert may not be in breach of his duty in respect of this possible chemical reaction.

As an alternative to a negligence action, Jane personally and Susan's estate may have an action under Part I of the Consumer Protection Act (CPA) 1987. This purports to create a regime of strict liability in respect of defective products which cause physical harm to the person or to property (CPA 1987, s. 2(1)). As a producer of a processed product (the cider) Albert will be subject to the Act (CPA 1987, s. 1(2)(a)). However, in his capacity as the grower of the apples, it is unlikely that the 1987 Act will apply, since CPA 1987, s. 2(4) provides that the rules on defective products do not apply to primary agricultural produce which has not undergone an industrial process. There might be an outside chance that the process of spraying crops with an insecticide might be regarded as an industrial process, but since the definition of the latter in the CPA 1987, s. 1(2)(c) requires the process to have changed the essential characteristics of the product, it is unlikely that spraying will have rendered the fruit anything less than apples. It seems to follow that the only product for which Albert is likely to be responsible under the 1987 Act is the cider.

The Act renders the producer liable for the defectiveness of his product. Under CPA 1987, s. 3(1) a product is defective if it is not as safe as persons generally are entitled to expect. Moreover, in determining what level of safety can be expected, s. 3(2) provides that regard may be had to the manner in which the product has been marketed, the purposes for which it has been marketed, any instructions or warnings as to use, what can reasonably be expected to be done with the product and the time at which the product was put into circulation.

A bottle of cider is presumably marketed as a beverage intended for adult human consumption and as such it should be safe to drink. However, the warning about excessive consumption is one the manufacturer can expect the consumer to heed. On the other hand, particularly since Albert is aware of the hallucinogenic properties of a preservative he has used in the cider, it may be that the cider is defective, particularly in relation to the death of Susan, although not necessarily in relation to Jane.

In relation to Jane, there is the further problem that the risk of chemical reaction between strong cider and curry is little known to the scientific world. While the 1987 Act purports to introduce a regime of strict liability, there is a possible defence under s. 4(1)(e) in relation to development risks. Section 4(1)(e) provides that it is a defence for the producer to show that the state of scientific and technological knowledge was not such that a producer of products of the same description as the product in question might be expected to have discovered if the defect had existed in his products while they were under his control. This rather complex wording might appear to differ in certain important respects from that used in the EC Product Liability Directive, which the 1987 Act was intended to implement, since the Directive appears to ask, rather more simply, what was the state of scientific and technical knowledge at the time the product was put into circulation. In particular, it was thought by some that s. 4(1)(e) imported a test based on the subjective knowledge of the producer whereas the Product Liability Directive set an objective test of knowledge. However, the European Court of Justice has ruled in *EC Commission* v *United Kingdom (Re The Product Liability Directive)* (Case C-300/951) [1997] 3 CMLR 923 that there is nothing wrong in the wording used in the 1987 Act and that in their opinion it does not set a subjective standard. Conversely, the European Court of Justice did opine that in order for a producer to be able to take into account the relevant state of scientific and technical knowledge, that knowledge had to be accessible. It may be the case that since the only reference to the possible reaction is in an obscure journal, it may not be regarded as accessible knowledge, especially if Albert is a very small-scale producer. Conversely, the relevant journal specialises in apple science and this might be regarded as a publication of which an apple and cider producer ought to have been aware. However, in *EC Commission* v *United Kingdom*, the point was made that some relevant information might only be available in a confidential memorandum, in which case it would be unreasonable to expect a producer to be aware of something regarded as entirely confidential. Similar considerations may also apply to a journal regarded as obscure.

QUESTION 2

Koffman Latrash plc manufacture a pharmaceutical product called 'Offenden' which is marketed as a cure for morning sickness suffered by pregnant women, subject to a warning that the drug should not be used by people who suffer from high blood pressure. Extensive trials have failed to reveal any other defect in the drug despite the fact that an obscure article published in a New Zealand medical journal has established that the principal ingredient in 'Offenden' may be capable of causing severe foetal limb abnormalities in rats in 1 per cent of cases in which the drug is used.

Alice, who knows herself to be pregnant, attends the surgery of Dr John who recommends the use of 'Offenden'. Alice has high blood pressure, a fact of which she is aware but which is not known to Dr John since he failed to make appropriate enquiries.

Alice suffers a heart attack in the course of giving birth to her son, Ronald, but she survives. The heart attack is shown to have been caused by high blood pressure exacerbated by ingredients in 'Offenden'. Ronald is born with shortened arms and severe sight defects. Two months after the birth of Ronald, a major scientific journal establishes incontrovertibly that one of the ingredients in 'Offenden' is likely, in more than 50 per cent of cases of use, to cause sight defects in newborn children.

Advise Alice and Ronald.

Commentary

This question requires consideration of the liability of a pharmaceuticals manufacturer for injuries caused to the immediate consumer of a drug and the effect of such consumption on an unborn child. The major areas for consideration are:

    (a)   is there a breach of duty to exercise reasonable care and how does the issue of a warning affect liability?

    (b)   is the doctor in breach of a duty of care?

    (c)   does the Consumer Protection Act 1987 apply to the drug and, if so, is it defective and what defences are available?

    (d)   is the unborn child protected by the Congenital Disabilities (Civil Liability) Act 1976?

Suggested Answer

Alice is a consumer of the drug 'Offenden'. As such she is owed a duty of care by the manufacturer of the drug, Koffman Latrash plc, under the narrow rule in *Donoghue* v *Stevenson* [1932] AC 562. This states that a manufacturer of products which he sells in such a form as to show that he intends them to reach the ultimate consumer in the form in which they left him with no reasonable possibility of intermediate examination, and with the knowledge that the absence of reasonable care in the preparation or putting up of the product will result in an injury to the consumer's life or property, owes a duty to the consumer to take reasonable care.

Koffman Latrash plc have warned that the drug should not be used by persons with high blood pressure. If a manufacturer is aware that his product may cause harm if used in a particular way or by particular people, the best way he can discharge the duty of care he owes is by giving a warning or by issuing detailed instructions as to use (*Kubach* v *Hollands* [1937] 3 All ER 907). Moreover, where a warning of this kind has been issued, the manufacturer may have a reasonable expectation that an intermediary will check to ensure that the instructions are complied with. For example, in *Holmes* v *Ashford* [1950] 2 All ER 76 the manufacturer of a hair dye warned that before it was used, the dye should be patch tested to ensure that it did not have any adverse effect on customers. A hairdresser failed to heed this warning and the plaintiff contracted dermatitis. Since the manufacturer had done all that was reasonable in the circumstances, he was not in breach of the duty of care he owed. Moreover, the hairdresser's failure to take note of the warning rendered him liable for his negligence. So far as Alice is concerned she is unlikely to succeed in an action against Koffman Latrash plc, since there is a specific warning against the use of 'Offenden' by patients with high blood pressure. However, she may have an action against Dr John on the basis that, under the principle in *Bolam* v *Friern Hospital Management Committee* [1957] 2 All ER 118, he has failed to act in the way that reasonable medical practitioners, in making enquiries, would act, having regard to Alice's blood pressure and the warning issued with the drug.

Ronald may also want to bring an action for negligence. Despite some uncertainty, an unborn child does have a potential common law action (*Burton* v *Islington Health Authority* [1992] 3 All ER 833). However, for practical purposes, this applies only to children born before 22 July 1976, because from that date the provisions of the Congenital Disabilities (Civil Liability) Act (CD(CL)A) 1976 supplant the common law. Under s. 1(1) of that Act, if a child is born disabled as a result of an occurrence before its birth and a person other than the child's mother is answerable for those disabilities, then the child may sue for the wrongful damage. The occurrences to which the Act applies include those which affect the mother during pregnancy, so that the child is born with disabilities which would not otherwise have been present (CD(CL)A 1976, s. 1(2)(b)). The defendant is answerable only however, if he is or would have been liable in tort to the parents had actionable damage been sustained (CD(CL)A 1976, s. 1(3)). The problem this creates is whether Alice could have maintained an action against Koffman Latrash plc had she suffered any injury.

The facts of the problem indicate that the propensity of 'Offenden' for causing sight defects is established only after the drug is put into circulation. It is important that in a fault-based enquiry the defendant is judged only by reference to information available to him at the time of the alleged breach of duty (*Roe* v *Minister of Health* [1954] 2 QB 66). This would seem to suggest that no action would have been available in this respect as negligence on the part of the producer cannot be established. However, there is evidence to show that the drug has caused foetal abnormalities in 1 per cent of rats on which the drug has been tested. If this converts into a similar percentage risk in relation to human beings it may be evidence of negligence on the part of Koffman Latrash plc, but the information must have been reasonably available to the manufacturer and since the relevant research is contained in an obscure journal, it may not amount to a failure to exercise reasonable care not to have been aware of it.

As an alternative to a negligence action, both Alice and Ronald may seek to bring an action under the Consumer Protection Act (CPA) 1987. Koffman Latrash plc are producers of the drug by virtue of CPA 1987, s. 1(2)(a). Drugs, being substances which are not otherwise excluded from the scope of the Act, are products (CPA 1987, s. 45(1)). For the purposes of the Act, a product is defective if it is not as safe as persons generally are entitled to expect (CPA 1987, s. 3(1)). In deciding what persons generally are entitled to expect by way of safety, CPA 1987 s. 3(2) provides that regard may be had to the manner in which the product has been marketed, the purposes for which it has been marketed, any instructions or warnings as to use, what can reasonably be expected to be done with the product and the time at which the product was put into circulation.

If the time the product was put into circulation is a relevant consideration, this would seem to suggest that 'Offenden' is not a defective product in relation to the sight defects affecting Ronald. Other factors which may be relevant in relation to Alice and Ronald include the manner in which the product has been marketed. Presumably since this appears to be a drug available on prescription, there may be less danger to the public than if it were available over the counter. Given this assumption, it may not be a defective product if it is kept under the close control of responsible medical practitioners. In relation to Alice's heart attack, the warning issued by Koffman Latrash plc will also be relevant in determining whether the drug is defective, since a danger which is warned against may cease to be a danger at all. Moreover, since the court may consider what can reasonably be expected to be done with the product, it may be concluded that a responsible medical practitioner would take appropriate measures and not give this drug to a person with high blood pressure.

The one area where Koffman Latrash plc may be liable is in relation to the foetal abnormality which results in Ronald's shortened arms. The question shows that the manufacturer may have been aware of the propensity of the drug for causing this variety of harm. Although the 1987 Act is supposed to have introduced a regime of strict liability, it also provides a 'state of the art' or development risks defence in s. 4(1)(e). This provides that it is a defence for the producer to show that the state of scientific and technical knowledge was not such that a producer of products of the same description as the product in question might be expected to have discovered if the defect had existed in his products while they were under his control. The manner in which s. 4(1)(e) is worded suggests that the test set is not purely objective, but rather requires consideration of subjective elements such as the resources of the particular manufacturer in question. The rather complex wording of s. 4(1)(e) might appear to differ in certain important respects from that used in the EC Product Liability Directive, which the 1987 Act was intended to implement, since the Directive appears to ask, rather more simply, what was the state of scientific and technical knowledge at the time the product was put into circulation. In particular it was thought by some that s. 4(1)(e) imported a test based on the subjective knowledge of the producer whereas the Product Liability Directive set an objective test of knowledge. However, the European Court of Justice has ruled in *EC Commission v United Kingdom (Re The Product Liability Directive)* (Case C-300/951) [1997] 3 CMLR 923 that there is nothing wrong in the wording used in the 1987 Act, and that in their opinion it does not set a subjective standard. Conversely, the European Court of Justice did opine that in order for a producer to be able to take into account the relevant state of scientific and technical knowledge, that knowledge had to be accessible. It may be the case that since the only reference to the possible reaction is in an obscure journal, it may not be regarded as accessible knowledge. However, as the defendants Koffman Latrash plc appear to be a large pharmaceutical company, they might have the resources to be aware of up-to-the-minute scientific research, even if reported only in an obscure journal. Accordingly, it may be argued that the defence would not be available to Koffman Latrash plc in relation to Ronald's limb defects.

(2)   Liability for animals

QUESTION 3

Desmond, a farmer, takes his prize bull to market in a lorry. Instead of using the market lorry-park, Desmond parks outside a nearby china shop owned by Patricia. While leading the bull from the lorry to the marketplace, it breaks away and runs into Patricia's shop. It causes considerable damage to Patricia's stock of china and glassware and completely destroys a priceless Ming vase on loan, for exhibition purposes, from the Victoria and Albert Museum.

Advise Patricia.

Would your answer differ if the damage had been caused in the following circumstances:

(a)   by a gorilla which had escaped from a local circus?

(b)   by a customer's Labrador dog?

Commentary

This question is designed to test the candidates' knowledge of the Animals Act 1971. The question is primarily concerned with:

(a)   the difference between liability for dangerous and domesticated species of animal;

(b)   the strictness or otherwise of the duty imposed upon the keeper of different kinds of animal;

(c)   the relevance of defences at common law and under the Animals Act 1971.

Suggested Answer

Desmond's prize bull

A bull is a type of cattle, and all types of cattle are 'livestock' within the meaning of the Animals Act 1971, s. 11. The expression 'livestock' covers most farmyard animals including horses, pigs, sheep, goats and poultry as well as cattle.

The general rule under the Animals Act 1971, s. 4 is that a person who has possession of livestock is responsible for any damage which it may cause to land or other property, but not for personal injuries. This liability does not depend on proof of negligence and is a statutory replacement of the old common law rules relating to 'cattle trespass'. Liability under s. 4 extends to all of the damage caused, not just to that which is reasonably foreseeable. Nevertheless, the defendant will be able to disclaim liability under s. 5(1) for any damage which was wholly due to the plaintiff's own fault and he (the defendant) will also be able to rely on the Law Reform (Contributory Negligence) Act 1945 if the plaintiff was partly responsible for any of the damage caused. However, on the facts, there seems to be little to suggest that Patricia is, in any way, to blame for the damage caused by Desmond's bull, except in so far as leaving a Ming vase exposed may amount to contributory negligence.

Under the Law Reform (Contributory Negligence) Act 1945, the court has a power to reduce the plaintiff's damages in accordance with the plaintiff's share of the responsibility for the damage he has suffered. Under the 1945 Act, the defence will be available where the damage to the plaintiff is reasonably foreseeable (*Jones* v *Livox Quarries Ltd* [1952] 2 QB 608). Moreover, the plaintiff's conduct must be, in some way, a cause of the harm suffered, although it does not have to be a cause of the accident which results in that harm (*Jones* v *Livox Quarries Ltd*). Desmond may contend that the damage to the Ming vase was caused by Patricia's fault in leaving it in such an exposed position, thereby disregarding its priceless value. However, since the damage would not have occurred but for the trespassing of Desmond's bull, it is difficult to see how Desmond can argue that the Animals Act 1971, s. 5 applies, although there might be an arguable case based on contributory negligence.

Desmond may argue that under the Animals Act 1971, s. 5(5), strict liability for the trespassing livestock does not extend to cases in which an animal strays from the highway on to adjoining land, if their presence on the highway constitutes a lawful use of the highway. Here, Desmond will be liable only if there is proof of negligence. In this regard, much will depend on expert evidence as to how bulls should be handled when being taken to market, but it does seem reasonable to assume that the use of the highway in a market town for the passage of livestock will be regarded as a lawful use of that highway.

Conversely, there may be some evidence of negligence in that Desmond has not used the lorry-park at the market, but has chosen to park in the street.

The gorilla

Gorillas do not fall into the definition of livestock, but will be regarded as a dangerous species under the Animals Act 1971, s. 6(2), since the gorilla, as a species, is not normally domesticated in the British Islands and because a fully grown gorilla may cause severe damage unless it is restrained. By analogy, an elephant, albeit ruminant and placid, is nonetheless a dangerous species, largely due to its size and potential for causing damage (*Behrens* v *Bertram Mills Circus Ltd* [1957] 2 QB 1).

If the damage to Patricia's shop was caused by an escaped gorilla, the Animals Act 1971, s. 2(1) provides that the keeper of that animal will be liable for any damage caused. For the purposes of the 1971 Act, a keeper is a person who owns or has the animal in his possession (s. 6(3)). This liability is not confined to damage to land and other property, but also extends to cover personal injury, including psychiatric damage. Moreover, liability is strict in that s. 2(1) does not require proof of negligence. For the purposes of s. 2(1), what matters is whether the species to which the animal belongs is dangerous. Thus it will be no defence to argue that the particular gorilla was friendly, not known to be dangerous or unpredictable in its behaviour or not fully grown, since an adult gorilla has characteristics which make it dangerous. The key issues will therefore be those of causation and remoteness of loss. The Animals Act 1971 does not state whether any particular remoteness test applies to its provisions and, historically, liability for animals has set a very high standard, requiring the keeper to keep an animal (especially one belonging to a dangerous species) at his peril. More recent developments in other areas of supposed strict tortious liability seem to suggest a shift towards a greater use of the reasonable foresight of harm test established in the *Wagon Mound (No. 1)* [1961] AC 388 (see *Cambridge Water Co. Ltd* v *Eastern Counties Leather plc* [1994] 1 All ER 53 in relation to the rule in *Rylands* v *Fletcher*). However, in *Behrens* v *Bertram Mills Circus Ltd* statements by Devlin J to the effect that the keeper of an escaped, but amiable tiger would remain liable for injury to a plaintiff who suffered a heart attack on witnessing the tiger sitting on his bed. This would seem to suggest that liability is very strict and that there is not a remoteness test based upon reasonable foresight of harm. Conversely, in *Brook* v *Cook* (1961) 105 SJ 684, the keeper of a monkey was held not to be liable for the plaintiff's broken wrist when she took fright at the sight of a monkey and fell in her panic. Apparently, the reasoning behind this decision rested on the fact that the keeper would be liable only if his animal were to attack the victim.

The customer's dog

A dog is not a dangerous species, because it is 'commonly domesticated in the British Islands'. Strict liability does not, therefore, arise. It is not clear whether the damage to the china and glassware was caused by some abnormal characteristic of the dog (e.g., excitability, nervousness or vice). If this is the case, and if the keeper of the dog knew or ought to have known of that characteristic, he will be liable for the damage under s. 2(2) of the 1971 Act. If the keeper was unaware of the characteristic or could not be reasonably expected to have known of it he will not be liable without proof of some other negligence or actionable nuisance on his part. For example, in *Pitcher* v *Martin* [1937] 3 All ER 918, it was held that there was an actionable nuisance where a dog had been allowed to run around the streets with a long, trailing lead. Similarly, the keeper might be guilty of negligence if he were to allow his dog loose in a shop full of china and glassware, especially if the dog is large and clumsy.

The precise wording of s. 2(2) is extremely cumbrous or even inept with the result that it is somewhat difficult to follow (See *Cummings* v *Granger* [1977] QB 397; *Curtis* v *Betts* [1990] 1 WLR 459). What seems to be required is that the damage caused by the animal must be something likely to be caused by the particular animal unless it was restrained or that the damage, if caused by that animal, was likely to be severe. Secondly, there must be a causal link between the damage caused and the special characteristic of the animal which results in the damage suffered by the plaintiff. (Note that the precise language of s. 2(2)(b) refers to the 'likelihood of the damage or of its being severe', but the Court of Appeal considered this form of words to be inept and that the wording of the Act as written were probably not intended.) In determining whether the damage caused by the animal is likely to be severe it seems to be sufficient that the damage is such as might well happen (*Smith* v *Ainger, The Times*, 5 June 1990). Thirdly, the particular characteristic which resulted in the damage being caused must be known to the keeper. On the facts, there appears to be no particular characteristic present in the Labrador dog which causes the damage to the china shop and the particular species is, generally, known to be very friendly and docile. It may be that the damage caused is simply due to the size of the animal, but this is not a feature which will set this particular dog apart from the rest of its species. However, if the dog is suffering from an illness which makes it short-tempered or otherwise mischievous and the keeper is aware of this, liability may attach under s. 2(2). However, on balance, it is likely that because of the docile nature of the Labrador breed, the keeper will have little idea that the dog is likely to cause severe damage, in which case, no liability will attach.

QUESTION 4

Alice, a professional trapeze artiste, is engaged to appear at Bronco Bill's Circus at Blackpool for an eight week summer season. Alice's act includes, inter alia, a mid-flight trapeze exchange with Mickey, a monkey owned by Bronco Bill's Circus, but specially trained by Alice. During a rehearsal, Alice and Mickey attempt to exchange trapezes in mid-flight, but both fail to catch their target and fall into the safety net. Being frightened, Mickey bites Alice's big toe and runs out of the circus tent into a neighbouring garden owned by Tilly, an 80-year-old pensioner. As Tilly is hanging out her washing, Mickey screams at her, baring his teeth, still being very frightened after his fall. Tilly suffers serious shock, resulting in heart palpitations which require extensive medical treatment.

As Alice is making her way to the first aid caravan after her fall, she encounters Humpy, the pregnant camel, normally a very docile animal, but who because of her delicate state is apt to be aggressive. Humpy spits at Alice and kicks her in the stomach. Subsequently, Humpy sprints at high speed out of the main entrance to the circus compound and collides with a passing petrol tanker which swerves into a house owned by Donald, catching fire and causing serious fire damage to Donald's property.

Oblivious to these events, Alice enters what she believes to be the first aid caravan, but which is, in fact, Bronco Bill's personal caravan. Bronco Bill's pet dog (a cross between an Alsatian and a bull mastiff) immediately attacks Alice, believing its own territory to have been invaded by a stranger. Alice is seriously injured as a result of this attack and requires extensive hospital treatment.

Advise Alice, Tilly and Donald.

Commentary

This question raises a number of issues relevant to the liability of the keeper of an animal for injuries caused by that animal. Important issues are:

(a)   who is a keeper?

(b)   do any of the animals belong to a dangerous species, in which case is the liability of the keeper strict?

(c)   how does the liability of the keeper of a domesticated animal differ from that applicable to a dangerous species?

(d)   what remoteness test, if any, applies to the Animals Act 1971?

Suggested Answer

The facts of the problem reveal a number of possible actions. Tilly is frightened by Mickey the monkey. Donald's property is damaged indirectly as a result of the escape of a camel. Alice is injured when she mistakenly strays into a private area and is attacked by a dog.

Tilly v Alice and/or Bronco Bill

Tilly, an 80-year-old pensioner suffers, shock and heart palpitations as a result of being frightened by Mickey the monkey. The first question to consider is whether a monkey is a domesticated or a dangerous animal. Under the Animals Act 1971, s. 2(1) the keeper of a dangerous animal is strictly liable for damage caused by an animal which belongs to a dangerous species under the definition given in s. 6(2) of the 1971 Act. Section 6(2) provides that an animal is dangerous if it belongs to a species which is not commonly domesticated in the British Islands and, secondly, that fully grown animals of the species concerned have characteristics that, unless restrained, are likely to cause severe damage or that any damage they may cause is likely to be severe.

A monkey is often seen in captivity in a zoo, and some people even keep them as pets, but this probably will not be sufficient to amount to domestication. Moreover, monkeys, in their wild state, may bite or attack if threatened. Under the common law rules which applied before 1971, a monkey was regarded as *ferae naturae* (*Brook v Cook* (1961) 105 SJ 684). Since the 1971 Act was passed it seems reasonable to assume that a monkey will continue to be regarded as a dangerous species, which means that Mickey will be dealt with under the provisions of s. 2(1) regardless of how tame or domesticated the particular animal might be. Mickey bares his teeth at Tilly and might have gone on to bite her. Such characteristics must be regarded as likely to cause severe damage within the meaning of s. 6(2).

On the facts, Tilly has suffered serious shock and resultant heart palpitations. On the basis that this is more than mere emotion and constitutes actionable damage in the form of physical harm (*Hinz v Berry* [1970] 2 QB 40) Tilly may be able to bring an action for damages against the person responsible for control of Mickey, provided the damage suffered is not too remote. The fact that liability under the 1971 Act is strict might suggest that the defendant will be liable regardless of the foreseeability of the harm suffered. However, in recent years, the courts have demonstrated a general unwillingness to impose strict liability and also to hold the defendant liable for remote losses (see, e.g.,

Cambridge Water Co. v *Eastern Counties Leather plc* [1994] 2 WLR 53 applying the same remoteness test to actions under the rule in *Rylands* v *Fletcher* as applies to a nuisance action).

The Animals Act 1971 makes no provision for what remoteness test should apply, although the position at common law seems to have been that the keeper of a dangerous animal was liable for all damage caused by it. Moreover, the Animals Act 1971, s. 2(1) states that the keeper is liable for 'any damage', which would seem to suggest that the position has not changed and that the keeper will be liable for any damage which is directly caused by the animal. The position is a little more complicated in that for the purposes of domesticated animals, the keeper is liable under s. 2(2) only for damage which can be expected of that particular animal in the light of characteristics which it possesses and which are known to the keeper. If similar reasoning is applied to a dangerous species, it ought to follow that the keeper will be liable only for damage which flows from the special risks associated with the species to which the animal belongs. However, there are cases at common law which suggest a stricter approach. For example, in *Behrens* v *Bertram Mills Circus Ltd* [1957] 2 QB 1 the keeper was liable where a frightened elephant ran after a barking dog and in so doing injured the plaintiff. In the same case, Devlin J stated obiter that if a man woke up to find an escaped tiger in his bedroom and suffered a heart attack as a result, the keeper would be liable no matter how tame or docile the tiger might have been. To the contrary, in *Brook* v *Cook* the plaintiff, a 61-year-old lady, saw a monkey jump on to her garden wall. As a result of this she took fright, ran indoors and in so doing, tripped and injured her wrist. Despite the fact that the monkey was regarded as *ferae naturae*, Lord Evershed MR considered that the keeper would be liable only for injuries resulting from an attack by the monkey. In the present case, Mickey does appear to demonstrate a characteristic which might be expected of a wild monkey and the baring of his teeth might suggest he is about to attack. On this basis the keeper of Mickey may be liable for the harm suffered by Tilly.

The final issue relevant to Mickey the monkey is to determine who is his keeper. For these purposes, the Animals Act 1971, s. 6(3) states that a keeper is someone who (a) owns the animal or (b) has it in his possession or (c) is the head of a household in which a person under the age of 16 owns or possesses the animal. On the facts of the question, it is stated that Mickey is owned by Bronco Bill's Circus, but is specially trained by Alice for the purposes of their circus act. Also, Mickey's escape occurs when he and Alice are engaged in a training session. What is important is that the list of keepers in s. 6(3) is stated in the alternative, so that it is possible that more than one person may be regarded as a keeper. This would seem to suggest that Tilly may choose between Bronco Bill and Alice as possible defendants, but the more likely of the two to be insured against injury caused by circus animals is Bronco Bill.

Donald v *Bronco Bill*

Donald's property is damaged by a petrol tanker which swerves to avoid Humpy the camel who has escaped from the circus for no apparent reason. The first question to consider is whether a camel is a domesticated animal or not. The position at common law was that because camels were widely domesticated in other parts of the world, they should be regarded as *ferae mansuetae*, that is domesticated animals (*McQuaker* v *Goddard* [1940] 1 KB 697). However, the definition of a dangerous animal under the Animals Act 1971, s. 6(1) appears to preclude this reasoning, since what matters is whether the camel species is commonly domesticated in the British Islands and whether a fully grown camel generally has characteristics which make it likely that any damage they cause will be severe. As a result, it has been held that a camel is now to be regarded as a dangerous species to which s. 2(1) applies (*Tutin* v *Mary Chipperfield Promotions Ltd* (1990) 130 NLJ 807). It will follow from this that Bronco Bill, as owner of Humpy, will be liable for 'any damage' caused as a result of the actions of Humpy, especially since adult camels are well known to spit, may kick if threatened and, in any case, because of their size can be regarded as a species which due to their characteristics are likely to cause severe damage. The question informs us that Humpy is normally very docile, but if an animal is classified as belonging to a dangerous species, the characteristics of the particular animal under consideration become irrelevant (*Behrens* v *Bertram Mills Circus Ltd*).

The remaining issue regarding Humpy, is whether the harm suffered by Donald is too remote. It has been observed already, in relation to Tilly's action, that the 1971 Act does not make specific reference to a remoteness test and that a literal reading of s. 2(1) suggests that the keeper will be liable for any damage. The problem with the present case is that the particular features of a camel which may need to be guarded against are spitting and kicking, but perhaps not colliding with petrol tankers. It has been noted that in *Brook* v *Cook* a sympathetic view was taken where an animal caused damage not associated with the special risk which needed to be guarded against. However, it may be that the stricter approach is that which applies in English law and that a keeper will be liable for any damage caused by the animal, no matter how remote it might be. On this basis, Donald may succeed in an action against Bronco Bill so long as a causal link can be forged between Humpy's escape and the damage to Donald's house.

Alice v *Bronco Bill*

Alice is seriously injured as a result of an attack by Bronco Bill's pet dog when she inadvertently strays into Bronco Bill's personal caravan. The dog, as a species, is commonly domesticated in the British Islands and, as such, it will not be regarded as a dangerous species. Instead, the liability of the keeper falls to be considered under s. 2(2) of the 1971 Act.

This very cumbrously worded provision states that a keeper of a non-dangerous animal will be liable if:

1.   the damage caused by the particular animal is of a kind which

    (a)   the animal, unless restrained, was likely to cause; or

    (b)   if caused by that animal, was likely to be severe; and

2.   the likelihood of the damage or its severity was because the particular animal had characteristics which are

    (a)   not normally found in members of its species; or

    (b)   not normally so found except at particular times, or in particular circumstances; and

3.   those characteristics were known to the keeper, a member of his household under the age of 16 or anyone employed by the keeper who is in charge of the animal.

What is clear from this wording is that liability under s. 2(2) is not strict, since the keeper will not be responsible for a dangerous characteristic of which he was not aware. It is also important to emphasise that for the purposes of s. 2(2) the court is concerned with the characteristics of the particular animal (in this case a cross between a bull mastiff and an Alsatian dog) rather than the characteristics displayed generally by the species to which the animal belongs.

In order to interpret s. 2(2) it has been held in *Curtis* v *Betts* [1990] 1 All ER 769 that each separate part of the section has to be taken in turn. Thus s. 2(2)(a) requires the court to consider simply the kind of damage likely to be caused by the animal or the likelihood that such damage, if caused, would be severe. Thus there will be no need to relate this issue to the specific characteristics referred to in s. 2(2)(b) (but c.f. *Jaundrill* v *Gillett, The Times*, 30 January 1996 contra). Given the size of bull mastiffs and Alsations, unless they are restrained, they are likely to cause damage (*Curtis* v *Betts*; *Cummings* v *Granger* [1977] 1 All ER 104). Moreover, when they cause damage, such as by biting or attacking a person, it is reasonable to assume that it will be severe damage. The principal difficulty with the wording of s. 2(2)(a) is that the Court of Appeal, on two occasions, has encountered difficulty in determining what is meant by the phrase 'the likelihood of the damage or of it being severe'. In *Curtis* v *Betts* the court took the view that what the draftsman probably intended was that the court should consider whether there is a causal link between the characteristic of the animal and the damage caused by it. Thus in *Curtis* a normally docile and friendly bull mastiff which had been familiar with the plaintiff for all its life attacked the plaintiff when he came towards the dog when it was in the back of an estate car. The particular characteristic which proved crucial was that, according to experts, bull mastiffs are very territorial and will attack if they believe their territory is being invaded. This particular animal regarded the back of the car as his territory, since he was often taken some distance in the car before being allowed out for exercise. Moreover, this was a characteristic of which the keeper was aware, since the dog had been known to bark at passers-by in the street.

Given that bull mastiffs, generally, have these characteristics, this might be a fact known to Bronco Bill and if the animal has previously displayed territorial tendencies, this is damage for which he may be liable.

Section 2(2)(b) may be relevant on the facts stated, since the dog has attacked because it believes its own territory to have been invaded. This may be regarded as a special times or a special circumstance. For example, it was regarded as a special circumstance in *Cummings* v *Granger* [1977] 1 All ER 104 that an Alsatian dog was being used as a guard dog and might therefore savage an intruder. Assuming Bronco Bill is using the dog to guard his private premises, this, taken with the territorial nature of bull mastiffs, should suffice to satisfy the requirements of s. 2(2)(b).

The knowledge required by s. 2(2)(c) is actual knowledge. Generally, this will require the animal to have displayed characteristics in the past which show that it is likely to act in the way in which it did on the occasion under consideration. On the facts of the question, there is no evidence to show that this is the case and, if this is the first time the dog has attacked a human being, it may be that Alice will be unable to recover damages from Bronco Bill.

Apart from the question of initial liability under s. 2(2), it is possible that Alice may be met by one of a number of defences provided for in the Animals Act 1971, s. 5. Under s. 5(1), it is a defence for the keeper of an animal to show that the harm suffered by the plaintiff is due 'wholly to the fault of the person suffering it'. This would seem to involve the plaintiff in taking some conscious, risky decision such as entering a leopard's cage to pick up a dropped cigarette (*Sylvester* v *Chapman Ltd* (1939) 79 SJ 777). On the facts of the question, we are informed that Alice believed she was entering the first aid caravan, and it may be that it cannot be regarded as entirely her fault that she inadvertently encounters the dog. Under s. 5(2), the keeper may treat voluntary assumption of risk as a defence, except where the person injured is an employee who incurs a risk incidental to his or her employment. This would rule out the possibility of pleading this defence in relation to the initial bite to Alice's toe while she is performing with Mickey the monkey, provided Alice can be regarded as an employee. The only questionable issue is whether a specialist trapeze artiste engaged for an eight week season is an employee or an independent contractor. However, assuming that Alice may be regarded as an employee, the defence under s. 5(2) will not be available.

In relation to the attack by the dog, it may be reasonable to assume that an employee is still 'employed' while seeking first aid following a work injury. However, the problem will be whether the risk of being bitten by a dog in a private caravan is a risk incidental to Alice's employment. In any event, the defence is one of voluntary assumption of risk, and it may be that because Alice inadvertently strays into the private caravan, she is taken not to have voluntarily accepted the risk.

While Alice will clearly have permission to be on circus premises, she may become a trespasser when she strays into Bronco Bill's private caravan. In these circumstances, s. 5(3) provides that a keeper will not be liable for harm caused to a trespasser where the animal is (a) not kept there for the protection of persons or property and (b) it is not unreasonable to keep the animal where it is kept. The question does not specifically inform us that the dog was kept there as a guard dog. If it is not, the defence will not help Bronco Bill, but even if it is kept as a guard dog, its presence may be regarded as perfectly reasonable, as was the case in *Cummings* v *Granger*. If the keeping of the dog in the caravan is regarded as reasonable, the effect of this will be to leave Alice, as a trespasser, to rely on the provisions of the Occupiers' Liability Act 1984.

8   Torts in Relation to Land

INTRODUCTION

This chapter is concerned with the competing interests of landowners and other miscellaneous matters concerned with landownership. Public and private nuisance are both actionable as torts, although the former is also a crime. Public nuisance is concerned with interferences which affect a class of Her Majesty's subjects and generally the interference must have a wide ranging effect. Private nuisance is concerned with private property rights and is based on the unreasonableness of the defendant's interference with his use or enjoyment of land. The principal underlying theme is one of give and take. Landowners can expect to put up with some inconvenience from their neighbours, but not to an unreasonable extent. For the purposes of private nuisance it is not the actions of the defendant which matter but the activity or state of affairs which has been allowed to continue. While damages may be an appropriate remedy, nuisances may frequently attract the remedy of an injunction, since the nature of many nuisances is that they are liable to continue.

The rule in *Rylands* v *Fletcher* (1868) LR 3 HL 330 is ostensibly a rule of strict liability based on the notion of escape. However, as a rule of strict liability it has not survived well, because of the judicial hostility which seems to exist to the imposition of liability in the absence of fault. It now appears that the rule in *Rylands* v *Fletcher* is little more than a special application of rules of nuisance in the context of an isolated escape, thus reducing any impact the rule might have had in terms of environmental protection. This is especially so in the light of the defences to liability under the rule and the interpretation of the concept of non-natural user in *Cambridge Water Co.* v *Eastern Counties Leather plc* [1994] 1 All ER 53.

The third of the 'land torts' torts is that of trespass to land which is concerned with deliberate invasions of the plaintiff's right peacefully to enjoy property in his possession. The questions which follow attempt to show how each of these land-related torts operates and how they can overlap.

QUESTION 1

Peter buys a farm house and the surrounding farm buildings in Toadington. He plans to convert the house into a 50 bed private hospital, retaining an apartment for his private use. Planning permission to convert the land from agricultural use has been granted by Toadington District Council.

Desmond, a neighbouring landowner, who is annoyed that Peter was able to buy the land on which the hospital is built, frequently fires guns, day and night, on his own land. Desmond claims this is necessary in order to control the rabbit population and to frighten off birds. Desmond also complains that dust produced by Bashitt Ltd, the building contractors employed by Peter to convert the farm buildings, has clogged up the engine of his, Desmond's, car.

Some weeks after Peter's private hospital receives its first patients, Desmond lets some of his outbuildings to John, who organises a 'rave' on one night only. Many of the patients at the hospital are unable to sleep and one of these patients, Mary, suffers a broken arm when she falls down some stairs on her way to complain to Peter about the noise. Many patients ask to be transferred elsewhere, resulting in loss of income to Peter.

Electrical discharge from generators installed by John to power amplifiers for the rave causes interference with Peter's television reception. As a result Peter cannot view an Open University transmission forming part of his part time degree studies.

Advise Peter, Bashitt Ltd, Desmond and John of their liability in tort and how, if at all, can Peter prevent raves from taking place in the future?

Commentary

This question deals with the problem of disputes between neighbouring landowners and requires consideration of both public and private nuisance. The key issues to consider are:

(a)   is there a public nuisance and has special damage been suffered so that it is actionable as a tort?

(b)   who has standing to sue for a private nuisance and who is a potential defendant?

(c)   what criteria identify an unreasonable state of affairs?

(d)   what is the most appropriate remedy?

Suggested Answer

A public nuisance is generally a crime, which is actionable as a tort on proof of special damage and is defined as an act or omission which materially affects the reasonable comfort and convenience of life of a class of her Majesty's subjects (*Attorney General* v *PYA Quarries Ltd* [1957] 2 QB 169). It is concerned with 'public rights', but those rights are not clearly defined, although interferences with public health appear to be covered. A class of people has to be affected — the 50 patients and Peter probably will be a sufficiently large group. Private rights are irrelevant, thus there is no need for a plaintiff to have an interest in land in order to be able to sue for a public nuisance. This will be important to Mary, in particular.

If a person is to be able to succeed in public nuisance as a tort, it must be shown that there is special damage, i.e., damage over and above that suffered by others. What is unclear is whether the special damage must be different in kind to that suffered by others or whether a difference in terms of extent will suffice. Here the inconvenience caused by the noise is suffered by everyone, but there are items of damage specific to particular individuals, for example, Mary's broken arm and the loss of income to Peter caused by the departure of patients. But according to *Walsh* v *Ervin* [1952] VLR 361, the damage must be substantial, direct and not consequential, although it may cover general damage. Personal injury is covered (*Castle* v *St Augustines Links* (1922) 38 TLR 615), but Mary's broken arm may be consequential and not direct damage, and in any case some element of fault will probably have to be proved. Economic loss such as loss of income is also recognised as special damage (*Benjamin* v *Storr* (1874) LR 9 CP 400). The dust produced by Peter's contractors may also give rise to public nuisance liability, since it causes damage to property (*Halsey* v *Esso Petroleum Co. Ltd* [1961] 2 All ER 145). However, in this last instance, there is no evidence that anyone other than Desmond has been affected in which case there is no adverse effect on a class of people.

A private nuisance is an unlawful interference with the use or enjoyment of land. In order to be able to sue for a private nuisance, the plaintiff must have an interest in the land affected (i.e., be owner, tenant or have a right of occupation (*Malone* v *Laskey* [1907] 2 KB 141; *Hunter* v *Canary Wharf Ltd* [1997] 2 All ER 426). Peter and Desmond have no problems in this respect as they are both owners. But Mary, as a patient, is likely to be no more than a contractual visitor. In any case, all she complains of is personal injury and there is no English authority which recognises this as a recoverable head of damage in private nuisance, since the tort is concerned with land interests.

An action for private nuisance may be brought against the creator of the nuisance and the occupier of the land from which the nuisance emanates. Thus John and Bashitt as creators may be sued and it does not matter that they have no interest in the land (*Southport Corp.* v *Esso Petroleum Co. Ltd* [1953] 3 WLR 773). The occupier can also be sued in respect of a nuisance committed by an independent contractor, but only where the employer's duty is non-delegable. Where the nuisance is an inevitable consequence of the work undertaken (e.g., dust from a building operation) the occupier cannot escape responsibility by passing the work to a contractor (*Matania* v *National Provincial Bank* [1936] 2 All ER 633). This would suggest that Peter can be sued in respect of the damage to Desmond's car. A landlord can be sued where he lets premises and in so doing authorises an activity which amounts to a nuisance. This covers a local authority granting permission for the use of land for go-karting (*Tetley* v *Chitty* [1986] 1 All ER 663) so the same should apply to Desmond in letting premises for the purposes of holding a rave at which loud music is played.

Private nuisance is based on the principle of give and take and the role of the court is to try to reach a balance between the competing interests of neighbours. The relevant factors in this process are whether there is a substantial interference with use or enjoyment and whether the defendant can show that his use of land is reasonable. Liability turns on whether the interference (rather than the acts which cause the interference) is reasonable or not.

Factors relevant to this balancing process are:

(a) *Malice* While malice is not usually relevant to liability in tort, it may convert an otherwise reasonable act into one which is unreasonable. This covers deliberately making noise with a view to annoying one's neighbour (*Christie* v *Davey* [1893] 1 Ch 316) or in a manner calculated to cause damage (*Hollywood Silver Fox Farm Ltd* v *Emmett* [1936] 2 KB 468). This may mean that Desmond, in deliberately firing guns day and night, has created an unreasonable state of affairs.

(b) *Locality* So far as inconvenience nuisance (e.g., noise) is concerned, it is relevant to consider where the alleged nuisance takes place. Thus it was said in *Sturges* v *Bridgman* (1879) 11 Ch D 852 that what is a nuisance in Belgrave Square would not necessarily be so in Bermondsey. Here the standards expected of a rural area would have to be considered, and a noisy rave might not be regarded as acceptable. However, regard also has to be had to the fact that planning permission has been granted by the local authority to develop the property. The granting of planning permission does not amount to a defence of statutory permission, but it may have the effect of altering the character of the neighbourhood so that what was once an intolerable interference may, over the passage of time, become an acceptable state of affairs in the locality affected. Thus in *Gillingham Borough Council* v *Medway (Chatham) Dock Co. Ltd* [1992] 3 WLR 449 planning permission was granted to convert a naval dockyard into a commercial port with the result that there was a substantial increase in heavy traffic, especially at night. Although the case was complicated by the fact that the plaintiffs who were seeking an injunction were also responsible for having granted planning permission in the first place, it was held that no nuisance was committed on the basis that the character of the neighbourhood had changed. However, this should not be taken to mean that the granting of planning permission will, in all cases, prevent an action for nuisance. For example, in *Wheeler* v *J. J. Saunders Ltd* [1995] 2 All ER 697 planning permission had been granted to a farmer to build two pig housing units on land next to that owned by the plaintiff. An inevitable consequence of this was that the plaintiff suffered as a result of the smell produced by the increased number of pigs on the neighbouring land. In contrast with the approach adopted in the *Gillingham* case, it was held that there was no more than a more intensive use of land for a purpose for which it had previously been used. In the light of this the character of the neighbourhood had not changed so that the plaintiff was still able to object to the inconvenience caused by the defendant's activities. Here if Desmond complains about the noise resulting from building operations, it may be that the granting of planning permission affects his ability to enjoy his land as he did previously. Unlike *Wheeler* v *Saunders* what appears to have been sanctioned by the local authority is a complete change of use, which Desmond might have to put up with.

Locality is irrelevant where material property damage is caused by the alleged nuisance (*St Helens Smelting Co.* v *Tipping* (1865) 11 HL Cas 642). In this instance the only relevant issue is the over-sensitivity of the plaintiff (see below). Material property damage, namely, clogging of the car engine, has been suffered by Desmond, but this is unlikely to raise the issue of sensitivity.

(c) *Sensitivity* If property damaged by an alleged nuisance is over-sensitive, there is no nuisance (*Robinson* v *Kilvert* (1889) 41 Ch D 88) because the defendant's interference would not have affected a person of ordinary susceptibilities. The same general arguments may also apply to interference with television reception since it was considered in *Bridlington Relay Ltd* v *Yorkshire Electricity Board* [1965] Ch 436 that the reception of TV pictures was not an ordinary use of property. But regard should be had to Peter's particular use, namely self education, which might turn television use into an ordinary use of property. Moreover, there is Canadian authority which suggests that widespread interference with television reception is actionable in private nuisance (*Nor-Video Services* v *Ontario Hydro* (1978) 84 DLR (3d) 221). However, it appears that the House of Lords has turned its back on this possibility. In *Hunter* v *Canary Wharf Ltd* [1997] 2 All ER 426 it was held that no action in private nuisance would lie in favour of residents of properties in the shadow of the Canary Wharf Tower if all they complained of was interference with television reception. The mere presence of a building, in the absence of some specific nuisance emanating from the defendant's land, did not disclose a cause of action. However, in the problem, it is not the presence of a static structure which causes the television interference, but electrical discharge from generators on Desmond's land. This might be taken to suggest that an action for private nuisance cannot be ruled out. However, Lord Lloyd in *Hunter* v *Canary Wharf Ltd* was of the opinion that damages for nuisance must be measured by reference to the diminution in the value of the land and that there is no cause of action in private nuisance for personal injury or interference with personal enjoyment. If television viewing is taken to be no more than a matter of personal enjoyment, this might suggest that there will be no cause of action in private nuisance.

(d) *Duration of the interference* Generally a 'one-off' event will not be sufficient to establish a nuisance since this is likely to indicate its triviality. What matters for private nuisance is the state of affairs created by the defendant. It may be the case that there is a state of affairs which manifests itself in an isolated occurrence but which could be repeated for the future (*Castle* v *St Augustines Links* (1922) 38 TLR 615). In this case, there is an isolated occurrence — the noisy rave — but it may be difficult to regard this as part of a wider state of affairs, unless there is some indication that a similar event will be arranged in the future, or if the interference it causes is substantial (*Matania* v *National Provincial Bank* [1936] 2 All ER 633). There is also authority to suggest that a temporary nuisance carried on at night, thereby causing sleep loss is unreasonable (*De Keyser's Royal Hotel* v *Spicer Bros* (1914) 30 TLR 257). All this may be sufficient to allow the rave to be regarded as an unreasonable interference.

(e) *Public utility* Although this is not a defence *per se*, the utility of the defendant's activity relates to the issue of reasonableness in the sense that a person is expected to put up with operations which are necessary for trade, the enjoyment of property and for the benefit of the public at large (*St Helens Smelting Co.* v *Tipping* (1865) 11 HL Cas 642). Generally, the courts are more concerned with private rights than public interests when considering the primary question of whether there is a nuisance (*Bellew* v *Cement Co.* [1948] IR 61) but the more useful the defendant's activity, the less likely it is that the court will grant an injunction.

The remedies available in the event of a private nuisance are twofold — either damages or an injunction. The question asks whether Peter can prevent raves from taking place in the future — this will require an injunction which is a discretionary remedy, but is readily granted where there is a continuing nuisance. In general there are four guiding principles (*Shelfer* v *City of London Electric Lighting Co.* [1895] 1 Ch 287). These are that damages will be awarded instead of an injunction if the injury to the plaintiff's legal rights is (i) small; and (ii) can be estimated in money terms; and (iii) can be adequately compensated by a small money payment; and (iv) it would be oppressive to grant an injunction. It may be that the public interest is relevant to the grant of an injunction, although the cases are divided on this issue. For example, the fact that heavy job losses might result from the closure of a factory has been ignored in granting a temporary injunction on a factory (*Bellew* v *Cement Co.* [1948] IR 61). But in *Miller* v *Jackson* [1977] QB 966 an injunction was refused against a cricket club on the ground that there was a public interest in preserving playing fields for recreation. This latter approach might help Desmond and John if holding a rave is seen as a useful method of keeping young people occupied — though this is extremely unlikely!

QUESTION 2

Cockroach plc produces chemicals. As part of their operation, they use a fume-suppression device which is extremely noisy. The device is widely regarded as efficient and reliable but, occasionally, noxious fumes are nonetheless discharged into the atmosphere. Numerous residents in the locality have complained of the noise and the fumes produced by Cockroach plc's operations. These residents allege that it is impossible to sleep with windows open and that they cannot now sunbathe in their back gardens.

Eileen, one of the local residents, complains that her highly sensitive African violets, grown in her greenhouse, have all died as a result of the pollution caused by Cockroach plc. Moreover, Tom, a lodger in Eileen's house, complains that the combined effect of the noise and the fumes has caused him to suffer from a respiratory illness and extreme fatigue brought on through loss of sleep so that he has become permanently incapable of work.

Advise Cockroach plc.

Commentary

This question is concerned, primarily, with private nuisance, but it also raises the possibility of an action in public nuisance, negligence and under the rule in *Rylands* v *Fletcher*. Answers should deal with the following issues:

(a) who can sue and who is a potential defendant in an action for private nuisance?

(b) what factors indicate whether a private nuisance constitutes an unreasonable state of affairs?

(c) for the purposes of private nuisance what is the relevant standard of care?

(d) is personal injury actionable damage in a private nuisance action and if not is an action in public nuisance a viable alternative?

(e) what remedies are available?

(f) does *Rylands* v *Fletcher* apply to intangible escapes?

Suggested Answer

A private nuisance is defined as an unreasonable interference with the use or enjoyment of land. In private nuisance either the creator of the nuisance or, in more limited circumstances, the occupier of the land from which the nuisance emanates, can be sued. Since Cockroach plc is both the creator and the occupier, they appear to be the only possible defendant.

Eileen v *Cockroach plc*

In order to be able to sue for a private nuisance, Eileen must have an interest in the land affected by the state of affairs (i.e., be owner, tenant or, possibly, have a right of occupation (*Malone* v *Laskey* [1907] 2 KB 141; *Hunter* v *Canary Wharf Ltd* [1997] 2 All ER 426). There is nothing to suggest that Eileen lacks such an interest.

Private nuisance is based on the principle of give and take and the role of the court is to try to reach a balance between the competing interests of neighbours. The relevant factors in this process are whether there is a substantial interference with use or enjoyment and whether the defendant can show that his use of land is reasonable. Liability turns on whether the interference is reasonable or not, but it is not necessary to prove that the defendant's acts are unreasonable. This is important in this context, since we are told that the fume-suppressing system is widely regarded as efficient and reliable.

Relevant in determining whether an interference is unreasonable is the issue of locality. In *St Helens Smelting Co.* v *Tipping* (1865) 11 HL Cas 642 a distinction was drawn between property damage and sensible personal discomfort. Locality is relevant to the latter, but not the former. Thus since Eileen complains of damage to property (her African violets), it will be irrelevant where she lives. In this instance the only relevant issue is the over-sensitivity of the plaintiff. If Eileen's violets are unusually sensitive and there is evidence that other plants would not be damaged in the same way, there is no nuisance (*Robinson* v *Kilvert* (1889) 41 Ch D 88). However, if Cockroach's activity would have interfered with ordinary land use in any event, the fact that the plaintiff is unusually sensitive will make no difference (*McKinnon Industries* v *Walker* [1951] 3 DLR 557). Plants which have to be grown in a greenhouse may appear to be sensitive, but many other plants require similar treatment. Moreover, if the extent of the pollution is such that other plant life also dies, the *McKinnon* approach seems to be the better one here.

A further issue is that of the duration of the alleged nuisance. What matters for private nuisance is that the defendant's activity must be capable of causing a continuing, unreasonable state of affairs. A state of affairs which manifests itself in an isolated occurrence is still capable of being repeated in the future (*Castle* v *St Augustines Links* (1922) 38 TLR 615). The fact that there has been one escape does not prevent this from being a continuing state of affairs, which will satisfy the duration requirement.

On balance, particularly in the light of the observations on sensitivity, there is probably a nuisance, but consideration must be given to the standard of care required of Cockroach. A negligence action will probably be unsuccessful because Cockroach's act in using the fume-suppression system is not sufficiently unreasonable to constitute a breach of any duty of care he may owe. But liability in nuisance differs. It was said in the *Wagon Mound (No. 1)* [1961] AC 388 that negligence in the narrow sense is not necessary in a nuisance action. But negligence in the wider sense of foresight of harm under the remoteness test is a requirement. Thus if it is foreseeable to Cockroach that Eileen might suffer damage through the emission of fumes, an action may lie (*Wagon Mound (No. 2)* [1967] 1 AC 617). On this basis, it is probably foreseeable that the fumes emitted from Cockroach's factory could cause damage of the kind actually suffered.

All of the factors considered above will also apply to the other local residents referred to in the question in respect of an action based on private nuisance.

Tom v Cockroach plc

Tom is a lodger. This creates the immediate problem of standing to sue — the plaintiff must have an interest in the land affected, but it is necessary to consider what is a sufficient interest. In *Hunter v Canary Wharf Ltd* [1997] 2 All ER 426 it was held that since the tort of private nuisance is directed at protecting the plaintiff's enjoyment of his rights over land, the action must be confined to a person with a sufficient interest. This was defined as including a freeholder, a tenant or a licensee with exclusive possession. However, none of these categories would seem to cover Tom in his capacity as a lodger. If Tom has a right of exclusive occupation of part of Eileen's house, he might have a sufficient interest, in which case Tom's action will be similar to that of Eileen, except that he has suffered personal discomfort and personal injury.

On the discomfort issue, locality is a factor. Where there is an inconvenience nuisance (e.g., noise, smells etc.), it is relevant to consider where the alleged nuisance takes place. Thus it was said in *Sturges v Bridgman* (1879) 11 Ch D 852 that what is a nuisance in Belgrave Square would not necessarily be so in Bermondsey. The facts reveal that others in the area have had to close their windows, which establishes that the interference is widespread. If Tom lives in a quiet residential area, the fumes will probably be a nuisance, but if there are a number of other factories in the area, it may be that Tom has to put up with the inconvenience caused. However, even in an industrial area, if the extent of interference is gross, it may still be a nuisance (*Rushmer v Polsue and Alfieri Ltd* [1907] AC 121).

The other important issue concerning Tom is that of personal injury. Generally, private nuisance is concerned with damage to an interest in land. Respiratory ailments and fatigue do not immediately come into this category, and it has been said that only land interests are protected (*Read v Lyons* [1947] AC 156). But it has also been held that if the personal injury is associated with damage to a land interest, it is actionable (*Hale v Jennings* [1938] 1 All ER 579). In *Hunter v Canary Wharf Ltd* the general rule established in *Read v Lyons* has been affirmed, namely that since private nuisance is a tort concerned with the plaintiff's enjoyment of land, there is no cause of action in nuisance if the basis of the plaintiff's complaint is that he has suffered personal injury. The cause of action in this respect lies in the tort of negligence and fault must be proved. Thus if negligence cannot be proved, the uncertainty concerning the status of personal injuries in a nuisance action may prove fatal to Tom's claim.

If Tom has no land interest or if personal injuries are not actionable in private nuisance, he may have a claim in public nuisance. A public nuisance is a crime, which is actionable as a tort on proof of special damage and is defined as an act or omission which materially affects the reasonable comfort and convenience of life of a class of Her Majesty's subjects (*Attorney General* v *PYA Quarries Ltd* [1957] 2 QB 169). It is concerned with 'public rights', but those rights are not clearly defined, although interferences with public health appear to be covered. A class of people has to be affected. The fact that other residents have complained suggests an effect on a class of people, but Tom also has to prove special damage, i.e., damage over and above that suffered by others. What is unclear is whether the special damage must be different in kind to that suffered by others or whether a difference in terms of extent will suffice. Here the inconvenience caused by the fumes is suffered by everyone, but there are items of damage specific to Tom, namely the respiratory illness and his consequent loss of earnings. According to *Walsh* v *Ervin* [1952] VLR 361, the damage must be substantial, direct and not consequential, although it may cover general damage. Personal injury is covered (*Castle* v *St Augustines Links* (1922) above). The loss of earnings looks like consequential loss, but it is included within the definition of general damage.

Remedies

Assuming a nuisance is established which is more likely in Eileen's case than in Tom's, the appropriate remedy must be considered. The alternatives are damages or an injunction, but an injunction would shut down a factory placing employees out of work. In general there are four guiding principles (*Shelfer* v *City of London Electric Lighting Co.* [1895] 1 Ch 287). These are that damages will be awarded instead of an injunction if the injury to the plaintiff's legal rights is: (i) small; and (ii) can be estimated in money terms; and (iii) can be adequately compensated by a small money payment; and (iv) it would be oppressive to grant an injunction.

It may be that the public interest is relevant to the grant of an injunction, although the cases are divided on this issue. For example, the fact that heavy job losses might result from the closure of a factory has been ignored in granting a temporary injunction on a factory (*Bellew* v *Cement Co.* [1948] IR 61). But in *Miller* v *Jackson* [1977] QB 966 an injunction was refused against a cricket club on the ground that there was a public interest in preserving playing fields for recreation. The fairness and utility arguments may prevent an injunction from being granted provided the interference is not excessive.

Rylands v *Fletcher*

There may be the possibility of an action under the rule in *Rylands* v *Fletcher* (1868) LR 3 HL 330, but generally this requires the accumulation of something tangible which is likely to do mischief if it escapes. Fumes and smells do not normally satisfy this requirement, which means that a *Rylands* action may not be of any use.

QUESTION 3

Chromoshine Ltd, a small-scale cleaning firm, stores quantities of a toxic industrial cleaning chemical on its land on an industrial estate close to a residential housing estate. The site used by Chromoshine Ltd has been occupied by various industrial cleaners for the past 25 years. Evidence shows that a group of badly behaved teenagers have been seen in the area on various occasions over the past two months. Mysteriously, a barrel of the toxic fluid is overturned and ruptures with the following results:

(a) Mary, a catering assistant who works in Chromoshine's canteen, steps in the spilled fluid. Her legs are badly burned and her shoes are seriously damaged.

(b) A quantity of the fluid seeps into an underground water supply used by the South Downs Water Company with the result that the latter must find an alternative source of supply in order to meet its statutory obligations to water consumers in the area.

(c) The fluid flows into the street outside Chromoshine Ltd's premises. Traffic passing in the street causes small quantities of the fluid to splash on to Alice's front garden and her display of summer flowers is destroyed and the smell caused by a chemical reaction between the fluid and the material from which her dustbin is made result in Alice having to vacate her house for two weeks while remedial action is taken.

Commentary

(a) The question centres principally on the tort known as the rule in *Rylands* v *Fletcher*, but also raises the possibility of private nuisance negligence and occupiers' liability actions.

(b) It must be asked if the substance that escapes is likely to do mischief.

(c) It is pertinent to decide whether the defendant company was engaged in a 'non-natural user' of its land.

(d) It must be determined whether personal injury is an actionable head of loss for the purpose of *Rylands* v *Fletcher*.

(e) It must be asked if the 'mysterious' cause of the escape is something for which the defendant company may be held liable if the true responsibility lies with the actions of a stranger.

(f) The relevant rules on remoteness of damage under the rule in *Rylands* v *Fletcher* have to be applied.

Suggested Answer

This problem centres upon the tort known as the rule in *Rylands* v *Fletcher* (1868) LR 3 HL 330 which requires that a defendant, in the course of the non-natural user of her land, must bring on to that land, or keep or collect there something which, if it escapes, is likely to do mischief. In jurisprudential terms, the tort is one of strict, but not absolute, liability. This means that where an escape takes place causing harm, the defendant is *prima facie* liable for that harm, but he may nevertheless successfully defend an action if he is able to raise one of several recognised defences.

For the purposes of clarity of analysis it is beneficial to discuss each of the heads of loss in turn. The first person likely to bring an action is Mary who has suffered both damage to her shoes and injury to her person. Since *Rylands* involved damage caused to a neighbour's land the question might be asked whether damage to chattels and personal injury are protected by the tort. These points have been mooted in the past. However, in Mary's case, both questions need not be asked given the decision of the House of Lords in *Read* v *Lyons* [1947] AC 156 for there, Viscount Simon LC insisted that a pre-condition of the tort was that there had been an 'escape from a place where the defendant has occupation of, or control over, land which is outside his occupation or control'. On this basis, it seems clear that Mary could not frame an action in *Rylands*, since, at the material time, she was still on the premises of Chromoshine Ltd.

The facts relating to how the toxic fluid got spilt are not clear but if the spillage could be attributed to the negligence of a fellow employee then an action might lie in negligence against that person (or Chromoshine Ltd via the principle of vicarious liability if the negligence occurred in the course of the other employee's employment). An action might also be framed in terms of a breach of Chromoshine's non-delegable duty, as Mary's employer, to provide her with a safe place of work (*Wilsons and Clyde Coal Co. Ltd* v *English* [1938] AC 57). Finally, an action may lie under the Occupiers' Liability Act 1957 in respect of the premises not being safe for the purposes for which Mary was on them.

With respect to the loss suffered by the Downs Water Company, an action could possibly be brought in private nuisance or under *Rylands* v *Fletcher*. With respect to the private nuisance action, it would be necessary to show that Chromoshine Ltd had occasioned an unreasonable interference with the land of the Downs Water Company. With respect to the *Rylands* action, it would be necessary to show that Chromoshine Ltd were, prior to the escape, engaged in non-natural user of the land. This issue would also be relevant to the nuisance action in so far as it would be one consideration that the court would take into account in deciding whether the interference caused to the water company was unreasonable (*Cambridge Water Co.* v *Eastern Counties Leather plc* [1994] 1 All ER 53).

The leading definition of non-natural user was supplied by the Privy Council in *Rickards* v *Lothian* [1913] AC 263 where it was said to entail 'some special use bringing with it increased danger to others'. In the *Cambridge Water* case (factually similar to the present scenario), Lord Goff said that *Rickards* v *Lothian* provided a useful starting point but went on to proffer a more literal construction of 'non-natural user'. His Lordship was of the view — and the rest of their Lordships agreed — that 'non-natural user' requires a strict construction that focuses simply on the artificiality of the user. Indeed, he was adamant that whether or not the chemicals were intended for industrial usage did not affect the fact that their storage was one of the most unnatural users of which he could think.

Thus, though it might have been at one time relevant that Chromoshine Ltd is, and its predecessors have been, located on an industrial estate (*Mason* v *Levy Auto Parts of England Ltd* [1967] 2 QB 530), it now seems irrelevant in the light of the *Cambridge Water* case. The duration of occupation of the site may, however, be relevant to the possible nuisance action. The fact that Chromo-shine's site has been occupied for more than 20 years could be argued to support a claim for a prescriptive right to carry on the cleaning business (*Sturges* v *Bridgman* (1879) 11 Ch D 852). This would depend on whether the nuisance was viewed as being the actual escape or the continuation of a state of affairs which threatened pollution of the Downs Water Company's water supply and upon whether the user in question had not been complained about for 20 continuous years. It is clear in the light of the *Cambridge Water* case that the test for the remoteness of damage in *Rylands* is the same as that in negligence (the *Wagon Mound (No. 1)* [1961] AC 388 test of reasonable foresight of the kind of harm suffered). It is probable, with this in mind, that all the losses that Alice suffered would be regarded as too remote a consequence of the spillage of some of the toxic fluid. Were they not, however, it seems that the damage to the chattels (the flowers and dustbin) would be compensable (*Midwood* v *Manchester Corpor-ation* [1905] 2 KB 597), although it is not so clear whether her personal injury is recoverable under *Rylands* because of the doubt cast on this issue in *Read* v *Lyons*. (Note, however, that such loss is recoverable in nuisance (*Halsey* v *Esso Petroleum* [1961] 2 All ER 145 from which tort Lord Goff held *Rylands* to derive in *Cambridge Water*).) Finally, subject to the remoteness point made above, it might well be that the economic loss that Alice has probably incurred (the cost of temporary accommodation) is recoverable, because of her interest in the land affected (*Weller* v *Foot and Mouth Disease Institute* [1966] 1 QB 569).

As regards the defences that may be open to Chromoshine Ltd we have already seen that prescription might apply in the nuisance context. With respect to the *Rylands* actions, the only defence that might avail itself is that of 'act of a stranger'. According to this defence, a defendant may avoid liability where the escape is attributable to the act of a third party over whom the defendant had no control unless the plaintiff can go on to show that the act which caused the escape was an act of the kind which the owner could reasonably have contemplated and guarded against. The facts do not illuminate the point beyond saying that the spillage occurred mysteriously, yet it is arguably reasonable to suppose an element of human instrumentality, in which case the defence may well be available.

QUESTION 4

A strong case can be made for the view that the rule in *Rylands* v *Fletcher* is but an application or instance of liability in nuisance.

(Salmond, Heuston & Buckley, *Law of Torts*).

Discuss the interrelationship between the two torts in the light of this statement.

Commentary

In particular this question requires discussion of the House of Lords' decision in *Cambridge Water Co. Ltd* v *Eastern Counties Leather plc* [1994] 2 WLR 53 in which Lord Goff subjected the interrelationship between these two torts to detailed examination. It also requires consideration of the principles underlying the imposition of liability in nuisance and under the rule in *Rylands* v *Fletcher* with emphasis being placed upon both common and distinguishing features. Reference will also be made to the recent decision of the House of Lords in *Hunter* v *Canary Wharf Ltd* [1997] 2 WLR 684, which addressed a number of important issues about the scope of the tort of nuisance.

Suggested Answer

The interrelationship between the tort of nuisance and the rule in *Rylands* v *Fletcher* (1866) LR 1 Exch 265 received substantial consideration by the House of Lords in *Cambridge Water Co. Ltd* v *Eastern Counties Leather plc* [1994] 2 WLR 53 in which Lord Goff concluded that foreseeability of damage should be regarded as a prerequisite of liability for the recovery of damages under the rule in *Rylands* v *Fletcher*, as is the case with nuisance. Before turning to this recent decision for a fuller examination, the constituent elements of the respective torts will be surveyed. Liability under the rule in *Rylands* v *Fletcher* is imposed on a defendant where in the course of non-natural use of his land he accumulates upon it for his own purposes anything likely to do mischief if it escapes. Briefly, the facts of the case were that the defendants had employed independent contractors to construct a reservoir on their land in order to supply water to the defendants' factory. Due to the contractors negligently failing to discover and block a disued mine shaft, water from the reservoir burst through the shafts and flooded the plaintiff's mine. The defendants were held personally liable despite the absence of fault on their part. The existing law did not provide redress in this situation. There was no trespass as the flooding was not direct and immediate, and neither was there a nuisance given that at the time when Blackburn J formulated the rule, an isolated escape was insufficient to found liability under this head. More recently, however, it has been recognised that a single escape may constitute a nuisance, although the nuisance must arise from a state of affairs (*SCM (United Kingdom) Ltd* v *Whittall (W. J.) & Son Ltd* [1970] 1 WLR 1017, *per* Thesiger J). Indeed it is this requirement in nuisance that the defendant permits a 'state of affairs' which puts the plaintiff's property interests at risk which in itself allows for recovery for an isolated escape (*Spicer* v *Smee* [1946] 1 All ER 489).

There are numerous instances where the overlap between this rule and the tort of nuisance is clearly apparent. Liability in the tort of nuisance arises where there has been an unreasonable interference with the plaintiff's proprietary interest in land. In *Read* v *Lyons* [1947] AC 156, Lord Simonds pointed to Blackburn J's original formulation of the rule as recognising that in most cases the law of nuisance and the rule in *Rylands* v *Fletcher* may be 'invoked indifferently'. Also, the principle of reasonable user in nuisance under which a defendant will not be liable for consequent harm to his neighbour's enjoyment of his land equates with the similar principle of natural use found in the rule in *Rylands* v *Fletcher*.

However, there are marked distinctions between the torts. *Rylands* v *Fletcher* is founded upon the non-natural accumulation of something by the defendant on his land which is likely to do damage if it escapes. By definition this excludes things naturally on the defendant's land. Thus, an occupier is not liable for damage caused by ordinary trees on his land given that growing a tree is a natural use of soil (*Noble* v *Harrison* [1926] 2 KB 332). On the other hand, in *Crowhurst* v *Amersham Burial Board* (1878) 4 Ex D 5, a yew tree on the defendants' land projected over land belonging to the plaintiff on which cattle grazed. The leaves of yew trees are poisonous, and the plaintiff's horse died after eating some of them. The defendants were held liable under the rule in *Rylands* v *Fletcher* on the basis that it was not a natural use of land to plant on it a poisonous tree.

In contrast, liability in nuisance may arise from the state of the land itself. Thus, in *Goldman* v *Hargrave* [1967] AC 645 the Privy Council held that an occupier of land was under a duty to abate a fire started by lightning striking a tree on his land which had spread to his neighbour's property. This was followed by the Court of Appeal in *Leakey* v *National Trust for Places of Historic Interest or Natural Beauty* [1980] QB 485 where the defendants, who owned a hill which had slipped due to weathering, were held liable in nuisance to the plaintiff for damage caused to his contiguous property.

In *Rylands* v *Fletcher* the water had been brought on to the land by the defendants. Where water is naturally on the land, the defendant will not be liable if it escapes. Thus, in *Smith* v *Kendrick* (1849) 137 ER 205 rain water had formed a subterranean lake surrounded by a coal seam. When the coal was mined the water escaped and flooded the plaintiff's mine. It was held that the defendant was not liable given that the adjoining mine owners each had a 'natural' right to work their respective mines in the manner best suited to them, even though the natural consequence of their work could be prejudicial to the other.

A further distinction is that nuisance covers damage caused by intangible escapes such as noise and so in *Rushmer* v *Polsue and Alfieri Ltd* [1906] 1 Ch 234 the plaintiff successfully brought an action in respect of noise at night caused by printing presses, even though he lived in the printing area of London. *Rylands* v *Fletcher* is confined to the accumulation of a tangible object on land which is likely to cause damage, either upon its own escape or upon its giving off fumes, electricity or gas which escape.

A major distinction that can be drawn between the rule in *Rylands* v *Fletcher* and the tort of nuisance relates to 'standing to sue'. With respect to the former, it was stated by Lawton J in *British Celanese* v *Hunt (A. H.)* [1969] 1 WLR 959 that once an escape is established, anyone who suffers damage as a consequence may claim irrespective of whether or not they are occupiers of adjoining land. As we have seen, nuisance is premised upon protecting proprietary interests in land and is therefore narrower in its scope of protected interests. Since the plaintiff must satisfy the requirement of having either a possessory interest or some other proprietary interest in order to bring an action in nuisance, members of his family who lack this interest will be precluded from suing even though they have suffered personal injuries as a result of the defendant's activity. Accordingly, in *Malone* v *Laskey* [1907] 2 KB 141 it was held that the tenant's wife, who was injured when a toilet cistern fell on her as a result of vibrations caused by the defendant, had no claim in private nuisance. The decision in *Malone* was applied by the House of Lords in *Hunter* v *Canary Wharf* [1997] 2 WLR 684 in which two questions of law were addressed by their Lordships. First, whether interference with television reception signals could constitute an actionable nuisance. It was held that since the interference was the result of the presence of a building, the Canary Wharf office block, on the defendants' land, no action in private nuisance lay. An owner was entitled to build on his land as he wished, subject to planning control, and was not liable in the absence of an easement or agreement if his building interfered with his neighbours' enjoyment of their land. The second question was whether it was necessary to have an interest in land to sue in private nuisance. It was held by a majority of their Lordships that an action in nuisance can be brought only by a person in 'exclusive possession' of the affected land, or by an owner without exclusive possession.

Finally, it has been said that neither the rule in *Rylands* v *Fletcher* nor the tort of nuisance require proof of fault on the part of the defendant. Yet it is apparent, particularly in more recent decisions culminating in the *Cambridge Water* case, that the judges are steadily eroding non-fault based liability. In his speech in *Read* v *Lyons* [1947] AC 156 Lord Porter alluded to the concepts of 'justice' and 'reasonableness' when reviewing the judicial process for determining whether liability under the rule should be imposed. He pointed to the fact that judges have regard to all the surrounding circumstances including the time, place and practice of mankind so that what might be regarded as non-natural may vary according to the circumstances. In *Mason* v *Levy Auto Parts of England Ltd* [1947] 2 QB 530 MacKenna J in equating 'non-natural' user with unreasonable risk recognised the similarities inherent in this approach with those considerations applicable in negligence. Moreover, the concept of 'unreasonableness' is central to the tort of nuisance, and fault is concomitant with unreasonableness. Further, the importance of fault-based liability in nuisance was recognised by Lord Reid in *Wagon Mound (No. 2)* [1966] 1 AC 617 when he stated that 'fault of some kind is almost always necessary and fault involves foreseeability.'

Against this background the decision of the House of Lords in *Cambridge Water Co.* v *Eastern Counties Leather plc* has done much to clarify the confusion which has marked the development of the torts under consideration. The defendant operated a tanning business and up until 1976 had used large quantities of chemical to degrease raw skins. Much of this chemical had been spilt and had seeped into the ground; however, its effects at that time were considered to be innocuous. The plaintiffs purchased a well located over a mile away from the defendant's factory. At the time of purchase the plaintiffs had had the water tested and it was found to be perfectly fit for consumption. Subsequently, as a result of an EEC Directive in 1985 governing water purity standards, it became illegal to supply water from this source due to chemical contamination. At first instance the plaintiffs' claim failed, but on appeal, the Court of Appeal held that the defendant was strictly liable for the contamination of the water percolating under the plaintiffs' land. Not surprisingly this decision was heavily criticised by the commentators (see for example, Weir [1993] CLJ) 17). The defendant successfully appealed to the House of Lords where, following the restrictive approach adopted in *Read* v *Lyons* with respect to the imposition of strict liability, it was held that strict liability under the rule in *Rylands* v *Fletcher* arose only if the defendant knew or ought reasonably to have foreseen that the escape would cause damage. Liability under the rule is strict only in the sense that the defendant could be held liable for an escape resulting from the non-natural use of land notwithstanding that he had exercised all due care to prevent the escape occurring. Given that the defendant could not have reasonably foreseen that the seepage of the chemical through the factory floor would cause the pollution to the plaintiffs' borehole, it was not liable under the rule in *Rylands* v *Fletcher*.

The judicial trend noted above which has heralded the erosion of non-fault based liability was further reinforced by the trial judge and by the House of Lords in *Cambridge Water*. The first instance judge and Lord Goff shared the view that the imposition of strict liability in respect of high risk operations should be left to Parliament. It was stated that statute would be the appropriate means of ensuring that precise criteria were laid down governing the incidence and breadth of such liability.

QUESTION 5

Petronella owns a farm in the country and a disused plot of land in central London. The farm is situated near to an airfield used by a gliding club. Some of the gliders have occasionally landed in the fields of surrounding farms, damaging the crops, but the gliding club has always paid compensation to the farmers in such circumstances. The plot of land in central London is adjacent to a building site and the jib of a tall crane, owned by the developers of the site, constantly oversails into the air space above Petronella's plot. The developers have offered to buy the plot of land from Petronella, but she has always asked for more than they are prepared to pay.

Petronella is now seeking to obtain an injunction against the gliding club, preventing them from flying over her farm, and against the developers of the building site, preventing them from intruding into the air space above her land with their crane, even though it will be very difficult for them to redevelop their land without doing this.

Advise Petronella.

Commentary

This question is concerned with the difference between the tort of trespass to land (and air space) and the tort of private nuisance, and the rules which apply to the discretionary remedy of an injunction.

The fact that Petronella's farm is affected by overflights from a nearby gliding club raises the question of statutory immunity for gliders and other aircraft.

Suggested Answer

Petronella's farm

If the launching of gliders involves the generation of unreasonable levels of noise, Petronella might be able to commence an action in the tort of private nuisance. However, the most immediate source of grievance appears to be overflying and crash landing.

Overflying and possible noise nuisance may be subject to immunity under the Civil Aviation Act 1982, ss. 76 and 77. This immunity extends to both trespass to air space and to nuisance, but it arises only if the club was complying with an air navigation order made under s. 60. There is no such immunity against claims arising from damage caused by an aircraft falling from the air, or by people or things falling from aircraft on to land below, even where negligence cannot be proved (Civil Aviation Act 1982, s. 76(2)). Any such claim would equate to a claim for trespass to land, although it is probably a statutory cause of action in its own right.

In *Bernstein* v *Skyviews & General Ltd* [1978] QB 479, it was held that, even if an aeroplane overflies too low and too unreasonably to be protected by the Civil Aviation Act 1982, the cause of action will lie in nuisance rather than the tort of trespass to air space, unless the aeroplane flies so low that it interferes with the 'normal user of the land'. A distinction is drawn between direct interference, which constitutes a trespass, whereas an indirect interference is more likely to amount to a nuisance. Thus in *Mann* v *Saulnier* (1959) 19 DLR (2d) 130 a nuisance only was committed where a fence had been erected, but, through the passage of time, began to lean over and intrude into the space above the plaintiff's land.

If the cause of action lies in the tort of nuisance, as opposed to trespass, Petronella will not be able to succeed unless she can prove that she has suffered some actual or apprehended damage to her land, or some interference with her use and enjoyment of that land. Even in such a case, the remedy will normally be that of damages, or an injunction restraining the repetition of the unreasonable methods of flying, but it is unlikely that a court will grant an injunction forbidding the gliding club from continuing to make use of the airfield since this use is presumably permitted by an air navigation order, and therefore sanctioned by statutory authority. Where a person acts under statutory authority, the defendant must prove that the interference with the plaintiff's land is inevitable and the only possible source of liability will lie where the defendant has acted without taking reasonable care (*Manchester Corporation v Farnworth* [1930] AC 171). For these purposes, negligence is taken to mean that the defendant has failed to carry out the authorised work and to conduct the operation without reasonable regard and care for the interests of other persons (*Allen v Gulf Oil Refining Ltd* [1981] AC 1001).

Since there seems to be no dispute about the club's liability or willingness to pay compensation for any damage actually caused by the gliders, there would not be anything to be gained by Petronella in commencing an action for actual or apprehended damage to her fields or crops. If it were not for the Civil Aviation Act 1982, the answer might have been a different one. It is no defence to an application for an injunction against trespass that it will be difficult to avoid a future trespass on the plaintiff's land (*League Against Cruel Sports v Scott* [1986] QB 240).

Petronella's land in London

Petronella seems to be using her land in London as a 'ransom site', i.e., a strip of land which frustrates development on neighbouring land unless it is bought for whatever price the owner cares to name. There is no remedy against this at common law, since a man may make whatever lawful use of his own land he choses (*Bradford Corporation v Pickles* [1895] AC 587). The only statutory remedies are those which relate to the compulsory purchase of land by a local authority and those procedures made available to private landowners by the Access to Neighbouring Land Act 1992. The developers in this case do not possess any powers of compulsory purchase, because the price would not then have been one dictated by Petronella. The Access to Neighbouring Land Act 1992 is confined to cases in which access is necessary for the purpose of the preservation of neighbouring or adjacent land. The Act does not apply to works for the alteration, adjustment, improvement or demolition of any buildings or other land unless those operations are incidental to works of 'preservation'. In any event, even if the developers are entitled to rely on the 1992 Act, they cannot go ahead with any entry on to the neighbouring or adjacent land without first obtaining a court order. We may assume, therefore, that the developers in this case are building something completely new, and are not in a position to make any application to the court for rights of entry on to, or over, Petronella's land.

The question arises whether the intrusion of the jib of the developers' crane into the air space above Petronella's plot amounts to a trespass to that air space, or merely to nuisance. The distinction is an important one, because trespass is actionable per se, i.e., there is no need to prove that damage has been suffered. Nuisance is actionable only if there is proof that some damage, actual or apprehended, has been or will be suffered or if it can be shown by the plaintiff that there has been or will be some unreasonable interference with the plaintiff's right to use and enjoy his land. In *Anchor Brewhouse Developments Ltd* v *Berkley House Developments Ltd* [1978] 2 EGLR 173, it was held that the jib of a crane, or any other intrusion emanating from a structure (rather than from an aeroplane), amounted to a trespass to air space. The court also held that in such a case the plaintiff was entitled to an injunction as a matter of course, if the trespass was going to be repeated. It does not seem to matter that the plaintiff might be acting as a 'dog in a manger' (per Scott J in *Anchor Brewhouse*). This represents an exception to the general rule that an injunction, being an equitable remedy, can be denied to a plaintiff whose conduct meets with the disapproval of the court (he who comes to equity must do equity).

There was an earlier decision of the High Court in *Woolerton & Wilson* v *Costain* [1970] 1 WLR 411 in which an injunction to restrain a developer from trespassing with a crane was effectively denied to a plaintiff who had adopted a wholly unreasonable attitude. However, that decision has been disapproved of in later cases, including *Anchor Brewhouse*.

Assuming the proper action is one for trespass, the ingredients of this tort are that the defendant must have acted intentionally and there must be an interference, but this does not have to cause damage. Relevant defences are those of right of entry and of licence to trespass, but neither of these would appear to be relevant. Strangely, the tort can be committed unintentionally, since the required intention needs only relate to the voluntariness of the defendant's act in entering in the plaintiff's land, and there need be no intention to trespass (*Conway* v *George Wimpey & Co. Ltd* [1951] 2 KB 266). On the basis that a crane driver is not likely to have involuntarily trespassed on Petronella's air space, this would seem to suggest that the essential requirement of an action for trespass to land is made out.

So far as invasion of air space is concerned, it is necessary that the invasion occurs at a height at which the intrusion might interfere with the full use of the land. Thus an advertising sign which intrudes by only eight inches on to the plaintiff's land (*Kelsen* v *Imperial Tobacco Co. Ltd* [1957] 2 QB 334, but an interference as high as a crane jib will also amount to a trespass (*Anchor Brewhouse Developments Ltd* v *Berkley House Developments Ltd* [1978] 2 EGLR 173). Conversely, interference from overflying aircraft seems to occur at such a height that it is unlikely that there will be any available action in the tort of trespass (*Bernstein* v *Skyviews & General Ltd*).

It would appear, therefore, that Petronella is likely to be successful in her claim for an injunction against the property developers, but she is unlikely to be successful in her proceedings against the gliding club.

9   Liability for Statements not made Negligently

INTRODUCTION

This chapter is principally concerned with the torts of defamation and injurious falsehood. Both torts allow a person to clear his name where a statement has been made by the defendant which either attacks the plaintiff's reputation or attacks the plaintiff's economic interests by tending to undermine a business interest.

Defamation requires a publication of a statement which tends to subject the plaintiff to ridicule or contempt or tends to lower the plaintiff in the minds of right-thinking members of the public. For the most part, it is a tort which does not require proof of damage unless the statement is made in a merely transitory form.

Defamation does not attract legal aid, with the result that a person who wishes to protect his reputation but who cannot afford to fund a defamation action may choose to sue for injurious falsehood. However, this tort is not primarily concerned with protecting reputation, but it may sometimes be used to clear the plaintiff's name. The ingredients of injurious falsehood differ in a number of respects from the elements of defamation. In the first place, injurious falsehood protects a person's economic interests, and does require proof of economic damage. Secondly, the defendant's statement must be false, whereas a defamatory statement may be literally true, but may contain some actionable innuendo. For the purposes of injurious falsehood, there must be an intention to disparage, whereas there can be an entirely innocent defamation.

QUESTION 1

Alice is employed by Genial George, a spendthrift film actor, as nanny to George's children. One evening, while George has taken responsibility for the care of his children, he trips with the result that he falls on his head and is rendered unconscious. Alice returns some time later and tenders first aid. By chance, a photographer employed by the *Daily Scum* observes Alice removing George's wallet from his pocket while cradling him in her arms. Alice has removed the wallet in order to relieve any obstruction to his breathing.

The following morning, the photograph is published in the *Daily Scum* together with the headline, 'Genial George Gropes Thieving Nanny'. As a result of this publicity, Genial George advises Alice that her services are no longer required. It transpires further that no one else will employ Alice as a nanny. Genial George is also upset that he has been prevented from telling his own version of what happened by virtue of the invasion of his privacy.

Neither Alice nor Genial George can afford to bring an action for defamation.

Advise Alice and Genial George.

Commentary

This question requires a discussion of the elements of the tort of injurious falsehood, namely:

(a)   does the plaintiff have a protectable financial interest?

(b)   is there any disparagement?

(c)   is the statement false?

(d)   what was the defendant's state of mind?

(e)   has damage been caused?

Suggested Answer

In normal circumstances an action for defamation is the most obvious way of clearing a person's name, but the facts of the question make it clear that neither Alice nor Genial George is able to afford to bring proceedings for defamation.

Moreover, since defamation actions are not legally aided, some alternative source of redress must be found if this is permitted. The decision in *Joyce* v *Sengupta* [1993] 1 All ER 897 shows that although the principal means of protecting reputation is the tort of defamation, sometimes an action for injurious falsehood may serve to clear a person's name. Since actions for injurious falsehood also attract legal aid, this may be the appropriate avenue for impecunious litigants such as Alice and Genial George. This is not to say that the two torts do not have their differences. For example, injurious falsehood always requires proof of damage, whereas some varieties of defamation are actionable *per se*. Also, in an action for injurious falsehood, the plaintiff must prove that the statement made by the defendant was untrue, whereas in a defamation case, it is a defence for the defendant to prove the truth of his statement.

Injurious falsehood was originally called slander of title, because it was generally confined to the protection of a person's interest in his title to land. In later years the tort was extended to cover a person's interest in goods or his business provided the statement has been maliciously published (*Ratcliffe* v *Evans* [1892] 2 QB 524). It is now established that the tort also protects an individual's economic interests whether or not they are also commercial interests (*Kaye* v *Robertson* [1991] FSR 62; *Joyce* v *Sengupta*).

The basis of the tort is that the defendant's false statement has caused the plaintiff economic damage. In *Kaye* v *Robertson* a television actor was seriously injured in a freak storm. While recovering in hospital, he was photographed and a story was run in the defendant's newspaper, suggesting that the plaintiff had authorised publication. The plaintiff argued that this had caused economic loss as he had been prevented from marketing his own story. This was held to be sufficient to disclose an action for injurious falsehood. Oddly, there is no right, in law, to privacy, which is the true interest the plaintiff in *Kaye* was seeking to protect. It follows that a perverse interest in the desire to make a pecuniary gain had to be realised in order to protect the plaintiff's interests.

A key feature of the decision in *Kaye* was that the plaintiff was prevented from telling his story because the defendant had suggested the story was printed with the plaintiff's authority. In the present case, there is no such suggestion by the *Daily Scum*. Moreover, the essence of the newspaper headline is an attack on Genial George's reputation which is probably best dealt with by means of an action for defamation, in the absence of an action for the invasion of privacy.

In *Joyce* v *Sengupta* a newspaper article falsely suggested that the plaintiff had abused her position as an employee of a member of the Royal Family by stealing personal letters. The Court of Appeal held that there were sufficient grounds for allowing an action for injurious falsehood to proceed as the plaintiff's employment prospects had been prejudiced, thereby damaging an economic interest. This appears similar to Alice's position as the question states that no one will now employ Alice as a nanny. What is clear from *Kaye* and *Joyce* is that the tort is no longer confined to business interests and may be used in order to protect individual economic interests as well.

Apart from establishing that there has been damage to an economic interest, the plaintiff in an action for injurious falsehood must also prove that there has been some disparagement. Thus in *De Beers Abrasive Products Ltd* v *International General Electric Co. of New York* [1975] 2 All ER 599 the defendants published a report, as a sales promotion device, which falsely suggested that a rival product marketed by the plaintiffs had not been scientifically tested. Since a reasonable person would have regarded the statement as disparaging, the tort was committed. The key test in this regard is to ask if a reasonable man would take the statement made by the defendant as a disparagement of the plaintiff's economic interests (*De Beers Abrasive Products Ltd* v *International General Electric Co. of New York*).

Conversely, a mere 'puff' will not suffice (*White* v *Mellin* [1895] AC 154). If Alice is unemployable elsewhere, it would appear that there has been some disparagement relevant to her economic interests.

Before an action for injurious falsehood will lie, it must be shown that the defendant's statement is false. The onus of proof rests on the plaintiff (*Royal Baking Powder Co.* v *Wright, Crossley & Co.* (1900) 18 RPC 95). Here the truth is that Alice did not steal the wallet, therefore to call her a thief is a falsity.

The state of mind required on the part of the defendant is that he must have intended to disparage the plaintiff. However, recent cases have insisted that the plaintiff must prove malice (*Loudon* v *Ryder (No. 2)* [1953] Ch 423). The difficulty this raises is to determine what is meant by malice. Malice has been used variously to indicate an improper motive (*Balden* v *Shorter* [1933] Ch 427) or a mere want of honest belief in the truth of the statement (*Greers Ltd* v *Pearman & Corder* (1922) 39 RPC 406) or a want of bona fides or the presence of mala fides (*White* v *Mellin*). In order to discharge the burden of proof, it is sufficient for the plaintiff to show knowledge of the falsity of the statement or recklessness on the defendant's part (*Spring* v *Guardian*

Assurance [1993] 2 All ER 273). It would appear to be reckless, at least, on the part of the *Daily Scum* to go ahead with the story without first checking the truth of the assertion that Alice is a thief.

Since injurious falsehood requires proof of damage, Alice will have to establish that she has suffered some pecuniary loss (*Ajello* v *Worsley* [1898] 1 Ch 274). It is no longer a requirement that the plaintiff should be able to prove special damage where words are published in a written or permanent form or where the words are calculated to cause pecuniary loss in relation to any office, profession, calling, trade or business carried on by the plaintiff at the time of the publication (Defamation Act 1952, s. 3). If the publication causes mental distress or injury to feelings, no action for injurious falsehood will lie, although such damage may be included in the assessment of general damages (*Joyce* v *Sengupta* [1993]).

QUESTION 2

Trilby is a student of the Du Maurier College of Melodrama. She believes that she is being sexually harassed by Svengali, one of the lecturers at the college. She writes a letter, addressed to all the governors and lecturers at the college, which includes the statement, 'Svengali sexually harasses female students'.

Trilby takes the letter to the public library, in order to make 200 copies of it. By mistake, she leaves the original letter in the photocopier, where it is found by Nosey, who reads the letter and posts it, anonymously, to Svengali's wife.

Trilby sends copies of her letter to the governors and lecturers at the college, using the internal post. Each letter is in a brown envelope, addressed to the recipient and marked 'confidential'.

Two days later, one of these letters is found pinned to a notice board in the students' common room. Svengali denies the allegation of sexual harassment.

Advise Svengali.

Commentary

The main issues requiring consideration are:

(a)   is there a publication?

(b) what defences are available should defamation be established? More particularly, is the defence of qualified privilege available?

Suggested Answer

Svengali may wish to bring an action for defamation. He will have to prove that the words used were defamatory, that the statement referred to him and that it was published to a third party. The judge will first determine whether the words are capable of bearing a defamatory meaning. The accepted test for this purpose is whether the words in question would 'lower the plaintiff in the estimation of right thinking members of society' (*Sim* v *Stretch* [1936] 2 All ER 1237 at 1240, *per* Lord Atkin; see also *Berkoff* v *Burchill* [1996] 4 All ER 1008). It is for the jury to determine whether the words are actually defamatory. However, it should be noted that by virtue of the Defamation Act 1996, s. 7 either the plaintiff or the defendant may apply for an order to determine, before trial, whether the words are capable of bearing a defamatory meaning. It is suggested that given Svengali's profession, the statement that he sexually harasses female students is defamatory. It is in written form, and therefore an action will lie for libel which is actionable per se.

The requirement of publication is relatively straightforward in the present case. Svengali will wish to allege that the letter has been published to Nosey who, by chance, found the original letter in the public library and read its contents. Further, it has also been published to Svengali's wife who received the original letter in the post, to the governors and lecturers at the college who received copies of the letter in the internal post, and to the students and other users of the students' common room who have read the copy of the letter pinned to the notice board. Each publication is new libel and will be a major factor for the jury to take into account when assessing the amount of any damages to be awarded.

Trilby will admit to the publication of the letter to the governors and lecturers of the college. She will doubtless deny that she is responsible for any of the other publications. If Trilby has limited means, Svengali may wish to allege that the college is in some way responsible for the publication of the copy letter on the students' notice board (whether or not Trilby shares responsibility for that incident).

The library authorities will not be liable despite the discovery of the letter on their photocopier. They have not published the libel, but in any case they could argue that there is an innocent dissemination (*Vizetelly* v *Mudie's Select*

Library Ltd [1900] 2 QB 170). This defence will be replaced by the so-called 'distributor's defence' contained in the Defamation Act 1996, s. 1. As with innocent dissemination, it will be available only if the defendant did not know that his act involved or contributed to the publication of the defamatory statement in question.

Nosey has published the letter to Svengali's wife, but Trilby may share some responsibility for this incident. This does not provide Svengali with any additional defendant to sue, because of the anonymity of the sender. It may be noted in passing that, although there is no 'publication' of a statement between a husband and wife when they communicate with each other, the law does not take the same approach when the communication is made by a third person to one partner about his or her spouse (*Wenman* v *Ash* (1853) 13 Ch 836).

Trilby and Nosey

A publication occurs if the maker of a statement negligently allows a third party to read it. For example, in *Theaker* v *Richardson* [1962] 1 WLR 151 the writer of a letter was held to have published it to the addressee's spouse because he had sent it in a business envelope and did not make it clear that the contents were intended for the addressee only (c.f. *Huth* v *Huth* [1915] 3 KB 32). The negligent leaving of a letter in a public place is, therefore, an example of a publication of that letter to any member of the public who reads it.

Trilby, Nosey and Mrs Svengali

The sending of the letter by Nosey to Mrs Svengali (and the reading of that letter by her) amounts to a new publication of the defamatory statement. Although it does not amount to a publication of a defamatory statement to bring it to the attention of the person defamed, we have already seen that there is no legal right to bring it to the attention of his wife or her husband.

Since the Svengalis do not know the identity of the sender of the letter to Mrs Svengali, it must be asked if Trilby can be held responsible for this publication. In *Cutler* v *McPhail* [1962] 2 QB 292, it was held that the author of a defamatory letter sent to a newspaper was also responsible for its subsequent publication by that newspaper. In *Slipper* v *BBC* [1991] 1 QB 283, it was held that the makers of a defamatory television programme should have foreseen that it would be reviewed in a national newspaper, thereby spreading the allegations to a wider audience. The Court of Appeal, however, took the view that the actions of an unauthorised person could break the chain of causation, thereby releasing the original maker of the statement from any responsibility for its further publication. This argument may not apply, however, to a person who has negligently left a document in a public place.

In *Weld-Blundell* v *Stephens* [1920] AC 956, the plaintiff wrote a letter to his accountants about the financial affairs of a particular company. A member of the firm of accountants negligently left the letter at the offices of that company where it was seen by the manager who noted that it made defamatory remarks about two individuals. These individuals successfully sued the plaintiff for defamation. The plaintiff then successfully sued the firm of accountants for breach of contract in failing to take reasonable care of the letter.

Trilby and the Governors and Lecturers of the College

The governors and the lecturers of the college are the intended recipients of Trilby's letter. Trilby may invoke the defence of qualified privilege. This defence arises when A makes a statement to B, because she has a duty to make it to him, or because she (A) has a legitimate interest to protect in bringing it to his attention. Trilby has an interest to protect in complaining about Svengali to the proper authorities within the college. The question arises whether she has circulated her allegations too widely. In *Adam* v *Ward* [1917] AC 309 it was held that a publication to the public at large could be protected by the defence of qualified privilege if it related to a matter of the widest public importance. However, this is a rare situation. The general rule is that the defence of privilege will be lost if the defendant commits 'excess of privilege' by communicating the allegations to persons who have no legitimate interest in hearing them. Thus in *Chapman* v *Lord Ellesmere* [1932] 2 KB 431, it was held that the publication of a disciplinary decision of the Jockey Club was privileged when it appeared in *The Racing Calendar*, but not privileged when it appeared in *The Times* newspaper.

Any communication between a student and the governors of the college ought to entitle reliance on the defence of qualified privilege if it relates to the conduct of a member of staff. The fact that the governing body might be a large number of people does not matter. In *Horrocks* v *Lowe* [1975] AC 135 the House of Lords held that qualified privilege extended to a complaint made against a town councillor published to all the other councillors.

The vital question is whether Trilby had any right to circulate her allegations among the academic staff, most of whom would not have had any powers of management over Svengali. If the articles of government of the college show that all the lecturers have the right to participate in the running of the college, the net of qualified privilege will reach further. It will not be enough for Trilby to show that the allegations would be of some interest to the academic staff, in the sense of being newsworthy for their own sake.

However, the defence of qualified privilege will be defeated by malice. If Svengali can show that Trilby was motivated by malice, she will not be able to invoke the defence, no matter to whom the allegations were sent (*Horrocks* v *Lowe*; *Angel* v *H Bushel Ltd* [1968] 1 QB 813).

Trilby and the students

It is not clear how a copy of Trilby's letter appeared on the students' notice board. Trilby may argue that she is not responsible for this public display of the letter, but it will suit Svengali's purpose to allege that the college is responsible for this state of affairs.

Svengali may claim that the college authorities should have removed the copy of the letter from the notice board and that, by failing to do so, they adopted the defamatory statement and published it to the users of the common room. To remove the letter would involve no expense, and no damage to the structure of the building (*Byrne* v *Deane* [1937] 1 KB 818). Svengali must show, however, that the college authorities had a reasonable time to discover the letter and to remove it from the notice board. Svengali may also argue that the letter appeared on the notice board due to malice, negligence, or other fault of a lecturer at the college. He will therefore wish to hold the college vicariously liable for that conduct. He will have to show that the conduct in question was carried out during the course of the lecturer's employment, and that it did not amount to a 'frolic of his or her own'. The lecturer would not have been authorised to display defamatory material on student notice boards. In *Irving* v *Post Office* [1987] IRLR 289, the Court of Appeal held that the Post Office was not vicariously liable for the publication of racially offensive words on an envelope, written by a malicious sorter at a sorting office, even though it was part of the sorter's duty to re-direct mail and to write words and phrases on envelopes.

QUESTION 3

Alf Cheatem, the MP for Wessex North, is in the process of introducing a private members' Bill in Parliament authorising the redesignation of agricultural lands in his constituency for industrial development. This would allow

Wover Cars Ltd to build a manufacturing plant in the area. During the Parliamentary debate, the MP for a neighbouring constituency, Peter Green, emerged as the Bill's most vociferous opponent.

On hearing of the debate, Nick Whippet, the chairman and chief executive of Wover, wrote to Cheatem stating, 'No names, no pack drill, but our principal opponent in the House is a hypocrite whose opposition to the scheme has more to do with the fact that he has recently purchased several farms in Wessex North which he stands to lose, than with his apparent concern for the preservation of the countryside'.

Cheatem confronts Green with the allegations during a Parliamentary debate and accuses him of abusing his position by failing to disclose his personal interests. Cheatem has also written to the *Wessex Daily Globe* stating that 'Peter Green MP is a liar whose only interest is to protect his own property at the expense of bringing employment into the region'. Using this information, the newspaper prints an editorial criticising Peter Green in similar terms. In fact Peter Green does not own property in the Wessex North constituency.

Advise Peter Green.

Commentary

This question requires consideration of the Defamation Act 1952, the Defamation Act 1996 and the distinction between libel and slander. In particular the following aspects will be discussed:

(a)   the meaning of defamation;

(b)   publication;

(c)   defences, particularly justification, privilege and fair comment.

Suggested Answer

Peter Green may be able to bring an action in the tort of defamation against Nick Whippet, Alf Cheatem and the *Wessex Daily Globe*. A defamatory statement may be conveyed in any medium, but it is the choice of medium which determines whether Peter Green's action lies in slander or libel. If the defamatory statement is conveyed in a permanent form it is libel, whereas if it is in a temporary form, it is slander. The distinction between the two forms of action is important because libel is actionable per se (without proof of damage). Slander, on the other hand, is actionable only upon proof of actual damage. This requirement is subject to certain exceptions, the most important of which for the purposes of Peter Green's action is an imputation of unfitness or incompetence. The Defamation Act 1952, s. 2 provides that where the words are calculated to disparage the plaintiff in any office, profession, calling, trade or business carried on by him there is no need to prove special damage, 'whether or not the words are spoken of the plaintiff in the way of his office, profession, calling, trade or business'. It is therefore not necessary for Peter Green to prove defamation in the context of his office provided the words are likely to injure him within it. It should be noted that on grounds of public interest, the courts will not allow free speech to be fettered by permitting organs of government, whether local or central, to sue for libel (*Derbyshire CC* v *Times Newspapers* [1993] AC 534; *Goldsmith* v *Bhoyrul* [1997] 4 All ER 268). However, individuals such as MPs and party candidates may bring proceedings for defamation (*Goldsmith* v *Bhoyrul*, per Buckley J).

Having identified whether the particular statements can be categorised as slander or libel, it is necessary for Peter Green to prove the three elements of the tort of defamation, namely, that the particular words used were defamatory, that they referred to him and that they were published to a third party by the defendant.

Nick Whippet's letter is in permanent form and so the action against him will lie in libel. Peter Green will have to convince the court that the words are capable of bearing a defamatory meaning. The classic definition of defamation was promulgated by Parke B in *Parmiter* v *Coupland* (1840) 6 M&W 105 at 108, in which he said: 'A publication, without justification or lawful excuse, which is calculated to injure the reputation of another, by exposing him to hatred, contempt, or ridicule ...' is defamatory. This formula has been criticised as being too narrow since a plaintiff's reputation can be damaged without him or her being necessarily exposed to hatred, ridicule or contempt (see, for example, *Tournier* v *National Provincial Union Bank of England Ltd* [1924] 1 KB 461, Scrutton LJ). A wider test for determining whether the defendant's words are capable of being defamatory was formulated by Lord Atkin in *Sim* v *Stretch* [1936] 2 All ER 1237 at 1240. His Lordship said that the requisite question is: 'Would the words tend to lower the plaintiff in the estimation of right-thinking members of society generally?' Thus, there is no requirement that the defamatory statement should impute moral turpitude (*Youssoupoff* v *Metro-Goldwyn-Mayer Pictures Ltd* (1934) 50 TLR 581). In *Berkoff* v *Burchill* [1996] 4 All ER 1008, Neill LJ cited with approval the approach adopted in *Cropp* v *Tilney* (1693) 3 Salk 225, in which the plaintiff complained of a publication which he said had resulted in his failing to be elected as a member of Parliament. The defendant had alleged that the plaintiff was beaten by his wife. Holt CJ said that scandalous matter is not necessary to establish a libel but rather it is sufficient if the defendant induces an ill opinion to be had of the plaintiff.

If the judge considers that the words are capable of bearing a defamatory meaning they are put to the jury as 'right thinking members of society' to determine whether or not the words are in fact defamatory. By virtue of the Defamation Act 1996, s. 7 either party may apply for an order to determine before trial whether the words are actually capable of bearing a defamatory meaning. The description of Peter Green as a 'hypocrite' by Nick Whippet in his letter to Cheatem would appear to be libellous within the broader approach adopted by Holt CJ and subsequently by Lord Atkin. Although the words do not expressly refer to him this will not bar his action since he can introduce extrinsic evidence to show that he was identified (*Morgan* v *Odhams Press Ltd* [1971] 1 WLR 1239). Alf Cheatem's special knowledge would be relevant here. The third element of the tort is publication which has been defined as the communication of defamatory words to a third party, that is to some person other than the plaintiff (*Pullman* v *Walter Hill & Co.* [1891] 1 QB 524, CA). It is evident that Nick Whippet has in fact published the statement to Alf Cheatem (a third party).

The defence of justification is not available to Nick Whippet. Given that Peter Green does not own the farm land claimed, and therefore has no vested interest in opposing the scheme, there is no truth in the defamatory statement that he is a hypocrite seeking to protect his property (*Wakley* v *Cooke & Healey* (1849) 4 Exch 511). Similarly, fair comment is not available to him as a defence since the comment must be an opinion based on true facts (*London Artists Ltd* v *Littler* [1969] 2 All ER 193) and must be one that could honestly and recently be made (*Brooks* v *Lind* (1996) *The Times*, 26 March).

The allegation made by Alf Cheatem that Peter Green abused his position is prima facie slanderous in that it disparaged him in the conduct of his office. Further, on the basis of the Defamation Act 1952, s. 2, special damage need not be proved. However, given that the statement was made during a Parliamentary debate it enjoys absolute privilege (Bill of Rights 1688; *Ex parte Wason* (1869) LR 4 QB 573; the Defamation Act 1996, s. 13(4)), so that no action will lie in respect of it (although by s. 13 of the 1996 Act this privilege can be waived; this is unlikely on the given facts). Neither will an action lie against *Hansard* when Alf Cheatem's words are published, since any statement in a paper published by the authority of Parliament is privileged (Parliamentary Papers Act 1840). In *Church of Scientology of California* v *Johnson-Smith* [1972] 1 QB 522, the plaintiffs sued the defendant MP for a libel alleged to have been made on a television programme. The defence was fair comment. The plaintiffs pleaded malice which would negate this defence. To establish malice they wanted to use extracts from *Hansard*. It was held that this evidence could not be used because of Parliamentary privilege.

Cheatem's letter to the *Wessex Daily Globe* in which he expressly refers to Peter Green as a liar, is libellous in that it would tend to lower him in the estimation of right-thinking members of society. It has clearly been published to a third party, the newspaper and, as with Whippet, since the statement is based on the false assertion that Peter Green is motivated by protecting his property interests, the defences of absolute privilege, justification and fair comment are not available to him. Similarly, the newspaper will be liable for libel even if it has expressly stated in the editorial that it is merely reproducing what the editors have been told by Cheatem (*M'Pherson* v *Daniels* (1829) 10 B & C 263). Accordingly, the writer of the editorial, the newspaper proprietor and its printers will each be held liable for its publication. Also, in *Goldsmith* v *Sperrings Ltd* [1977] 2 All ER 566, it was held not to be an abuse of process for the plaintiff to pursue a claim arising from an article in a well known weekly satirical magazine against 37 different distributors with a view to making them settle his claim on the basis of their undertaking to cease distributing the magazine. As noted with respect to Nick Whippet and Alf Cheatem's letters, the defences of justification and fair comment will not be available. However, the newspaper may make an 'offer of amends' to Peter Green by offering to publish an apology or correction and pay him damages even before the writ is served (Defamation Act 1996, ss. 2–4). If Peter Green accepts such an offer the issue must be settled by an agreement between him and the newspaper. The court will only intervene, if necessary, to adjudicate as to the amount of compensation or on the nature of the apology or correction. Acceptance of an offer will operate to terminate the defamation proceedings.

The Defamation Act 1996, ss. 8–10 introduced significant reforms into the conduct of defamation proceedings. The so-called 'fast-track' procedure enables the court, in the absence of a jury, to dispose summarily of a case if it appears that the action has 'no realistic prospect of success'. Conversely, the procedure enables the court to provide 'summary relief' in a case if it appears that there is no defence and the claim has 'a realistic prospect of success'. By s. 9(1)(c) of the Act, summary relief is restricted to actions which can be adequately compensated by an award not exceeding £10,000. It is suggested that Peter Green may wish to opt for a jury trial given that by the nature of his vocation, he would hope for an award in excess of that figure. Juries are notoriously generous in assessing damages for libel or slander (see, for example, *Lord Aldington* v *Tolstoy and Watts* (1989) unreported, in which the plaintiff was awarded £1,500,000). Until recently the Court of Appeal lacked the power to reduce jury awards unless they were completely 'divorced from reality'.

QUESTION 4

During a local radio phone-in programme Bill Birch, the leader of the majority party on the council for the city of Bilchester, announces that he intends to push through his plans to deregulate gambling in the city and its suburbs. He explains that he wishes to see Bilchester become a second Las Vegas.

Mary Priggish, a well known member of the 'Moral Crusade Party', telephones the programme and is put on the air. She states that 'Birch is an immoral clown who wants to see law and order disintegrate in our city. If he were to marry he might give up his hedonistic lifestyle and start pushing for family virtues'.

In fact Bill Birch is married to Primrose, a charity worker who is also a governor of the local primary school. Shortly after the broadcast, Bill's wife is told that the chairman of the school governors wishes her to resign. He feels that it is inappropriate for someone who is co-habiting outside of wedlock to hold such a position.

Advise Bill Birch and Primrose.

Commentary

This question requires consideration of the three elements of the tort of defamation but with particular emphasis on:

(a)   the Broadcasting Act 1990, s. 166;

(b)   innuendo;

(c)   reference to the plaintiff;

(d)   the defence of unintentional defamation (the Defamation Act 1952, s. 4; and the Defamation Act 1996, ss. 2–4).

Suggested Answer

Both Bill Birch and Primrose may have an action in defamation against Mary Priggish and the radio company. The Broadcasting Act 1990, s. 166 provides that the publication of any words during the course of a broadcast programme, on television or radio, shall be treated as publication in permanent form. Their action will therefore lie in libel which is actionable per se (without proof of actual damage), and thus the request for Primrose to resign from the school governors is not material to her claim. Accordingly, it is necessary for them to prove the constituent elements of the tort, namely that the statement was defamatory, that it referred to them and that it was published to a third party by the defendants.

Bill Birch has two possible claims. Firstly, that the statement that he is an 'immoral clown' is capable of being defamatory since it would 'tend to lower him in the estimation of right thinking members of society' (*Sim* v *Stretch* [1936] 2 All ER 1237, per Lord Atkin), or the words could expose him to 'hatred, contempt or ridicule' (*Parmiter* v *Coupland* (1840) 6 M & W 105, per Parke B). Whether or not the statement is capable of bearing a particular meaning or meanings is a question for the judge to determine. The judge will therefore lay down the limits of the range of the possible defamatory meanings of which the words are capable (*Mapp* v *News Group Newspapers Ltd* [1998] 2 WLR 260 at 262, per Hirst LJ). It is for the jury to decide the actual meaning of the words within that permissible range (*Slim* v *Daily Telegraph Ltd* [1968] 2 QB 157 at 174, per Diplock LJ). It is submitted that an imputation of immorality is capable of being defamatory within the tests laid down by Parke B and Lord Atkin, particularly given the nature of Bill Birch's public office. Recourse to the Defamation Act 1952, s. 2 (slander affecting official, professional or business reputation) is not necessary given that Bill Birch's action lies in the tort of libel. Secondly, although the suggestion that he is unmarried is not *prima facie* libellous, it must be considered against the fact that he is married to Primrose. It is immaterial if the people who know that he lives with Primrose conclude that they are unmarried but nevertheless do not think any less of him, since the test for determining whether the statement is defamatory is dependent upon its effect on 'right thinking members of society'. Although the courts do not favour actions for defamation brought by organs of local or central government since there is a public interest in free speech (*Derbyshire CC* v *Times Newspapers* [1993] AC 534), proceedings by individuals such as councillors, MPs and candidates are nevertheless allowed (*Goldsmith* v *Bhoyrul* [1997] 4 All ER 268).

Bill will need to introduce extrinsic evidence to establish the meaning of this true innuendo. The decision of the Court of Appeal in *Cassidy* v *Daily Mirror Newspapers Ltd* [1929] 2 KB 331, is clearly pertinent to his claim. The defendant newspaper published a picture of Mr Cassidy, also known as Michael Corrigan, and a woman. The caption stated that it was 'Mr M. Corrigan, the race horse owner, and Miss X, whose engagement has been announced'. Mrs Cassidy sued for libel claiming that the caption and photograph were capable of meaning that her husband was a single man, and that therefore she was living in immoral co-habitation with him. It was held that in the light of the extrinsic evidence that Mr Cassidy was in fact married, the publication was defamatory. It was immaterial that the defendant was unaware of the extrinsic facts, provided that the paper had been read by those who did and who knew that it applied to the plaintiff.

With respect to the action by Primrose, the suggestion that Bill is unmarried carries the imputation that she is living with him outside of wedlock and similarly the decision in *Cassidy* v *Daily Mirror Newspapers Ltd* is apposite. The fact that she is not referred to does not bar her claim given that ordinary sensible people, proved to have special knowledge of the facts, might reasonably believe that the statement referred to her. In *Morgan* v *Odhams Press Ltd* [1971] 2 All ER 1156, the House of Lords held that there was no requirement that the words themselves expressly referred to the plaintiff and extrinsic evidence could be adduced to show that she was referred to. Thus the key factor is the inference which an 'ordinary sensible' listener would draw from the statement.

When making her statement on the phone-in Mary knew that it would be broadcast contemporaneously and is therefore liable for its publication (*Adams* v *Kelly* (1824) Ry & M 157). Similarly, the radio company as the 'publisher' of the statement is also liable (*M'Pherson* v *Daniels* (1829) 10 B & C 263). Further, the programme's production staff may also be found liable on the basis that they disseminated the defamatory statement. The defendants may raise the defence of unintentional defamation provided by the Defamation Act 1952, s. 4, in relation to the innuendo. However, the defence is available only if a person innocently publishes words alleged to be defamatory and has exercised all reasonable care in relation to the publication. As a public figure it would not be difficult to ascertain Bill's marital status, and therefore reasonable care had not been taken to avoid defaming him and, by implication, Primrose. In the absence of reasonable care, it is immaterial that the defendants were unaware of the external facts which turned a presumptively innocent statement into one which is defamatory (*Newstead* v *London Express Newspaper Ltd* [1940] 1 KB

377). The defence of unintentional defamation may now become more widely used due to the reforms contained in the Defamation Act 1996. An 'offer of amends' procedure was introduced by ss. 2–4 of that Act. A defendant may make a written offer to the plaintiff to publish an apology or correction and pay damages even before the action is commenced. The offer may be in relation to the defamatory statement generally or to a specific defamatory meaning within it, in which case it is called a 'qualified offer'. The offer must be made before a defence is served. If Bill Birch and Primrose accept the offer then the matter is settled by agreement and the court will only intervene, if necessary, to adjudicate on the amount of compensation or on the nature of the apology or correction to be published by the radio broadcasting company. Their acceptance of an offer will terminate the defamation proceedings against the company. If, however, they do not accept the offer of amends, it can be withdrawn by the broadcasting company and either a new offer can be made in its place or the original offer can be left to stand and used as a defence.

10   Interference with Chattels and Business Interests

INTRODUCTION

One purpose served by the law of tort is to protect members of society against harm to the person, but it also protects property rights and, to a much lesser extent, a person's legitimate business interests.

The first of the questions which follow is primarily concerned with the tort of conversion which requires consideration of the plaintiff's right to possession of goods. Both conversion and the tort of trespass to goods require proof of an intention, on the part of the defendant, to interfere. Moreover, since these are intentional torts, the remedies available to the plaintiff differ from torts which require a lesser state of mind.

The other two questions consider the economic torts of conspiracy and inducement to breach of contract. While these provide some protection against intentional interference with economic interests, they both illustrate a strain in the law in that they compete with the right of another to make a living. A balance has to be struck between legitimate business competition or hard bargaining and unacceptable interference with the interests of another. In some way, the law has to attempt the difficult task of identifying those unlawful acts which interfere with the trade or business of another without unduly restricting the right of others to engage in free competition. As the development of the tort of conspiracy and inducement to breach of contract illustrate, this is not easy.

(1)   Trespass to goods and conversion

QUESTION 1

Tom, a keen golfer, while looking for a lost golf ball, finds a heavy gold chain at the bottom of a shallow lake on the Victoria Park Golf Course, a site owned and run by Graspshire County Council. The clasp on the chain is imperfect with the result that Tom asks Harold, a jeweller, to carry out repairs. Harold sells the chain to Deborah for £500, claiming that it belongs to a friend of his who has given him authority to obtain the best possible price. Deborah then gives the chain to her boyfriend, Albert, as a birthday present. Albert, a dealer in jewellery, has now displayed the repaired chain in his shop window at a price of £1,500.

Advise Tom.

Commentary

(a)   Define conversion and trespass to goods.

(b)   Is a finder of goods someone who has standing to sue?

(c)   What effect does the existence of a bailment relationship have on the liability of the bailee?

(d)   What effect does the common law defence *jus tertii* have in the light of the Torts (Interference with Goods) Act 1977, s. 8?

(e)   What remedies are available in respect of the tort of conversion in the light of the Torts (Interference with Goods) Act 1977, s. 3?

(f)   What are the rights of an improver under the Torts (Interference with Goods) Act 1977, s. 6?

Suggested Answer

Conversion is the intentional dealing with goods which is seriously inconsistent with the possession, or right to immediate possession, of another person (*Street on Torts*). However, there is no tort of conversion where what is interfered with is no more than an equitable interest (see *MCC Proceeds Inc* v *Lehmar Bros* [1998] 4 All ER 675). Trespass to goods involves a direct interference with goods in the possession of the plaintiff, whether the interference is intentional or careless.

Since Tom has found the chain at the bottom of a lake on a golf course owned by someone else, it has to be established from the outset that he has a right to possession of the chain which is capable of protection by the torts of conversion or trespass. It appears that there is truth in the common assertion 'finders keepers' since the fact of simple possession is sufficient to create an interest in the goods. In *Parker* v *British Airways Board* [1982] QB 1004 it was held that the finder of a chattel acquires rights over it if the true owner is unknown, the chattel appears to be abandoned or lost and he takes the chattel into his care or possession. In such a case, the finder acquires a right to the goods which is valid against everyone except the true owner, or a person who asserts a prior right to the goods which subsisted at the time the finder took possession. Similarly, if a customer finds banknotes on the floor of a shop, the customer will have a better claim to the notes than the shopkeeper, since until informed of their presence by the customer, the shopkeeper is unaware that they are there (*Bridges* v *Hawkesworth* (1851) 21 LJQB 75).

In *Amory* v *Delamirie* (1722) 1 Stra 505, a boy found a ring containing a jewel and handed it to a goldsmith for valuation. When the goldsmith declined to return the jewel, now removed from its setting, it was held that the boy was entitled to succeed in an action for conversion. The facts of the question suggest that the chain has been found below the surface of the water but on the bed of the lake. This may suggest that Graspshire County Council has a superior interest. For example, a prehistoric boat embedded in soil, six feet below the surface, was held to belong to the landowner rather than the finder on the basis that the landowner owns not just the surface of the land but also everything which lies beneath the surface down to the centre of the earth (*Elwes* v *Briggs Gas Co.* (1886) 33 Ch D 562). Similarly, in *Waverley Borough Council* v *Fletcher* [1995] 4 All ER 756 the defendant, using a metal detector, found a mediaeval gold brooch some nine inches below the surface of a public park owned by the plaintiff authority. The authority subsequently claimed a declaration that the brooch was their property, but the defendant relied on the defence of 'finders keepers'. Although the trial judge found in favour of the defendant on the basis that the owner of a public park impliedly licensed members of the public to go to the park to engage in recreational activity, the Court of Appeal found in favour of the plaintiff authority on the basis that they had a superior right to the brooch than did the finder of it. While recreational activity was impliedly permitted, the license was considered not to extend to the right to dig up the ground, which could be regarded as a variety of trespass.

However, the problem in the present case is that Tom has not had to dig in order to find the chain, but on the other hand the surface of the water may be regarded as the top of the County Council's land, in which case the chain may be regarded as equivalent to being buried.

In *South Staffordshire Water Co.* v *Sharman* [1896] 2 QB 44 an employee was instructed by a landowner to clean out the bottom of a pool. At the bottom of the pool, two gold rings were discovered. The Divisional Court concluded that the rings were found 'in' the land rather than simply 'on' it. Accordingly, the landowner had the better claim to possession. Unfortunately, in the course of giving judgment, Lord Russell seems to have said that whether a chattel is found in or on land, the chattel will still belong to the landowner if he has a manifest intention to exercise control, which might be taken to undermine the position adopted in cases like *Parker* v *British Airways Board.*

Conversely, the finder has a better interest in the goods if they are merely on the land rather than being attached to it, provided the owner has not shown an intention to exercise control over the land and things upon it. Thus in *Parker* v *British Airways Board* there was no evidence to show that the defendants had any intention to exercise control over a bracelet found by the plaintiff on the floor of the departure lounge at an airport. In contrast in *London Corporation* v *Appleyard* [1963] 2 All ER 834, the discovery of banknotes in a box in a wall safe showed that the owner of the land did have an intention to exercise control over the property. In the present case, there appears to be little evidence of an intention to control the chain on the part of Graspshire County Council, which may be taken to suggest that Tom has a greater interest. However, there still remains the problem that if the chain, like the rings in *South Staffordshire Water Co.* v *Sharman*, is taken to have been found in the land, then the County Council may have the stronger claim.

After finding the chain, Tom hands it to Harold for repair. As a repairer, Harold is a bailee who has a lien over goods entrusted to him for the purposes of repair, but only in respect of his right to payment for the work he has done. However, if the bailee wrongly parts with possession, he loses his lien. By selling the chain to Deborah, Harold loses his lien. Moreover, his act also amounts to conversion, thereby entitling the owner to sue him (*Mulliner* v *Florence* (1878) 3 QBD 484).

At common law many conversion actions succeeded even where the defendant could show that a third party had a better title than the plaintiff, because the defendant was not allowed to plead *jus tertii*. However, following the enactment of the Torts (Interference with Goods) Act 1977, s. 8(1), the common law rules on *jus tertii* were abolished so that the better title of a third party at the date of the alleged conversion (*De Franco* v *Metropolitan Police Commissioner, The Times*, 8 May 1987) may be pleaded as a defence to conversion. It follows that if Graspshire County Council have a better title to the chain, an action in conversion against Harold, Deborah or Albert is likely to fail.

For a person to be liable for an act of conversion, there must be an intentional act which results in an interference with the plaintiff's goods (*Ashby* v *Tolhurst* [1937] 2 KB 242). However, if the defendant intends to deal with the goods in such a way as to interfere with the plaintiff's right of control, it does not matter that he is unaware that he has challenged the true owner's right to property or possession (*Caxton Publishing Ltd* v *Sutherland Publishing Ltd* [1939] AC 178). It follows that there is no defence of mistake or good faith (*Hollins* v *Fowler* (1875) LR 7 HL 757). Clearly, Harold intends to deal in the chain in a manner which is inconsistent with Tom's right of possession. Since Harold is given possession only for the purposes of repair rather than sale, it is unlikely that there will be a sale with the consent of the owner for the purposes of the Factors Act 1889, ss. 1(1) and 2(1) (*Pearson* v *Rose & Young* [1951] 1 KB 275). Moreover, Deborah has also acted intentionally by delivering the chain to Albert and the fact that she is unaware that she has challenged Tom's right to possession is irrelevant.

Albert presents a slightly different problem since he has merely invited offers for the purchase of the chain. As such he has not sold the chain nor is there any agreement to sell, with the result that there is no transfer of possession and, therefore, no conversion (*Lancashire Wagon Co.* v *Fitzhugh* (1861) 6 H & N 502). However, Albert may have 'used' the chain as his own. For example, it has been held that merely wearing a pearl is an act of conversion (*Petre* v *Hemeage* (1701) 12 Mod Rep 519). Purporting to sell an article may be similarly treated with the result that Albert may have converted the chain as well.

The remedies for conversion are such that the plaintiff is entitled to compensation to the extent of the value of the goods converted. This will normally be the market value of the converted goods, which in this case is £1,500, if Albert's price for the chain represents its market value. However, the relevant date for assessment of damages is the date of conversion (*BBMB Finance Ltd* v *Eda Holdings Ltd* [1991] 2 All ER 129).

By repairing the chain, Harold may have increased its value. Generally, it is not open to the plaintiff to recover that enhanced value (*Caxton Publishing Ltd v Sutherland Publishing Ltd*). If the act of conversion occurs after the improvement, as in Harold's case, the Torts (Interference with Goods) Act 1977, s. 6(1) applies. This provides that if the defendant has improved the goods in the mistaken belief that he has a good title, an allowance can be made. Under s. 6(2) a similar allowance may also be made in favour of subsequent purchasers provided they act in good faith. It seems unlikely that Harold will be able to argue that he honestly believed he had a good title, but Deborah may be able to show that she did purchase in good faith, having been told that Harold was selling the chain on behalf of a friend. Albert is unlikely to be able to use s. 6 in his favour, since it applies only to a subsequent purchaser, and as Deborah gave him the chain as a present, he is a volunteer.

(2)   Conspiracy

QUESTION 2

Although no branch of the law of torts has a higher proportion of decisions of the House of Lords ... the scope of the tort is as obscure as its history.

(Salmond, Heuston & Buckley, *The Law of Torts*.)

How far is this an accurate reflection on the tort of conspiracy?

Commentary

This question requires a critical examination of the scope of the tort of conspiracy, including where it came from and the present range of unlawful acts capable of falling within the definition of the tort. Answers should:

(a)   define the tort;

(b)   show its links with the criminal law;

(c)   differentiate between a conspiracy to injure and unlawful means conspiracy.

Suggested Answer

Conspiracy amounts to the commission of a tort when two or more persons agree to commit an act which would be lawful if committed by one person acting alone. In order for there to be an actionable conspiracy, there must be an intention to cause damage and actual damage must result from the acts of the conspirators.

Conspiracy takes one of two forms: conspiracy to injure or conspiracy to carry out an unlawful act such as the commission of a crime or a tort.

The origins of the tort are unclear, but a conspiracy can be both a crime and a tort, although the extent to which conspiracy is now a criminal offence is substantially reduced by virtue of the Criminal Law Act 1977. Moreover, why the deeds of two people acting in combination should be actionable when the actions of a multinational corporation, as a single juristic person, are not, has attracted criticism. Indeed, for this very reason, doubts have been expressed by the House of Lords as to the rationale of the tort of conspiracy, although on each occasion, the existence of the tort has been confirmed (see *Lonrho Ltd v Shell Petroleum Ltd (No. 2)* [1982] AC 173; *Lonrho plc v Fayed* [1992] 1 AC 448). The connections between the tort of conspiracy and its criminal law origins may also explain the non-availability of the general defence of contributory negligence. What seems to have persuaded the courts to regard conspiracy as an actionable wrong is that the wilful nature of the actions of the defendants acting in combination, if it causes actual pecuniary loss, should be actionable in itself and that the mere fact that the plaintiff had the opportunity to investigate and take action, but failed to do so, will have no effect on the remedy ultimately awarded to the plaintiff (*Corporacion Nacional del Cobre de Chile v Sogemin Metals Ltd* [1997] 2 All ER 917).

A conspiracy to injure occurs where there is a wilful act which is intended to and does cause damage to the plaintiff in the course of his trade or business. For these purposes, there is still a conspiracy if the defendants know all the facts and intend to cause damage even if they are unaware of the illegality of their actions (*Pritchard v Briggs* [1980] Ch 388). It is important to emphasise that the gist of the action is actual pecuniary loss. Accordingly, it has been held that injury to reputation, including injury to business reputation in the form of damage to goodwill, is not a recoverable head of damage in an action for conspiracy (*Lonrho plc v Fayed (No. 5)* [1994] 1 All ER 188). Such losses are the proper province of the tort of defamation in which justification may be pleaded by the defendant.

For the purposes of 'unlawful act conspiracy', it appears that the unlawful act relied on by the plaintiff must have been actionable at his suit. (*Generale Bank Nederland v Export Credits Guarantee Department* (1997) (unreported);

Yukong Line v *Rendsburg Corp. (No. 2)* [1998] 4 All ER 82). Thus if the unlawful act would have been actionable at the suit of a third party, but not the plaintiff, the plaintiff cannot plead the agreement to commit the unlawful act as a conspiracy.

One of the earliest developments in relation to the tort of conspiracy is to be found in *Quinn* v *Leathem* [1901] AC 495 in which the plaintiff employed workers who did not belong to the trade union of which the defendants were officials. The defendants maliciously threatened to compel the plaintiff's most important customer not to deal with the plaintiff unless he dismissed the non-union employees. The combined actions of the defendants were held to be an actionable conspiracy since there was actual damage in the form of lost custom.

Following *Quinn* v *Leathem* it was thought that malice was an ingredient of the tort, but it is clear since *Crofter Hand-Woven Harris Tweed Co. Ltd* v *Veitch* [1942] AC 435 that spite or malevolence is not a necessary requirement, although it may actually be present in some cases. The decision in *Crofter* made it necessary to consider the predominant purpose of the defendants' actions. Thus in *Crofter* the defendants' (a trade union) predominant purpose in placing an embargo on the importation of woollen yarn to the Isle of Lewis was the protection of the interests of its members.

If the predominant purpose of the defendants is to injure the plaintiff in his trade or business or his other legitimate interests and damage results, there is an actionable tort. What is important is that the defendants should have acted *in order that*, not *with the result that* the plaintiff should suffer damage (*Crofter*). Accordingly a very selfish act may still be justified. Thus if the defendant's intention is to benefit the sellers rather than to injure the plaintiff, no action for conspiracy will lie (see *Yukong Line* v *Rendsburg Corp. (No. 2)* [1998] 4 All ER 82). The burden of proving absence of justification for the defendants' actions may lie on the plaintiff if the analogy between conspiracy as a crime and as a tort is maintained. However, in modern civil law it may be better to require the defendant to justify his actions, especially since the basis of the tort is that the defendant has intentionally caused the damage complained of.

The second kind of actionable conspiracy, namely unlawful means conspiracy, requires a combination between two or more people to commit a crime or a tort, with the result that the plaintiff suffers damage. In this case, it is irrelevant that the defendants' object is legitimate (*Metall & Rohstoff AG* v *Donaldson Lufkin & Jenrette Inc* [1990] 1 QB 391). Moreover, proof of a predominant intention to injure the plaintiff is not an essential element of the tort (*Lonrho plc* v *Fayed* [1992] 1 AC 448).

In *Lonrho Ltd* v *Shell Petroleum Co. (No. 2)* [1982] AC 173 the defendants intentionally agreed to import oil into Southern Rhodesia from South Africa, in breach of a statutory prohibition. By acting in this way, the defendants substantially increased their profits at the expense of the plaintiffs. On these facts, it was held that there was no intention to injure the plaintiffs since there was no tort unless the defendants acted for the purpose not of protecting their own interests but of injuring the interests of the plaintiffs. However, since *Lonrho plc* v *Fayed* [1992] 1 AC 448 the fact that a reason or even the predominant reason for acting unlawfully is the furtherance of one's own interests is not to be regarded as a defence.

(3)   Inducement to breach of contract

QUESTION 3

While the tort of inducement to breach of contract may have started its life in the form of an action for enticing the services of the employee of another, it is better now to regard the tort as one concerned with contractual relations of any kind.

Discuss.

Commentary

This question is concerned with the scope of the tort of inducement to breach of contract and how its use has spread beyond interference with employment relations into other areas. The principal issues for consideration are:

(a)   the origins of the tort in the field of employment contracts;

(b)   the development of the notion of secondary action and the effect of this on the activities of trade unions in labour disputes;

(c)   the necessary state of mind required on the part of the defendant;

(d)   the characteristics of the contractual relations interfered with in order to allow the application of the tort.

Suggested Answer

If the defendant intentionally and without lawful justification induces or procures a person to breach a contract he has made with the plaintiff, the latter may recover damages in respect of the inducement, provided he, the plaintiff, has suffered actionable damage. Moreover, the remedy of damages apart, there is a judicial willingness to grant an injunction in order to restrain threatened breaches of contract (*Swiss Bank Corporation* v *Lloyd's Bank Ltd* [1979] 2 All ER 853).

The origins of the tort lie in actions flowing from the inducement of an employee to leave the services of his employer. In *Lumley* v *Gye* (1853) 2 E & B 216 it was held that for the defendant to be liable, he must maliciously induce a person to break a fixed-term contract for the provision of exclusive personal services consisting of either a single act or a course of dealing. However, since that time, it has become apparent that other contractual relations may fall within the scope of the tort. For example, a threat by a trade union to cause labour difficulties to a building materials supplier if he did not refrain from dealing with the plaintiff, was actionable as an inducement to breach of contract despite the fact that there was no approach to the plaintiff's own employees (*Temperton* v *Russell* [1893] 1 QB 715). From this, it became possible to recognise the notion of the secondary action, namely a threat to interfere with the plaintiff's commercial dealings with others as a means of furthering an industrial dispute. However, the principle in *Lumley* v *Gye* concerned not merely an expectation of performance by third parties, but the actual advantage of a promised performance by a person with whom the plaintiff has contracted. In the light of this it has been held that interference with the economic advantages to be gained from a contract, as opposed to interference with the contract itself, is not actionable (*RCA Ltd* v *Pollard* [1983] Ch 135).

Conversely, if the defendant has broken his contract with the plaintiff and seeks to interfere with that contract and with other similar contracts made by the plaintiff at a later stage, the court may grant an injunction to prevent interference with all contracts concerned (*Torquay Hotel Co. Ltd* v *Cousins* [1969] 2 Ch 106). This is said to be justifiable because it is not the same thing as ordering a person not to make a contract (*Midland Cold Storage Ltd* v *Steer* [1972] Ch 630).

Assuming the contract is of a type to which the tort applies, the interference must be unlawful. The decision in *Lumley* v *Gye* suggests that the defendant's actions must be malicious. However, it is now clear that ill-will is not a necessary requirement and that it will be sufficient if the defendant's violation is committed knowingly, or if there is no lawful justification for the interference (*Quinn* v *Leathem* [1901] AC 495). Accordingly, it is no defence for the defendant to argue that he acted without malice (*Greig* v *Insole* [1978] 1 WLR 302), or that he acted in good faith (*Pratt* v *British Medical Association* [1919] 1 KB 244). It is sufficient to establish that the defendant has done an act which must damage the plaintiff and there is no need to prove that he intended to do so (*Lonrho plc* v *Fayed* [1992] 1 AC 448).

While the action for inducement to breach of contract may lie where there is an interference with a contract of service, the contract itself must be valid in law. Thus no action will lie where the relevant contract is void, made in restraint of trade (*Greig* v *Insole*), or even where the contract is unenforceable (*Smith* v *Morrison* [1974] 1 WLR 659). However, where a secondary contractual duty to pay damages is ineffective, a tort action for inducement to breach the contract of which that provision is a part may still lie (*Merkur Island Shipping Corporation* v *Laughton* [1983] 2 AC 570). It remains the case that so long as there is a direct and deliberate interference with a contract, it does not matter that there has been no breach of that contract (*Torquay Hotel Co. Ltd* v *Cousins*). Thus action which merely hinders performance of primary obligations under a contract will suffice (*David Dimbleby & Sons Ltd* v *National Union of Journalists* [1984] 1 WLR 427). Conversely, merely making the performance of a contract less valuable than it might otherwise have been does not, in itself, amount to an inducement to breach of contract. Moreover, it has also been held that the tort may extend beyond interference with the plaintiff's right to primary performance by a third party and may also cover cases of interference with the plaintiff's secondary right to relief against a third party for breach of contract, provided the violation of that right is, in itself, an actionable wrong (*Law Debenture Trust Corp plc* v *Ural Caspian Oil Corp Ltd* [1995] 1 All ER 157). However, if what the defendant does is lawful at the time, there is no actionable tort. Thus in *Law Debenture Trust Corp plc* v *Ural Caspian Oil Corp Ltd* [1995] 1 All ER 157, the defendants were a number of companies which had traded in Russia prior to the 1917 revolution and had had their assets expropriated without receiving any compensation. Shares in those companies were sold on condition that all subsequent transferees would be required to covenant that they would pay to the plaintiff any government compensation which might subsequently be paid. Shares were later transferred in breach of one such covenant to a company which subsequently sold the shares to another purchaser. The last of these transfers was effected at a time when the transferor had full legal and beneficial rights of ownership. As such the transfer was one which had to be regarded as not being unlawful, with the result that no tort was committed.

According to the decision of the Court of Appeal in *DC Thompson Ltd* v *Deakin* [1952] Ch 646, if the defendant's action is to be regarded as an inducement, it must satisfy one of five possible criteria. First, it may directly persuade, procure or induce a breach of contract as in *Lumley* v *Gye*. Secondly, the defendant's action may physically prevent performance of the relevant contract, for example, by destroying the tools of a man's trade (*DC Thompson Ltd* v *Deakin*). Thirdly, dealings between the defendant and the other contracting party may be inconsistent with the terms of the contract made between the plaintiff and that other, to the knowledge of the defendant (*F* v *Wirral Metropolitan Borough Council* [1991] 2 All ER 648, 677 *per* Ralph Gibson LJ). Fourthly, an action by the defendant which would amount to a breach of contract if performed by one of the parties to the contract, will be an actionable wrong if done with knowledge of the contract and without the knowledge of either of the contracting parties (*GWK Ltd* v *Dunlop Rubber Co. Ltd* (1926) 42 TLR 376). Finally, there may be an indirect interference with contractual relations where unlawful means are used, the defendant has knowledge of the relevant contract and intends to secure breach or interference with its performance.

Since the tort is concerned with unlawful interference with contractual relations, an interference which is justified will not amount to the commission of an actionable wrong. Thus if the defendant seeks the performance of another contract which is inconsistent with the contract, inducement to breach of which is alleged, it is probable that no tort is committed (*Pratt* v *British Medical Association*). It may also be the case that where the defendant acts under some moral duty he commits no tort, for example, where the claims of a family relationship take precedence (*Midland Bank Trust Co. Ltd* v *Green* [1979] 3 All ER 28).

11   General Defences

INTRODUCTION

This chapter is concerned with the general defences available to a defendant who is faced with an action in tort. While a number of torts carry with them a range of specific defences, there are defences which apply across the whole range of tortious liability. In particular, this chapter considers the application of the defences of contributory negligence, *volenti non fit injuria* (otherwise known as the defence of consent to the risk of harm) and the defence of illegality encapsulated in the latin maxim *ex turpi causa non oritur actio* (a man cannot benefit from his own misdeeds).

The first of the questions which follow considers the limitations placed on the scope of the defence of contributory negligence by the definition of fault in s. 4 of the Law Reform (Contributory Negligence) Act 1945. In particular, it examines the extent to which contributory negligence can be used as a defence in an action for breach of contract in the light of the development of the notion of concurrent contractual and tortious liability, and whether there is any tortious liability in respect of which the defence is not available.

Question two considers the confused state of the defence of *volenti non fit injuria* and considers what are its true requirements and whether the defence serves any useful purpose in the light of the other available defences which may adequately explain the plaintiff's lack of complete success.

The last of the questions in this chapter continues on similar lines and is a problem question which illustrates the extent of overlap between the defences of contributory negligence, *volenti* and public policy.

QUESTION 1

How far is the application of the Law Reform (Contributory Negligence) Act 1945, s. 1(1) affected by the definition of the term 'fault' in s. 4 of the same Act?

Commentary

This question requires a consideration of the meaning of fault as used in the Law Reform (Contributory Negligence) Act 1945, s. 4, and in particular whether the following constitute fault on the part of the defendant:

(a)   a breach of contract;

(b)   an intentional tort;

(c)   a strict liability tort.

Additionally, consideration must be given to the availability of the defence of contributory negligence before the 1945 Act was passed.

Suggested Answer

The defence of contributory negligence applies where a person suffers damage partly as a result of his own fault and partly as a result of the fault of the defendant. In such a case, the plaintiff's damages are reduced to the extent that the court thinks is just and equitable, having regard to the claimant's share in the responsibility for the damage (Law Reform (Contributory Negligence) Act 1945, s. 1(1)). For these purposes, fault is defined in s. 4 of the Act as negligence, breach of statutory duty or other act or omission which gives rise to a liability in tort or would, apart from the Act, give rise to the defence of contributory negligence.

The word fault in s. 4 is used in two contexts. First, the fault of the defendant is covered by the words negligence, breach of statutory duty or other act or omission which gives rise to a liability in tort. The fault of the plaintiff is adverted to by the closing words of s. 4 which raise the question whether contributory negligence was an available defence at common law prior to the passing of the 1945 Act.

The principal problems associated with the definition of fault in s. 4 of the 1945 Act are threefold. First, is a breach of contract on the part of the defendant fault within the meaning of s. 4? Secondly, do all torts attract the defence. Thirdly is the defence available under the 1945 Act where its availability was doubtful at common law?

The issue of contributory negligence as a defence in an action for breach of contract has been subjected to a wide-ranging review by the Law Commission (Law Com No. 219, 1993) in which it was recommended that contributory negligence should be a defence in all actions for breach of contract, except those involving the breach of a strict contractual duty, such as a breach of the implied terms in the Sale of Goods Act 1979 relating to the quality and fitness of goods. But this is certainly not the present law.

The present state of the law is affected by the nature of the defendant's breach. It has been observed that there are three different types of breach of contract on the part of a defendant which may attract different responses to the availability of the defence of contributory negligence (*Forsikringsaktiesel-skapet Vesta* v *Butcher* [1986] 2 All ER 488, Hobhouse J). First, the defendant may be in breach of a strict contractual duty such as the implied statutory obligation in a sale of goods contract which requires the goods to be of merchantable quality. In this case, it is clear that there is no fault on the part of the seller with the result that the defence of contributory negligence is not available (*Quinn* v *Burch Bros (Builders) Ltd* [1966] 2 QB 370; *Barclays Bank plc* v *Fairclough Building Ltd* [1995] 1 All ER 289).

The second type of breach of contract is one in which the loss is of a type not recoverable in the ordinary law of tort. This would include varieties of economic loss in respect of which no tortious duty of care is owed. If the wording of s. 4 is interpreted so that the word negligence is not qualified by the words 'which gives rise to liability in tort', a breach of such a contractual duty of care might be regarded as negligence in the wider sense (*De Meza & Stuart* v *Apple, Van Staten, Stena & Stone* [1974] 1 Lloyd's Rep 508). Conversely, the manner in which a contractual term is broken has been said to be immaterial (*Quinn* v *Burch Bros,* above) with the result that the phrase other act or omission should be taken to refer to potential tortious liability only (*AB Marintrans* v *Comet Shipping Co. Ltd* [1985] 3 All ER 442).

The third relevant variety of contractual breach is one where liability sounds concurrently in contract and tort. Examples include contracts for the supply of services in which there is an implied term requiring the exercise of reasonable care and skill and contracts entered into by an occupier of land who owes the common duty of care under the Occupiers' Liability Act 1957. In such cases, it is accepted, possibly controversially, that the defence of contributory negligence is available if there is fault on the part of both the plaintiff and the defendant (*Sayers* v *Harlow UDC* [1958] 1 WLR 623).

Even if it is the case that the fault of the defendant comprised in a breach of contract, in some circumstances, may give rise to the defence of contributory negligence, the definition of the plaintiff's fault may serve to deny the availability of the defence. The wording of s. 4 of the 1945 Act refers to an act or omission which would, apart from the Act, give rise to the defence of contributory negligence. This may mean that the plaintiff's conduct must be such that it would have given rise to the defence at common law. If this is so, there is authority which suggests that the defence was not available in such circumstances (*Forsikringsaktieselskapet Vesta* v *Butcher* [1988] 2 All ER 43). An alternative view is that if the defendant is concurrently liable in tort and contract and the defence of contributory negligence would have been available at common law had the action been framed in tort, then the defence should be available if the plaintiff sues for a breach of contractual duty.

Where the action is framed solely in tort, the definition of fault in s. 4 may still give rise to problems since the plaintiff's conduct must be such that the defence would have been available apart from the Act. If this means that the defence must have been available at common law, it follows that the defence is inapplicable where the tort committed by the defendant is that of deceit (*Redgrave* v *Hurd* (1881) 20 Ch D 1). Moreover, in cases of deceit, the defendant has intended the plaintiff to rely on his statement, in which case it is not open to the defendant to argue that the plaintiff should have avoided his loss by taking more care not to be duped by the defendant (*Alliance & Leicester Building Society* v *Edgestop Ltd* [1994] 2 All ER 38).

Historically, the defence of contributory negligence did not apply to the tort of trespass to the person. However, in *Barnes* v *Nayer, The Times*, 19 December 1986 it was said that there was no logical reason why the defence should not apply to cases of battery (see also *Watson* v *Chief Constable of the Royal Ulster Constabulary* [1987] 8 NIJB 34). Whether the defence applies to an action for negligent misstatement under the rule in *Hedley Byrne & Co. Ltd* v *Heller & Partners Ltd* [1964] AC 465 is not entirely clear. It might be argued that since a requirement of *Hedley Byrne* is that the plaintiff should have reasonably relied upon the advice given by the defendant, the defence will be unnecessary since if the plaintiff unreasonably fails to take care for his own interests, an ingredient of the rule in *Hedley Byrne* has not been complied with, so that no duty of care will be owed (*JEB Fasteners Ltd* v *Marks, Bloom & Co.* [1981] 3 All ER 289).

However, in *Gran Gelato Ltd* v *Richcliff (Group) Ltd* [1992] 2 WLR 867 the defence was considered relevant to an action brought under the Misrepresentation Act 1967, s. 2(1), in which case, in theory, at least, it might be argued that the defence should also apply to actions under the rule in *Hedley Byrne.*

It is clear that the defence did not and does not apply where the defendant commits the tort of conversion or intentional trespass to goods (Torts (Interference with Goods) Act 1977, s. 11). Where negligence is an element in the tort committed by the defendant, the defence would have been available at common law. On this basis, the defence applies where the defendant commits a breach of statutory duty or the tort of nuisance.

QUESTION 2

The confused state of the defence *volenti non fit injuria* is 'partly due to a considerable overlap with other conceptual techniques employed to limit or reduce a defendant's liability'. (Jones, *Textbook on Torts.*)

Discuss.

Commentary

This question requires an explanation of the main ingredients in the defence of *volenti non fit injuria*, namely:

  (a)   voluntary choice;

  (b)   agreement to accept the legal risk of harm;

  (c)   knowledge of the existence, nature and extent of the risk of harm.

Suggested Answer

Roughly translated, *volenti non fit injuria* means, 'to one who is willing, no harm is done'. As such, it is a defence based on consent and where it operates, it serves to displace the duty which would otherwise be owed by the defendant.

The principal ingredients of the defence are that the plaintiff must have made a voluntary choice amounting to an agreement to accept the legal risk of harm with full knowledge of the nature and extent of that risk.

The requirement of voluntary choice means that the plaintiff must be in a position to make a free choice and must be aware of the circumstances relevant to the exercise of that choice (*Bowater* v *Rowley Regis Corporation* [1944] KB 476). It follows from this that an employee is not *volens* to the risk of injury at work merely because he is aware of a dangerous practice (*Smith* v *Baker* [1891] AC 325) since there may be other reasons why he continues to work, such as economic compulsion. Moreover, policy may dictate that certain people such as rescuers act in a manner which exposes them to a risk of injury because of some social or moral duty rather than because they have voluntarily assumed the risk of injury (*Haynes* v *Harwood* [1935] 1 KB 146).

The defence of *volenti* requires agreement. If the notion of agreement is taken in its contractual sense, a person can be said to agree to the presence of certain terms in a contract only if he has been made aware of those terms before the contract is made and agreement is reached. If one were to substitute the notion of legal risk of harm for 'the terms of the contract' this would seem to suggest that in order to be *volens* the plaintiff must be aware of the risk of harm and consent to run that risk before it arises. Put this way, who but the most foolish would ever consciously 'agree' to run the risk of negligently inflicted injury?

The agreement required must amount to a waiver of legal rights that may arise from the harm which is risked — in effect a sort of estoppel. Thus it has been said that in the absence of express consent to the legal risk of harm, the defence of *volenti* should not be available (*Wooldridge* v *Sumner* [1963] 2 QB 43). Conversely, there are cases in which it has been held that the defence is available in cases where the plaintiff merely encounters an existing danger (*Titchener* v *British Railways Board* [1983] 3 All ER 770; *Dann* v *Hamilton* [1939] 1 KB 509). This trend is also borne out in a number of statutory provisions which allow a defence in the event of conscious acceptance of an existing risk of harm (Occupiers' Liability Act 1957, s. 2(5); Unfair Contract Terms Act 1977, s. 2(3)), but these are better viewed as varieties of 'statutory *volenti*', not necessarily reflecting the proper view of the common law defence.

If a plaintiff is to be met by the defence of *volenti* he must be aware of the nature and extent of the risk of harm, although this knowledge alone will be insufficient to establish the defence. Thus the mere knowledge that a driver is inexperienced is not sufficient to raise the defence (*Nettleship* v *Weston* [1971] 2 QB 691). The knowledge test is subjective with the result that it may be relevant to consider whether the plaintiff was in such a condition of intoxication as to be unable to appreciate the nature of the risk taken (*Morris* v *Murray* [1990] 3 All ER 801). Oddly, this means the more intoxicated is the plaintiff, the less likely that he will be met by the defence of *volenti* (*Barrett* v *Ministry of Defence* [1995] 3 All ER 87). If the plaintiff ought to have been aware of the risk of harm, the more appropriate defence is that of contributory negligence.

The difficulty created by the defence of *volenti* is that it sometimes appears to have been applied in circumstances in which some other limiting device might have been more appropriate. It must be appreciated that *volenti* is a defence which displaces the primary duty and that before it can be invoked, an actionable tort must have been committed. Thus, if a reduced standard of care is expected of the defendant, there may be no actionable tort and to use the language of *volenti* is misleading and unnecessary. Thus a photographer at a showjumping event who takes photographs from within the jumping arena is not *volens* to the risk of harm when he is struck by a horse, because it can hardly be said that he has consented to the risk that he might be injured (*Wooldridge* v *Sumner*). Instead, it is probably better to say that the event organisers owe a lesser duty of care to such people so that the standard of care is more easily satisfied. This reduced standard of care test also works in other contexts. Thus an explanation for the application of the defence *ex turpi causa non oritur actio* is that it is difficult or impossible to ascertain what standard of care is required of the defendant in the light of the plaintiff's own illegal or immoral conduct. In *Pitts* v *Hunt* [1990] 3 All ER 344 the plaintiff failed in an action for damages against the deceased's estate where he had encouraged the deceased in driving a motor cycle in a dangerous fashion. It was not that the plaintiff had consented to the injuries he suffered, but his involvement in the series of events which led up to the accident was such that it was impossible to say what level of care was required of the deceased. In contrast, neither defence seems to be available where a person commits suicide in police custody, especially if the police are aware that the deceased might commit suicide since this is a 'wrong' against which the police are required to take adequate precautions (see *Reeves* v *Commissioner of Police of the Metropolis* [1998] 2 All ER 381).

A further area where *volenti* may be confused with other defences is where a person takes a lift from a drunken driver. While it has been held that the defence of *volenti* is capable of dealing with such an occurrence (*Dann* v *Hamilton* [1939] 1 KB 509), it seems that the normal judicial response will be to treat the plaintiff as merely contributorily negligent (*Owens* v *Brimmell* [1977] QB 859 — 20 per cent reduction; see also *Donelan* v *Donelan and General Accident Fire & Life Insurance* [1993] PIQR P205 — 75 per cent reduction). It is suggested that the latter approach is legally correct since if *volenti* is properly understood, the plaintiff must assent to the legal risk that the defendant's actions will cause him harm but that he waives his right to sue for damages. If this is the case, the plaintiff's assent must come before any risk of harm exists. However, in the case of a drunken driver, the risk of harm is created by the act of consuming alcohol. If the driver is already drunk at the time the plaintiff accepts a lift from him, the risk is already present, in which case the plaintiff's assent is invalid. A better explanation is that the plaintiff has encountered a known and existing risk and is merely contributorily negligent. Only in extreme cases such as *Morris* v *Murray* [1990] 3 All ER 801 should the plaintiff be denied damages altogether. Moreover, if this is considered necessary, it is surely public policy rather than the fact that the plaintiff has assented to the risk of injury that justifies the failure of the plaintiff's action.

QUESTION 3

William and Tony, two students, having completed their final examinations, decide to spend a night out at the Mucky Duck, a public house. William meets Tony at the Mucky Duck. At the end of the evening, Tony offers William a lift home at a time when both of them are extremely drunk. Tony drives his car down the middle of the road, occasionally swerving to frighten other road users. William enthusiastically encourages Tony in this venture.

Tony drives through a red traffic light at speed and collides with a car driven by Gary. Gary who is not wearing a seatbelt is crushed behind the steering wheel of his car. William is also seriously injured in the collision.

When taken to hospital, Gary refuses a blood transfusion on religious grounds. Because of this refusal and the seriousness of his injuries, Gary must have a leg amputated.

Advise Tony of his potential liability in tort.

Commentary

This question concerns liability for negligently caused personal injury, the issues of causation and contributory negligence and the availability of the general defences in an action for negligence.

Relevant considerations are:

(a) whether and on what conditions the defence of *volenti non fit injuria* applies;

(b)   whether intoxicated driver cases are generally better dealt with under rules on contributory negligence;

(c)   what principles apply to the issues of foresight of harm, causation and apportionment under the Law Reform (Contributory Negligence) Act 1945;

(d)   the relevance of the defence, *ex turpi causa non oritur actio*.

Suggested Answer

William v *Tony*

There is no doubt that, as a road user, Tony, in normal circumstances, would owe a duty of care to William, since any person who uses the road owes a duty of care to other road users. Moreover, the manner in which Tony drives also suggests that he has failed to exercise reasonable care since he has not reached the standard ordinarily expected of a reasonably competent driver (*Nettleship* v *Weston* [1971] 2 QB 691). However, William's own involvement in the events of the evening may allow Tony to plead one of a number of possible defences which may serve to reduce or negative his potential liability.

Tony might argue that the defence of *volenti non fit injuria* applies. This defence requires a tort to have been committed, and where it operates, it serves to displace any duty which, otherwise, would have existed. What seems to be required is that the plaintiff should have assented to the legal risk of injury created by the defendant's negligence. Some cases go so far as to say that the plaintiff should expressly or impliedly agree to waive any claim against the defendant before any risk arises (*Nettleship* v *Weston*). Conversely, other cases take the view that it is sufficient that the plaintiff encounters a known and existing danger created by the defendant (*Dann* v *Hamilton* [1939] 1 KB 509). In a case such as the present, it may be difficult to find an express agreement to run the legal risk since at the time the lift is offered to William, he is extremely drunk and may not be in a state to be able to give a valid consent. However, there are instances in which the courts have been prepared to find an implied agreement from the parties' conduct that the defendant will not be liable for future negligent conduct which results in injury to the plaintiff. Most frequently, this type of case has involved a passenger accepting a lift from a drunken driver (*Dann* v *Hamilton* [1939]; *Morris* v *Murray* [1990] 3 All ER 801).

A further difficulty is that the plaintiff must have subjective knowledge of both the existence of the risk and its nature and extent (*Smith* v *Austins Lifts Ltd* [1959] 1 WLR 100). This might suggest that a passenger who is intoxicated does not have the necessary knowledge. In *Morris* v *Murray* the plaintiff went on a flight with a drunken pilot. At the time the plaintiff was drunk, but not so drunk that he did not realise what he was doing, so that the defence applied. It was accepted by the Court of Appeal that the question was whether the plaintiff was so drunk as not to realise what he was doing, which produces the paradox that a person is better off if he is extremely drunk rather than just a little!

The question states that William and Tony are both extremely drunk, which might mean that William is unable to give the necessary assent required for the purposes of the defence of *volenti*. In any event, William is injured in a road traffic accident and, in this regard, the Road Traffic Act 1988, s. 149 prevents reliance on the defence of *volenti* where the compulsory insurance provisions of that Act apply. Here Tony is driving on a public highway so that he is subject to the requirement of compulsory third party insurance. In this case, there can be no reliance on the defence of *volenti* (*Pitts* v *Hunt* [1990] 3 All ER 344).

Intoxicated driver cases are generally better dealt with under rules on contributory negligence (*Owens* v *Brimmell* [1977] QB 859). If William accepts a lift from a person who is incapable of driving safely, he appears to have acted in a way in which the reasonable man would not.

In order to establish contributory negligence, Tony must prove that William has not taken reasonable care for his own safety. In this respect, there are two principal issues. First, it must be asked whether harm to the plaintiff is reasonably foreseeable. The test is objective so that if William is so drunk as to be incapable of making a rational judgment, this will not matter for the purposes of this defence (*Owens* v *Brimmell*).

While the plaintiff's conduct does not have to be the cause of the accident, it must be causally relevant to the harm suffered. It will be sufficient if the plaintiff places himself in a dangerous position which increases the chance that harm will be caused (*Jones* v *Livox Quarries Ltd* [1952] 2 QB 608).

Where the defence applies, the court must apportion damages to such extent as it thinks just and equitable, having regard to the claimant's share in the responsibility for the damage (Law Reform (Contributory Negligence) Act 1945, s. 1(1)). The key factors here are those of damage causation and blameworthiness. The language used by the 1945 Act is said to be mandatory in that there must be an apportionment, which means that the court cannot hold the plaintiff wholly responsible for the damage (*Pitts* v *Hunt*).

However, there are instances in which the plaintiff's degree of blameworthiness is great, in which case a large percentage reduction may be justified. For example, in *Donelan* v *Donelan and General Accident Fire & Life Insurance Co. Ltd* [1993] PIQR P205 a 75 per cent reduction was considered appropriate where the defendant drove the car at the plaintiff's insistence when the plaintiff knew that the defendant was inexperienced and drunk. If the court wishes to extinguish William's claim altogether, the most likely way of doing this is through an application of the 'illegality' defence, *ex turpi causa non oritur actio* ('bad people get less' — Weir, *Casebook on Tort*).

In negligence cases the basis on which the defence works is that the plaintiff's 'illegal' involvement is such that the court may choose not to recognise the existence of a duty of care. For example, in *Ashton* v *Turner* [1981] QB 137 no duty of care was owed by the driver of a get-away car to his partner in crime. An alternative way of approaching the problem in negligence cases is to say that the plaintiff's action will fail where the illegal nature of the venture in which the parties are engaged is such that the court feels unable to set an appropriate standard of care (*Pitts* v *Hunt* [1990] 3 All ER 344). Thus in *Pitts*, the plaintiff was a pillion passenger on a motorcycle driven by the defendant, who was drunk. The vehicle was driven recklessly, but the plaintiff had encouraged him to drive in that fashion. The Court of Appeal held that the plaintiff's injuries arose directly out of the illegal venture and were not merely incidental. Accordingly, it was impossible to set an appropriate standard of care to be expected of the defendant. Alternatively, the court has to balance the adverse consequences of granting relief against the adverse consequences of refusing relief, which inevitably involves a value judgment (*Tinsley* v *Milligan* [1992] Ch 310, *per* Nicholls LJ).

On either test, it is arguable that William's claim in respect of his injuries might be rejected on the basis of the illegality defence.

Gary v *Tony*

Tony clearly owes Gary a duty of care and his driving is such that there is probably a breach of that duty, but problems may arise in relation to an award of damages. First, in relation to the injuries suffered in the traffic accident, it should be noted that Gary is not wearing a seatbelt. This is a well established example of contributory negligence since it involves a failure by Gary to take reasonable care for his own safety (*Froome* v *Butcher* [1976] QB 286). Moreover, the failure to wear the seatbelt is very likely to materially increase the risk of injury should there be a traffic accident, in which case it will be regarded as causally relevant to the harm suffered by the plaintiff (*Froome* v *Butcher*).

In determining how damages should be apportioned, the Court of Appeal has sought to lay down guidelines, since seatbelt cases are likely to be fairly common. In *Froome* v *Butcher* [1976] QB 286, it was held that if wearing a seatbelt would have prevented altogether the damage suffered, an appropriate reduction in damages would be 25 per cent. If the injury would have been less severe than it was in fact, the reduction should be 15 per cent, but if the injury would have been the same whether a belt was worn or not, there should be no reduction at all. The fact that this case was decided before the wearing of seatbelts was made compulsory will not matter, since the defendant's culpability in causing the accident is irrelevant (*Capps* v *Miller* [1989] 2 All ER 333).

Gary is crushed behind the steering wheel. Whether he was wearing a seatbelt or not, this is a kind of injury likely to be suffered by the driver of a car hit, at speed, by another vehicle. This would seem to suggest a maximum reduction in damages of 15 per cent, but if it is shown that the extent of injury would have been the same whether a seatbelt is worn or not, then Gary's damages should not be reduced at all.

When Gary is taken to hospital, he refuses a blood transfusion, with the result that his leg is amputated. It must be decided whether the cause of the amputation is the seriousness of Gary's injuries resulting from the traffic accident or whether Gary's refusal to have a blood transfusion is a *novus actus interveniens*.

The act of the plaintiff is capable of breaking the chain of causation (*McKew* v *Holland Hannen & Cubitts (Scotland) Ltd* [1969] 3 All ER 1621). Here the emphasis is on whether the plaintiff has acted reasonably in the circumstances. It is less important to consider whether the plaintiff's act is foreseeable or not. In *Wieland* v *Cyril Lord Carpets Ltd* [1969] 3 All ER 1006 it was said to be foreseeable that an injury caused by the defendant's negligence may affect the plaintiff's ability to cope with the vicissitudes of life and thereby be a cause of another injury.

The difficulty which arises in this case is that Gary's refusal is based on religious grounds. This will face the court with the daunting prospect of deciding whether it is reasonable for a person to hold a particular belief! The likely approach in these circumstances is that Tony will have to take Gary as he finds him and that Gary's refusal will not break the chain of causation. A similar approach has been taken in the criminal law, where a person has been found guilty of murder where his victim refused a blood transfusion on religious grounds (*R v Blaue* [1975] 3 All ER 446). The tort law equivalent of this approach is the eggshell skull rule under which unusual or unforeseeably extensive injury is not regarded as too remote where it results from some peculiarity of the plaintiff himself (*Smith v Leech Brain & Co.* [1962] 2 QB 405).

12 Remedies and Limitations of Actions

INTRODUCTION

This final chapter considers perhaps the most important issue so far as a tort plaintiff is concerned, namely what remedy is available in the event of a tort on the part of the defendant. The two major remedies in tort law are an award of damages and the grant of the equitable remedy of injunction. This chapter concentrates on the issue of damages, but questions concerning the rules which apply to injunctions can be found in **Chapter 8** (Torts in Relation to Land), where the injunction plays an important role in providing a remedy for continuing torts such as private nuisance.

So far as the remedy of damages is concerned, it is important to consider not just the issues raised in this chapter but also related issues such as the rules on causation and remoteness in negligence actions.

The three principal types of damage for which a remedy may be available include personal injury (which includes death and psychiatric harm), property damage and, in rare circumstances, economic loss. The primary purpose behind an award of damages is to compensate the plaintiff for the loss or damage actually suffered and not, generally, to punish or deter the defendant from his wrongdoing. The principle which lies behind an award of tort damages is, so far as money can do this, to return the plaintiff to the position he was in before the defendant's wrong was committed. In personal injury actions, it is sometimes difficult to achieve this result, particularly where harm such as pain and suffering is concerned, since these heads of loss are difficult to quantify in monetary terms.

In property damage cases there is sometimes a problem in identifying the appropriate basis for assessment of damages. For example, it might be appropriate to give the cost of repair, whereas in other cases the fairer measure of damages may be based on the diminution in value of the damaged property.

So far as the issue of limitation of actions is concerned, Parliament has seen fit to impose a time limit on bringing an action. As a general rule, the plaintiff must issue his writ within six years of the date on which damage is caused. The difficulty this can give rise to is that damage can be caused without the awareness of the plaintiff so that time is ticking away without the plaintiff's knowledge. In personal injury cases, this problem can be met through the exercise of judicial discretion to allow a claim to be commenced out of time. However, the same is not true in property damage cases, in which case the plaintiff may be time barred before he realises that he has a cause of action.

QUESTION 1

Hector has been warned by his doctor that he must not drive. Since his wife has been taken seriously ill, he decides to rush her to hospital by car rather than wait for an ambulance. Hector's daughter, Kiki has recently telephoned the police to inform them that Hector sometimes drives a car despite the fact that he has been advised not to, but the police have done nothing about this. On the way to the hospital, Hector collapses at the wheel, and the car swerves off the road. Dougal, who is painting a second floor window, is injured when he jumps from his ladder in an attempt to get out of the way of the car. The car comes to a halt after demolishing part of a shop owned by Zebedee. Twenty minutes later while the police are attempting to remove the car, part of a wall collapses on Florence and Ermintrude, two spectators.

Ermintrude, who has recently been divorced from her husband, Dylan, is crushed to death in the space of three minutes and Florence is so badly injured that she suffers from depression and commits suicide three months later. Florence's live-in lover, Brian, is distraught at the death of his partner. Ermintrude's ex-husband, Dylan, seeks to recover damages in respect of Ermintrude's death, including damages for the pain and suffering endured by her before she died.

Advise Dougal, Zebedee, Brian and Dylan.

Commentary

This question concerns the duty of care owed by a road user to other road users and the question whether there has been a breach of that duty. In relation to the remedy of damages, consideration has to be given to the effect of death on an award and how this affects dependants of the deceased and those representing the deceased's estate. In relation to pre-death injuries it is also necessary to consider the form of an award of damages for pain and suffering. The key issues to consider are:

(a)   is there a breach of duty?

(b)   how relevant is the dilemma which Dougal faces?

(c)   do the actions of the police amount to a *novus actus interveniens*?

(d)   who is a dependant and what damages may be recovered in respect of such dependency?

(e)   how do dependency damages differ from 'survival' damages?

(f)   is suicide a *novus actus interveniens*?

Suggested Answer

It is well established that all road users owe a duty of care to other road users (*Nettleship* v *Weston* [1971] 2 QB 691). It follows that there is a potential duty to Dougal and Zebedee in respect of the harm both suffer. That harm is, respectively, personal injury suffered by Dougal and property damage suffered by Zebedee, both of which appear to be foreseeable consequences of a road traffic accident.

Whether Hector is in breach of the duty of care he owes to Dougal and Zebedee requires consideration of the magnitude of risk, the seriousness of the harm suffered, the utility of the defendant's conduct and any precautions which might have been taken to guard against the risk. Since Hector has been warned by his doctor that he should not drive, it seems to follow that there is a substantial risk that he may be the cause of an accident in the event of his collapse while driving. However, regard should be had to the reason why he chooses this course of action, namely to ensure that his wife gets to hospital as early as possible in the light of her illness. In *Watt* v *Hertfordshire County Council* [1954] 1 WLR 853 the defendants required the plaintiff, a firefighter employed by them, to take up a potentially dangerous position so that life-saving equipment could be transported to the scene of a road traffic accident which threatened the life of another person. It was held that the utility of the defendants' conduct in seeking to save human life was justified and that the risk of harm to the plaintiff was acceptable in the circumstances. If this rule is applied to Hector, he has taken a risk by driving a car when advised not to do so, but he has done so in order to avert the risk of more serious harm to his wife. Conversely, the alternatives available to Hector also have to be considered. He could have waited for an ambulance to arrive or he could have ordered a taxi. Whether these alternatives are feasible depends on the seriousness of the risk to his wife's life, but it is generally accepted that the defendant must take only reasonable precautions to guard against the risk, not all possible precautions (*Latimer* v *AEC Ltd* [1953] AC 643).

In relation to Dougal, regard must be had to the 'dilemma principle' since he has taken the possibly foolish action of jumping from a ladder in the belief that he is about to be struck by an oncoming vehicle. In *Jones* v *Boyce* (1816) 1 Stark 493 the plaintiff jumped from a moving coach in the belief that it was about to overturn. In fact, the coach did not overturn, but the defendant was still fully liable for the harm suffered on the basis that his negligence had placed the plaintiff in a dilemma and that the plaintiff had acted reasonably in the circumstances. Applied to Dougal, if he reasonably believes that Hector's car is about to strike the ladder on which he is standing, it may be reasonable for him to jump, even though this may result in injury.

Whether Hector or the police are liable for the death of Ermintrude and the injuries to Florence will depend on whether the actions of the police amount to a *novus actus interveniens*. While there may be circumstances in which it has been held that for reasons of public policy the police should not be subject to a duty to take care in relation to the conduct of a criminal investigation (*Hill* v *Chief Constable of West Yorkshire* [1988] 2 All ER 238, it does not follow that the police cannot be liable for their negligence in the course of ordinary operations. Thus the police may be liable for harm caused by the negligent use of a CS gas canister (*Rigby* v *Chief Constable of Northamptionshire* [1985] 2 All ER 985) or where a traffic accident was caused by the negligence of a supervising police officer (*Knightley* v *Johns* [1982] 1 All ER 861). Similarly, the immunity suggested by some cases may be displaced for reasons of public policy, such as the proper protection of the public. Thus in *Swinney* v *Chief Constable of Northumbria Police* [1996] 3 All ER 449 the plaintiff supplied the police with confidential information about a group of known violent criminals, who obtained this information by breaking into a police vehicle. As a result of this, the plaintiff was subjected to violence and consequently suffered psychiatric harm. Because of the special relationship which existed between the plaintiff and the police, which set him apart from the general public, a duty of care was owed. The facts indicate that the police failed to take action after Kiki informed them that Hector was still driving his car. However, the principle in *Swinney* appears to be one which is personal to the informant, and since Kiki is not injured because of the failure of the police to take action, it is unlikely that the principle established in *Hill*, that a duty is not owed to the general public, will be displaced.

Although it is Hector's negligent driving which has caused the car to collide with the wall of Zebedee's shop, it may be that the manner in which the police conduct themselves amounts to a break in the chain of causation. Generally, if a third party is faced with a dilemma created by the defendant's negligence, a reasonable response by a third party will not break the chain of causation. This is so even where there has been time for reflection before the third party acts (*The Oropesa* [1943] P 32). Where the act of the third party is negligent, it is possible that it may amount to a *novus actus interveniens*, especially if it is characterised as a reckless act (*Wright* v *Lodge* [1993] 4 All ER 299), although no clear answer can be given. In *Knightley* v *Johns* [1982] 1 All ER 851 it was held that it should be asked whether the whole sequence of events is a natural or probable consequence of the defendant's negligence and whether it was more than just foreseeable as a mere possibility. In order to decide the question, it might sometimes be helpful to consider whether the third party's positive act is deliberate or whether he is guilty of no more than an omission or an innocent mistake or miscalculation. Thus in *Knightley* the defendant had caused a traffic accident at the exit to a tunnel. A supervising police officer did not immediately close the tunnel, as he should have done. The plaintiff was ordered to ride against the flow of traffic in order to close the tunnel and was struck by an oncoming vehicle. It was held that the defendant who caused the first accident was not liable for the injuries caused to the plaintiff since the collision with the driver coming in the opposite direction (the third defendant) was too remote a consequence of the first defendant's negligence, especially in the light of the numerous errors made by the supervising police officer (the second defendant). Accordingly, the second and third defendants were liable.

In the case of the accident caused by Hector, there does not appear to be any evidence of a negligent act on the part of the police, and the initial damage to the wall has resulted from Hector's driving. This might seem to suggest that the actions of the police do not amount to a *novus actus interveniens* and that Hector will also be responsible for the death of Ermintrude and the injuries to Florence.

There are likely to be two actions for damages. One will be brought by Florence's lover, Brian, and another is likely to be brought by Dylan, Ermintrude's former husband. Both Dylan and Brian may have an action of dependency damages under the provisions of the Fatal Accidents Act 1976, despite the fact that Dylan is no longer married to Ermintrude. This is because the list of dependants set out in the Fatal Accidents Act 1976, s. 1 includes spouses and former spouses, including those who have remarried (*Shepherd* v *Post Office, The Times*, 15 June 1995). Brian, as a co-habitee, will also be regarded as a dependant if he has lived with Florence for at least two years, although it is possible for a person to live in more than one household at the same time (*Pounder* v *London Underground Ltd* [1995] PIQR P217).

This is a new action which arises where death is caused by a wrongful act or default which is such as would have entitled the person injured to maintain an action and recover damages in respect of it. The person who would have been liable, had death not ensued, will be liable to an action for damages, notwithstanding the death of the person injured (Fatal Accidents Act 1976, s. 1(1)). The relatives covered by the action include spouses and persons who have lived with the deceased as husband or wife for a period of two years prior to the date of death (Fatal Accidents Act 1976, s. 1(2)), although persons falling into the latter category will be unable to recover set bereavement damages of £7,500, in the same way as a spouse may (s. 1A(2)). The action for dependency damages is brought by the executor or administrator of the deceased's estate on behalf of the dependant, or by the dependant if no action has been commenced within six months of the death. The action may be brought only if the deceased could have sued in his own right had he only been injured. The idea of damages under the Fatal Accidents Act 1976 is to give the dependant sufficient to represent the loss of a breadwinner. Accordingly, assessment of damages will start with a quantification of the wages the deceased was earning, subject to a deduction in respect of the deceased's own living expenses. This will produce a figure representing the deceased's earning capacity which is then subjected to a multiplier running from the date of death and representing the probable length of the deceased's earning period. The award is sub-divided into two parts covering, respectively, the period from death to the date of trial and from the date of trial on into the future. In order to be considered for dependency damages, the dependant must prove financial loss in consequence of the death, and in the case of Ermintrude, this will include the value of any domestic services she might have provided as a wife.

Brian and Dylan may also have a 'survival' action under the Law Reform (Miscellaneous) Provisions Act 1934 if they represent the estate of the deceased person. This is not a new action in favour of the survivor, but represents the pecuniary and non-pecuniary loss suffered by the deceased in consequence of the defendant's tortious act and is therefore dependent on whether the deceased could have maintained an action against the defendant had he survived. In order to bring an action under the 1934 Act, it is necessary that both Brian and Dylan represent the estate of the deceased, which will depend on the terms of the will of the deceased or relevant rules on intestacy. It may be that as an ex-husband, Dylan is not included in Ermintrude's estate, but this is not clear from the language of the question.

Regarding actions for damages in respect of pain and suffering, it appears that if the period between the defendant's initial tort and the subsequent death is so short as to be regarded as part of the death itself, no award in respect of pain and suffering may be made (*Hicks* v *Chief Constable of South Yorkshire Police* [1992] 2 All ER 65). This may suggest that the period of three minutes between the collapse of the wall while the police are attempting to remove Hector's car from Zebedee's shop and Ermintrude's death is too short to allow an award of damages for pain and suffering. Assuming Brian represents Florence's estate, it will have to be shown that had Florence lived she could have maintained an action against Hector. A difficulty in this regard is that, in a state of depression, she commits suicide three months after the date of the accident caused by Hector's negligence. It must be decided if Florence's suicide amounts to a break in the chain of causation, for if this is the case, Florence will have no claim against Hector, which will, in turn, prevent Brian from maintaining an action under the 1934 Act. There is authority in the decision in *Pigney* v *Pointer's Transport Services Ltd* [1957] 1 WLR 1121 which suggests that insane suicide does not amount to a *novus actus interveniens* so that an action under the 1934 Act by a surviving spouse will not be prejudiced. However, this was a case based on a test of remoteness of damage which rendered the defendant liable for all direct loss flowing from his negligence. Moreover, at the time, suicide was a criminal offence, which would have entitled an insurer to refuse to pay out under the terms of a life assurance policy. Since that time, a distinction appears to have been drawn between sane and insane suicide, the latter not affecting the defendant's liability (*Kirkham* v *Greater Manchester Police* [1990] 2 QB 283 cf. *Reeves* v *Commissioner of Police of the Metropolis* [1998] 2 All ER 381 *contra*). If Florence commits suicide in a state of depression, it is possible that this may be regarded as a variety of insane suicide which may not necessarily break the chain of causation, thereby allowing Brian to maintain an action for damages against Hector.

QUESTION 2

Donald, aged 35, is badly injured in a road traffic accident caused by the admitted negligence of Charles. Donald's car, valued at £10,000, is written off. The extent of his injuries is such that prior to the date of trial Donald incurs private medical expenses of £12,500, but has also spent a number of weeks in a National Health Service hospital at public expense, with the result that the household costs incurred by Rebecca, Donald's wife, are less than usual for part of the time, but greater than usual once Donald returns home for convalescence. During the period of hospitalisation and medical treatment, Donald is unable to work as a research chemist at a salary of £25,000 *per annum*.

The extent of Donald's injuries are such that for the future he will be unable to continue in his employment for a further three years after trial and will be unable to continue his pastime as an amateur cricketer. Moreover, there is a distinct prospect that his injuries may worsen in years to come, although this is by no means certain. Donald took out a personal accident insurance plan a number of years ago, which will pay substantial benefits following the accident. Moreover, Donald has also received social security benefits and will continue to do so after the date of trial.

Advise Donald.

Commentary

This question is concerned mainly with personal injury damages and the different heads of damage under which an award may be made. A distinction must be drawn between pre-trial expenditure and future loss. Account must also be taken of any deductions which should be made from an award of damages so as to ensure that the plaintiff is not over-compensated. There is also a minor issue in relation to damages for harm to property. The main points which should be considered include:

(a)   what pre-trial expenditure is recoverable and what off-sets must be made?

(b)   how is loss of future earnings to be quantified?

(c)   instead of a lump sum award, is there the possibility of an award of provisional damages?

(d)   what deductions from the award are to be made in respect of social security and insurance payments?

(e)   how are damages for pain and suffering and loss of amenity to be assessed?

(f)   is the appropriate basis for damages in respect of the car the cost of repair or the diminished value of the vehicle?

Suggested Answer

The question states that Charles admits negligence, therefore there is no need to consider whether a duty of care is owed or whether there is a breach of duty on Charles's part.

In an action for damages for personal injury, there are two distinct heads of damage. The first is expenditure incurred as a result of the tort of the defendant and the second is loss of earnings.

So far as pre-trial expenditure is concerned, any expenditure actually and reasonably incurred is recoverable against the defendant. This will include medical expenses such as the £12,500 private medical expenditure incurred by Donald, but there is a necessary deduction to be made in respect of any savings made through maintenance at public expense in a National Health Service hospital. Any savings made must be offset against any loss of income (Administration of Justice Act 1982, s. 5). Moreover, the household expenditure incurred by Rebecca is reduced compared with what is the norm. Thus it will be appropriate to make a deduction in respect of expenditure which would have been incurred in maintaining Donald (*Harris* v *Empress Motors Ltd* [1984] 1 WLR 212). However, it is also the case that after Donald returns home for convalescence, household expenses increase, in which case this increase may be taken into account. At one stage it was thought that the existence of a mere moral obligation to maintain the injured person was not sufficient to establish a pecuniary claim, but this is no longer the case (*Hunt* v *Severs* [1994] 2 All ER 385). Thus if Rebecca has to give up work in order to tend to Donald, an award may be made in respect of this expense, but Donald will hold such an amount in trust for Rebecca as a provider of the services.

Donald suffers loss of earnings as a result of his hospitalisation. It is well established that a plaintiff may recover the amount he would have earned between the date of the tort and the date of trial, subject to deductions in respect of taxation liabilities (*British Transport Commission* v *Gourley* [1956] AC 185).

Donald is entitled to damages which take into account his future pecuniary loss, which for the most part will consist of his lost future income. The way in which this is identified is by calculating the plaintiff's net annual loss which is then multiplied by a figure which, as far as possible and if properly invested, will produce an overall amount equivalent to the lost income. Taking account of investment is an important factor since the court must have regard for the fact that the damages are paid in the form of a lump sum. Accordingly, the multiplier used will not equate exactly with the number of lost working years. The fact that Donald's injuries may worsen in years to come may affect his earning capacity in the future. This is a factor which may be considered when assessing damages if it is likely to serve as a handicap in the job-market (*Moeliker* v *A Reyrolle & Co.* [1977] 1 WLR 132). However, the rule seems to be confined to complete loss of job prospects, whereas Donald will be unable to work for three years, but may be able to work thereafter. Nonetheless a person who is out of work for three years may find it difficult to find replacement employment after that period.

A well established problem with the lump sum system of paying damages is that it is not easy to deal with future uncertainties. It is now possible under the Supreme Court Act 1982, s. 32A for the court to award provisional damages, so that the plaintiff may return at a later stage to recover an additional payment if the circumstances warrant this. For the court to be able to make such an award, there must be a chance that at some definite or indefinite time in the future, the injured person will develop some serious disease or suffer some serious deterioration. It has been held that this means more than just some fanciful chance and must be capable of measurement (*Willson* v *Ministry of Defence* [1991] 1 All ER 638). The availability of this option is now a factor the courts will take into account in determining whether they should refuse to order a lump-sum payment, particularly if the degree of likely deterioration might result in death (*Molinari* v *Ministry of Defence* [1994] PIQR Q33).

The fact that there is no certainty that Donald's injuries will worsen may be an indication that the court will feel unable to make an award of provisional damages under s. 32A. Moreover, it is clear that continuing deterioration, such as the onset of osteo-arthritis after injuries consisting of broken limbs, will not fall within the ambit of s. 32A (*Willson* v *Ministry of Defence*).

When an award of damages is made in respect of pecuniary loss, the court must take account of any relevant offsets, so that the award does not over-compensate the plaintiff. As liability to taxation, the court will also have to have regard to sources of financial support other than the award of damages itself. The question states that Donald has received and will continue to receive social security benefits and that he is due to receive a payment under a personal accident insurance plan. The policy moneys under the personal accident insurance plan will not be deducted from the award of damages (*Bradburn* v *Great Western Railway* (1874) LR 10 Ex 1), since the plaintiff has paid for the benefit and it would discourage people from making such provision were there to be a deduction from any subsequent award of damages.

The rule on social security benefits is different since tort damages and these state benefits are designed to compensate the same losses. Not to deduct such payments would involve over-compensation. The Social Security Administration Act 1992, s. 81(5) now provides that when assessing damages the amount of any relevant benefit paid or likely to be paid to or for the plaintiff is to be disregarded. Relevant benefits include attendance allowance, disablement benefit or pension, family credit, income support, incapacity benefit, mobility allowance, reduced earnings allowance, retirement allowance, severe disable-ment allowance, statutory sick pay, disability living allowance, disability working allowance and job seeker's allowance. Under s. 82(1) of the 1992 Act the compensator is not permitted to pay any compensation until the Department of Social Security has issued a certificate detailing the total amount of benefit. Once this has been issued, the amount certified must be deducted in respect of a period of five years following the date of the accident and is payable to the Secretary of State. The deduction is made from the whole of the award which includes any element in respect of non-pecuniary loss. This remains the case even though social security benefits do not compensate for non-pecuniary losses such as pain and suffering.

In addition to pecuniary losses, an award of damages may also cover less easily quantifiable losses such as pain and suffering and loss of amenity. Provided it can be assumed that the plaintiff has endured pain, an award of damages for pain and suffering may be made. The one instance in which such an award is unlikely is where the plaintiff is and will remain permanently unconscious (*West (H.) & Son Ltd* v *Shephard* [1964] AC 326). Here there is nothing to suggest that Donald is comatose, in which case the award of damages may include an element in respect of pain and suffering. Donald is unable to continue his pastime as an amateur cricketer. This is a factor which may be reflected in any award of damages. Thus if the plaintiff loses the joy of life and cannot ride a bicycle or kick a football, he is entitled to damages representing his loss of enjoyment of life (*Heaps* v *Perrite Ltd* [1937] 2 All ER 60). It is important that Donald has played cricket before the date of the accident, since it is not open to a previously healthy person who has not engaged in a particular pastime to say that he has been prevented from pursuing that activity.

Finally, Donald's car is damaged in the accident caused by Charles's negligence. The question states that it has been written off and that it is valued at £10,000. Where a vehicle has been written off, it is considered uneconomic to repair it and the court is likely to treat this as a case of constructive total loss (*Darbishire* v *Warran* [1963] 1 WLR 1067). In the circumstances there is said to be no difference between the cost of repair and the reduction in market value of the damaged chattel. It follows that an award of damages will represent the replacement value of the damaged article (*Liesbosch Dredger (Owners)* v *Edison (Owners)* [1933] AC 449), in Donald's case, £10,000.

QUESTION 3

Tom through his admitted negligent driving damages a vintage Bentley car owned by Algernon. The car is so badly damaged that in normal circumstance it would be written off by an insurance company, but Algernon is so attached to it that he wants to have it repaired. Since Algernon is temporarily financially embarrassed, he cannot immediately afford to arrange for the necessary repairs, with the result that he waits for six months before doing anything. In the meantime Algernon hires a cheap alternative vehicle and discovers that the cost of repairing the car has risen by £250 compared with the cost of the car being repaired by a specialist in Bentley cars rather than taking the cheaper option of a general car repairer.

A further consequence of the collision between the two vehicles is that Tom's own car, after Tom was thrown from his vehicle, collided with a propane gas tank, causing an explosion which damages a derelict factory owned by Richmann Properties Ltd. Richmann had intended to clear this site for the purposes of future development.

Advise Tom of his potential liability in damages.

Commentary

This question concerns the rules on an award of damages for property damage. A car is badly damaged in circumstances in which it would be normal to see an award of damages based on market depreciation, but there is also the possibility of damages based on the cost of repair. Other factors such as consequential expenses, the impecuniosity of the plaintiff and rules on mitigation of damage must be considered. There is also a problem of damage to real property and the basis on which damages should be awarded. The principal issues for consideration are:

(a) the difference between repair costs and diminution in value in respect of damage to chattels;

(b) the effect of impecuniosity and the methods employed to avoid the harshness of the common law rule, including its relationship with the rule on mitigation of damage;

(c) whether the real property damage should be compensated on the basis of repair costs or diminution in value.

Suggested Answer

Since the question informs us that Tom has admitted to driving negligently, there is no need to consider the issues of duty of care and breach of duty.

Accordingly, the principal question concerns Tom's liability in damages for the harm suffered by Algernon and Richmann Properties Ltd.

The question states that Algernon's car is so badly damaged that in normal circumstances it would be written off by an insurance company. This is otherwise described as a constructive total loss (*Darbishire* v *Warran* [1963] 1 WLR 1067) and the award of damages will be based on the replacement value of the vehicle (*Liesbosch Dredger (Owners)* v *Edison (Owners)* [1933] AC 448). Thus in *Darbishire* v *Warran* the cost of repairing the plaintiff's car, including hire charges, was £192, but the car itself had a replacement value of only £85. It was held that the plaintiff should not have sought to repair the vehicle but should have purchased a replacement. The basis of the decision is that the plaintiff had not taken reasonable steps to mitigate his loss. Exceptionally, the plaintiff may be allowed the cost of repair where the damaged property is effectively unique. For example, in *O'Grady* v *Westminster Scaffolding Ltd* [1962] 2 Lloyd's Rep 238 the plaintiff had carefully looked after and maintained a car, a replacement for which would have been very difficult to purchase on the market. In the light of the plaintiff's close attachment to the vehicle and the difficulty in finding a replacement, the court was prepared to award the cost of repairing the vehicle even though this was substantially in excess of its market value. It would appear that Algernon's position is very similar to that in *O'Grady* and that the cost of repair might be the appropriate measure of damages.

Consequential losses suffered as a result of the damage inflicted by the defendant may also be recovered. Thus the cost of hiring a substitute until replacement or repair is effected (*Darbishire* v *Warran*) and any profits which would have been earned by the chattel had it been capable of use may be recovered (*The Argentino* (1888) 13 PD 191). Here Algernon has incurred the cost of hiring a replacement, but there is no evidence that there is any loss of profit.

A further relevant factor is that Algernon's ability to have his car repaired is impaired by reason of his impecuniosity. The general rule is said to be that losses resulting from the impecuniosity of the plaintiff are too remote to be recoverable (*Liesbosch Dredger (Owners)* v *Edison (Owners)* [1933] AC 449). However, this principle has been criticised and it appears difficult to reconcile with the rule that the defendant has to take the plaintiff as he finds him. In *Liesbosch* the plaintiff's dredger was destroyed by the defendant's negligence. Because the plaintiff's resources were tied up in the contract for which the dredger was being used, it was not possible to purchase an alternative vessel.

Instead, the plaintiff hired a replacement, but the total costs associated with this were considerably greater than the cost of buying a replacement vessel. The House of Lords held that the increased costs of hiring a replacement were not recoverable since they were consequent on the plaintiff's impecuniosity. The decision may be interpreted in one of two ways. The first is that the rule that the defendant must take the plaintiff as he finds him does not apply to 'business losses'. The second is that the plaintiff's impecuniosity in *Liesbosch* was an external factor which served to break the chain of causation linking the defendant's negligence to the plaintiff's loss. Alternatively, despite the fact that *Liesbosch* is based on a remoteness test of directness, it may be explained on the ground that it was not foreseeable that the plaintiff would be put in the difficulties he was by the defendant's negligence (*Perry* v *Sidney Phillips & Son* [1982] 1 WLR 1297).

The *Liesbosch* principle may be criticised on the ground that it is not sound in terms of policy, especially in the light of the contradictory rule of mitigation of loss that the defendant should take the plaintiff as he finds him. In view of this, it is not surprising that there have been attempts to get round the rule where possible. The first point is that the rule applies only where the reason for the increased loss is the impecuniosity of the plaintiff. Thus in *Martindale* v *Duncan* [1973] 2 All ER 355 a taxi driver whose cab had been damaged due to the negligence of the plaintiff chose to wait until he had obtained authorisation from his insurers before he had his vehicle repaired. While the vehicle was off the road, the plaintiff suffered loss of business profit. This loss was held to be recoverable despite the fact that one of the plaintiff's reasons for waiting was that he could not afford to have the repairs carried out himself. However, since there was another reason for the delay, namely than the plaintiff was awaiting the decision of his insurers, the *Liesbosch* principle was held not to apply. Similarly in *Perry* v *Sidney Phillips & Son* [1982] 1 WLR 1297, the plaintiff was able to recover damages for anxiety and inconvenience even though this anxiety arose principally from the plaintiff's inability to pay for the cost of repairs to the property concerned. Both of these cases are distinguishable from *Liesbosch* since in *Martindale* something other than the plaintiff's impecuniosity could be said to be the cause of the loss and in *Perry* the loss suffered by the plaintiff could not be described as a business loss, in which case the rule that the defendant must take the plaintiff as he finds him can be applied.

The *Liesbosch* principle was also distinguished in *Dodd Properties Ltd* v *Canterbury City Council* [1980] 1 WLR 433 where the cost of repairing a damaged building had risen sharply due to the effect of inflation. The plaintiffs had not had the property repaired immediately, partly because they claimed their resources would have been stretched and partly because they were awaiting the outcome of the trial before effecting the repairs. It was held that the increased cost was recoverable since the plaintiffs' impecuniosity was only one reason for the delay and that the case should be approached on the basis of mitigation principles rather than rules on remoteness of damage. On this latter basis, the plaintiff cannot reasonably be required to do something he cannot afford to do in order to reduce his losses. However, this approach can be criticised on the ground that the rule's on mitigation apply to steps taken to reduce losses for which damages are going to be awarded in the future. If the case is dealt with as one concerned with remoteness of damage, the defendant ought not to be held responsible for losses which result from an unreasonable failure by the plaintiff to act in his own best interests.

Applying all of this to Algernon, the *Liesbosch* principle may not apply to him since it may be a rule confined to business losses and Algernon appears to be a private individual. In such a case, it may well be foreseeable that such a person might not immediately be able to rectify the damage caused by the defendant's negligence. Assuming the delay in effecting repairs is reasonable, the cost incurred by Algernon in hiring a replacement will be recoverable. Moreover, the additional cost in employing the services of a specialist in Bentley cars does not seem out of the way, given the value of the vehicle.

The damage to the property owned by Richmann Properties Ltd also requires consideration. The basic principle which applies to harm to real property is that of *restitutio in integrum*, namely that the plaintiff should be put into the position he was in before the property was damaged. There are two ways in which this may be done. The first is to assess damages on the basis of the diminution in the capital value of the property and the second is to give the cost of effecting repairs. Generally, which is the appropriate measure will depend on the plaintiff's intended use of the property. For example, if the property is used by the plaintiff for the purpose of occupation or for the purposes of running a business, the appropriate measure will be the cost of repair, since it will be difficult for the plaintiff to sell the damaged property and purchase a replacement. This remains the case even where the cost of repairing the property is in excess of the depreciation in value and even where the effect of the repair is to give the plaintiff a better and more up to date set of premises (*Harbutt's Plasticine Ltd v Wayne Tank & Pump Co. Ltd* [1970] 1 QB 447). Conversely, if the property has been acquired as an investment, it seems that the appropriate measure of damages is to be based on the diminution in value of the property (*Taylor (C. R.) Ltd v Hepworths Ltd* [1977] 1 WLR 659). This appears to be the more appropriate measure in the case of Richmann Properties as the question states that the land is intended for future development.

QUESTION 4

Gregory, a surveyor, was asked by the Mid-Counties Building Society to carry out a valuation of a residential property which Damien was interested in purchasing using funds supplied under the terms of a mortgage offered by Mid-Counties. The property concerned was constructed two years earlier by Jerrybuild Ltd on behalf of South East Houses Ltd, but has been used by the latter since that time as a show house. Since the valuation requested by Mid-Counties did not attract a substantial fee, Gregory took only 15 minutes to look round the house, did not report any significant defect and valued the property at £85,000. In fact there was a serious defect in the foundations which resulted in minor cracking in an internal supporting wall between the garage and the main body of the house. Subsequent evidence shows that attempts have been made by Jerrybuild Ltd to disguise the defect in the hope that it will not be fully discoverable for many years.

Damien bought the house for £83,000, after seeing a copy of the valuation report given to him by the Mid-Counties Building Society. Five years after purchase the first signs of external cracking to the defective supporting wall begin to appear. Damien takes no action until two years later when the external cracks have become more prominent. After receiving the expert advice of a structural engineer, Damien consults his solicitor and a writ is issued seven years after the date of purchase and almost three years after the first external cracks began to appear in the supporting wall.

Damien claims that the foundation defects are such that he could sell the house for no more than £60,000, and only then to a professional builder and that in order to rectify the defects fully, if he is to remain in the house, the cost will be £28,000. Due to the fact that the value of the house is so diminished, the Mid-Counties Building Society has asked for additional security which Damien says he cannot provide.

Advise Damien.

Commentary

This question is concerned with the duty of care owed by a surveyor to a person he knows will rely on his advice, the duty of a builder to an occupier of the house he has built and the measure of damages applicable where economic loss has been suffered. The issue of limitation of actions is also relevant. The principal considerations are:

(a)   in what circumstances does a surveyor owe a duty of care to a person he realises will rely on his valuation of a property?

(b)   what duty is owed by a builder to a person who subsequently acquires a house he has built?

(c)   when is damage caused for the purposes of the accrual of a cause of action in tort and how does the common law rule differ from the position under the Defective Premises Act 1972?

(d)   what is the effect of an attempt to conceal a defect for the purposes of rules on limitation of actions?

Suggested Answer

The first issue to consider is the nature of any duty of care owed by Gregory to Damien. It is now established by the House of Lords in *Smith v Bush (Eric S.)* [1990] 1 AC 831 that a surveyor who fails to exercise reasonable care in the course of conducting a building society valuation owes a duty of care to a person he realises is likely to rely on that valuation. The general requirement of foresight of harm, proximity of relationship and justice are all satisfied where a person at the lower end of the housing market buys a house in reliance on a building society valuation. As was explained in *Smith v Bush*, at the lower end of the housing market it is now the norm for purchasers not to a commission a private, contractual survey of a house before purchase and the majority of buyers rely on the building society survey which they, in fact, pay for themselves through a payment to the building society. For this reason, surveyors who carry out such a survey should realise that their report is likely to be heavily relied upon. Since the valuation is for the comparatively small amount of £85,000 Damien is likely not to have commissioned a separate survey.

The valuation requested by the building society is not substantially remunerated, but it is clear from *Smith v Bush* that this is not a reason for cutting corners. Where a property is in reasonably good order, there is no need to take too long over the process of valuation. On the other hand, if a defect is reasonably discoverable, it is clear the surveyor is required to spend some time investigating it and if he does not do so with the result that the purchaser buys a house he might not have purchased had the true facts been known, there is a potential action for damages for negligence.

The risk which Gregory fails to report is one which had resulted in minor cracking in an internal wall. If this is considered sufficiently suspicious for a professional surveyor to suspect more serious future damage, it is a matter which might justify further investigation. Moreover, simply reporting that there are no defects at all might be evidence of negligence on Gregory's part.

If there is a breach of duty on Gregory's part, it must be decided what damages Damien is entitled to and whether he has brought his action in time. Where a person has bought a house for more than it is worth, in reliance on a surveyor's report, the general rule is that an award of damages should put the plaintiff in the position he would have been in before the report was negligently prepared (*Watts* v *Morrow* [1991] 4 All ER 937). This, it seems, is represented by the depreciation in value of the property and not the cost of repair, and this remains so even if the occupier decides to remain in occupation (*Watts* v *Morrow*). The difference between the £83,000 paid for the house by Damien and the £60,000 it is now worth is only £23,000, compared with the estimated £28,000 it will cost to effect repairs. However, the figure which is not provided in the question is the current market value of the property. What is clear from *Watts* v *Morrow* is that the cost of repair is not the appropriate measure of damages to apply.

Where property has been negligently over-valued as a result of which a lender of money has advanced more than the value of the building, it is possible that the lender may suffer loss. On the facts, the borrower (Damien) has not yet defaulted, but this may become a possibility. In *South Australia Asset Management Corporation* v *York Montague Ltd* [1996] 3 All ER 365 the House of Lords held that a valuer would not be liable for any part of the loss suffered by a lender as a result of a fall in the general value of the property market, but would remain responsible for such loss as was attributable to the act of over-valuation. On the facts, it would appear that the lender, as yet, has suffered no loss, but it is possible that they may do so in time.

As to the issue of limitation of actions, the general rule is that in an action for negligence the limitation period runs for six years from the date on which damage is caused (Limitation Act 1980, s. 2). In negligent advice cases, the date of damage is said to be the date on which the plaintiff relies on the advice given by the surveyor (*Secretary of State for the Environment* v *Essex, Goodman & Suggitt* [1986] 1 WLR 1432). This date will be that on which Damien contracts to buy the house. The problem states that a writ is not issued until seven years after the date of purchase, which would seem to suggest that the normal six-year rule has not been complied with and Damien is therefore out of time. Alternatively, if the damage suffered by Damien is not reasonably discoverable before the date on which the cause of action accrued (Limitation Act 1980, s. 14A(1)), namely the date on which damage is caused, an alternative limitation period may run for three years from the date on which the plaintiff acquired the relevant knowledge required for the purposes of bringing an action for negligence (Limitation Act 1980, s. 14(5)). The question states that the first signs of external cracking appear five years after purchase and that a writ is issued within three years of this date. Since economic loss in the form of diminution in the value of a building is actionable against a negligent surveyor, it would seem to follow that if the loss suffered by Damien is classified as latent damage, he may have brought his action in time.

Damien may have an alternative action against Jerrybuild Ltd. At common law, the builder only very exceptionally owes a tortious duty of care to the purchaser of defective premises if the nature of the complaint is that the property is not worth the amount paid for it, that is, where the purchaser has suffered economic loss (*D & F Estates Ltd* v *Church Commissioners for England* [1988] 2 All ER 992; *Murphy* v *Brentwood District Council* [1990] 2 All ER 908). The exceptional cases referred to above are that a duty of care may be owed in respect of economic loss in the form of diminution in property value where there is a uniquely close relationship of proximity and where there has been reasonable reliance on negligently prepared advice. However, neither of these seems to apply in these circumstances.

Jerrybuild Ltd may be liable under the Defective Premises Act 1972, s. 1 which provides that a person taking on work for or in connection with the provision of a dwelling owes a duty to see that the work is done in a workmanlike or professional manner, and with proper materials, so that as regards that work the dwelling will be fit for habitation when completed. The duty also applies not just to carrying out building work badly, but also to a failure to carry out remedial work (*Andrews* v *Schooling* [1991] 3 All ER 723). Moreover, the duty is owed to the person who orders the work and to any person who subsequently acquires an interest in the dwelling. Accordingly, even though the work may have been carried out for the benefit of South East Houses Ltd, the duty is also owed to Damien as a subsequent purchaser. The main problems with the provisions of the Defective Premises Act 1972, s. 1 is that they do not apply to a dwelling covered by an approved scheme which provides the owner with a remedy. This means that a dwelling covered by the National House Building Council insurance scheme does not fall within the scope of the Act. Since the

NHBC scheme covers the majority of newly built houses, the 1972 Act may not apply broadly. However, if it is assumed that the NHBC scheme does not apply to Damien's house, a duty will be owed under the 1972 Act.

Unfortunately, a further drawback with the 1972 Act is that the limitation period under it is particularly strict. The limitation period runs for six years from the date on which the building was completed (Defective Premises Act 1972, s. 1(5)). This contrasts with the normal limitation period in negligence actions which runs for six years from the date on which damage was caused. The date of damage is often many years after the date on which a building is completed. Moreover, had this been an action for negligence rather than one under the Defective Premises Act 1972, the fact that Jerrybuild Ltd had deliberately attempted to conceal the defect would have meant that the limitation period did not begin to run until the plaintiff did or could with reasonable diligence have discovered the concealment (Limitation Act 1980, s. 32(1)(b)).

However, that provision applies only to limitation periods prescribed by the 1980 Act and the special limitation period in defective premises cases is not one prescribed by the 1980 Act. Accordingly, it has to be decided if Damien has issued his writ within six years of the date on which the building was completed. The facts of the problem show that the house was constructed two years before the survey was carried out by Gregory. The first signs of damage appear five years after Damien purchased the property but Damien does not take action for a further two years after that. This suggests that Damien will issue his writ nine years after the date on which building was completed, in which case he is out of time.

Index